Foundations French

1

Second Edition

Dounia Bissar
French Co-ordinator on the Open Language Programme
at the London Metropolitan University

Helen Phillips
Deputy Director of Applied Foreign Languages
at the University of Bristol

Cécile Tschirhart
Deputy Head of the Department of Education and formerly Director of the
Open Language Programme at the London Metropolitan University

Series Editor
Tom Carty
Formerly Languages Programme Leader at Staffordshire University
and the University of Wolverhampton

Review Panel for the Second Edition

Judy Bailey, Lecturer, Department of Languages, Linguistics and Area Studies,
UWE, Bristol

Rachel Bower, Associate Lecturer in French, University
Language Scheme, Sheffield Hallam University

Fiona Haig, Associate Lecturer, School of Language and
Area Studies, University of Portsmouth

Alison Nader, IWLP Language Co-ordinator, School of Languages
and European Studies, University of Reading

palgrave
macmillan

First published 2001
Reprinted seven times
Second edition published 2008 by
PALGRAVE MACMILLAN
Houndmills, Basingstoke, Hampshire RG21 6XS and
175 Fifth Avenue, New York, N.Y. 10010
Companies and representatives throughout the world

PALGRAVE MACMILLAN is the global academic imprint of the Palgrave Macmillan division of St. Martin's Press, LLC and of Palgrave Macmillan Ltd. Macmillan® is a registered trademark in the United States, United Kingdom and other countries. Palgrave is a registered trademark in the European Union and other countries.

ISBN-13: 978–0–230–55304–0
ISBN-10: 0–230–55304–4

This book is printed on paper suitable for recycling and made from fully managed and sustained forest sources. Logging, pulping and manufacturing processes are expected to conform to the environmental regulations of the country of origin.

A catalogue record for this book is available from the British Library.

Audio production: University of Brighton Media Centre
Produced by Brian Hill

Voices: Hubert Liagre, Marie-Stéphanie Labattu, Jean-Louis Ropers, Micheline Maupoint, Dominique Le Duc, Thérèse Rosenfeld, Alix Huchet and Fabrice Bourgelle-Pyres

10 9 8 7 6 5 4 3 2 1
17 16 15 14 13 12 11 10 09 08

Printed and bound in China

CONTENTS

OVERVIEW

	Communication skills	Vocabulary	Grammar
1	• greetings • introducing yourself • asking/answering personal questions	• greetings • nationalities • occupations/studies • workplaces • numbers 1–70	• masculine/feminine • verbs: *être*, *faire*; verbs ending in *-er* (singular forms); negatives • asking questions
2	• giving/understanding information about friends and family • ordering snacks and drinks	• family • snacks and drinks	• verbs: *avoir*; verbs ending in *-er* (plural forms) • articles • possessive adjectives
3	• talking about everyday activities • asking for/giving the time • explaining what you like/dislike/have to do	• days of the week • expressions of time • meals • leisure activities	• prepositions *à* and *de* followed by *le* or *les* • verbs: *aller*; verbs ending in *-ir* and *-re*; verbs followed by the infinitive
4	• understanding street signs • asking for/giving directions • shopping for clothes and food • expressing preferences	• directions and locations • buildings and shops • clothes • colours • numbers 70+	• verbs: imperative • prepositions of location • pronouns *le*, *la*, *les* • demonstrative adjectives • descriptive adjectives • article *du*
5	• locating places on a map • explaining what you are going to do • requesting/giving travel information • understanding timetables	• countries and regions • trains: travel, tickets, etc. • other means of transport	• prepositions before towns and countries • verbs: *aller* + infinitive; *pouvoir*, *devoir* and *il faut* • pronoun *y*
6	• making a hotel booking • making complaints • understanding holiday brochures • describing accommodation	• months and seasons • hotel facilities • home: rooms and furniture	• verbs: reflexives • comparisons (with adjectives) • *pas <u>de</u>*

	Communication skills	Vocabulary	Grammar
7	<ul><li>making a telephone call</li><li>arranging to meet someone</li><li>describing physical appearances</li><li>ordering a meal</li></ul>	<ul><li>expressions used on the telephone</li><li>expressions used to make suggestions</li><li>physical appearance</li><li>restaurant dishes</li></ul>	<ul><li>verbs: introduction to conditional</li><li>pronoun *on*</li><li>pronouns *lui* and *leur*</li><li>pronoun *en*</li></ul>
8	<ul><li>talking about what you did last weekend</li><li>explaining why you are late</li><li>talking about your last holiday</li><li>describing places and the weather</li></ul>	<ul><li>types of holidays</li><li>holiday activities</li><li>vocabulary used to describe places</li><li>weather</li></ul>	<ul><li>verbs: perfect tense</li><li>*pendant* and *il y a*</li></ul>
9	<ul><li>talking about your background.</li><li>describing your education</li><li>describing your work experience</li></ul>	<ul><li>studies</li><li>exams and qualifications</li><li>vocabulary used to write a CV</li></ul>	<ul><li>*pendant* and *depuis*</li><li>verbs: reflexives in the perfect tense; agreement of the past participle</li></ul>
10	<ul><li>socialising and using colloquial language</li><li>asking for/giving help</li><li>asking permission/giving instructions</li><li>giving your opinion</li><li>describing your intentions</li></ul>	<ul><li>expressions used when saying goodbye</li><li>some common colloquial expressions</li><li>accidents and emergencies</li></ul>	<ul><li>object pronouns and the imperative</li><li>*ne ... pas* + infinitive</li><li>*qui* and *que*</li><li>*moi, toi, lui, ...*</li></ul>

CD TRACK LIST

Two CDs are supplied with this book. They contain all the audio material to accompany the exercises in this book.
- Where there is an audio element for an exercise it is marked with a icon.
- Every exercise has its own track which will help you locate the material very easily.
- All the audio for the **Exercices Supplémentaires** is on CD2.
- Tutors who require digital licences for this audio material should visit http://www.palgrave.com/modernlanguages/license.asp#Digital.

CD1

Track
01 L'abécédaire

Unité 1 – Toi et moi

02 Exercise 1a
03 Exercise 1b
04 Exercise 3 – 1
05 Exercise 3 – 2
06 Exercise 5
07 Exercise 7
08 Exercise 8
09 Exercise 9a
10 Exercice 9b
11 Exercice 10
12 Exercice 13
13 Exercice 18
14 Extra! Exercice 1 – a
15 Extra! Exercice 1 – b
16 Extra! Exercice 1 – c
17 Extra! Exercice 1 – d
18 Extra! Exercice 1 – e
19 Extra! Exercice 1 – f

Unité 2 – Les autres

20 Exercice 1
21 Exercice 3
22 Exercice 4
23 Exercice 5

24 Exercice 6
25 Exercice 9
26 Exercice 11
27 Exercice 12 – a
28 Exercice 12 – b
29 Exercice 12 – c
30 Exercice 13
31 Extra! Exercice 1

Unité 3 – La routine

32 Exercice 2 – a
33 Exercice 2 – b
34 Exercice 2 – c
35 Exercice 2 – d
36 Exercice 2 – e
37 Exercice 2 – f
38 Exercice 5
39 Exercice 8 – a
40 Exercice 8 – b
41 Exercice 8 – c
42 Exercice 8 – d
43 Exercice 8 – e
44 Exercice 8 – f
45 Exercice 10
46 Exercice 12
47 Exercice 14
48 Exercice 15
49 Exercice 16 – Archie
50 Exercice 16 – Thomas
51 Exercice 16 – Electra
52 Exercice 16 – Claudia

53 Exercice 17
54 Extra! Exercice 1

Unité 4 – En ville

55 Exercice 2 – a
56 Exercice 2 – b
57 Exercice 2 – c
58 Exercice 2 – d
59 Exercice 4 – a
60 Exercice 4 – b
61 Exercice 4 – c
62 Exercice 4 – d
63 Exercice 6
64 Exercice 9
65 Exercice 10 – madame
66 Exercice 10 – monsieur
67 Exercice 11
68 Exercice 12
69 Exercice 15
70 Extra! Exercice 2

Unité 5 – En train

71 Exercice 1
72 Exercice 4
73 Exercice 6
74 Exercice 7
75 Exercice 11 – 1
76 Exercice 11 – 2
77 Exercice 11 – 3
78 Exercice 12
79 Exercice 16

80 Exercice 17 – a
81 Exercice 17 – b
82 Exercice 17 – c
83 Exercice 17 – d
84 Extra! Exercice 1 – a
85 Extra! Exercice 1 – b
86 Extra! Exercice 1- c
87 Extra! Exercice 1- d
88 Extra! Exercice 1 – e
89 Extra! Exercice 1 – f
90 Extra! Exercice 1 – g

Unité 6 – A l'hôtel

01 Exercice 1
02 Exercice 2 – 1
03 Exercice 2 – 2
04 Exercice 2 – 3
05 Exercice 4
06 Exercice 5
07 Exercice 6
08 Exercice 7 – a
09 Exercice 7 – b
10 Exercice 10
11 Exercice 13
12 Exercice 15
13 Exercice 16
14 Extra! Exercice 2 – madame
15 Extra! Exercice 2 – monsieur

Unité 7 – Au restaurant

16 Exercice 1 – A
17 Exercice 1 – B
18 Exercice 1 – C
19 Exercice 1 – D
20 Exercice 2 – 1
21 Exercice 2 – 2
22 Exercice 3
23 Exercice 6
24 Exercice 7
25 Exercice 9
26 Exercice 10

27 Exercice 11
28 Extra! Exercice 1

Unité 8 – Vacances et loisirs

29 Exercice 1
30 Exercice 2
31 Exercice 5 – 1
32 Exercice 5 – 2
33 Exercice 5 – 3
34 Exercice 5 – 4
35 Exercice 5 – 5
36 Exercice 6
37 Exercice 7
38 Exercice 11
39 Exercice 12 – a
40 Exercice 12 – b
41 Exercice 14
42 Exercice 15
43 Extra! Exercice 1 – Muriel
44 Extra! Exercice 1 – Stéphane
45 Extra! Exercice 1 – Loulou
46 Extra! Exercice 1 – Bernard

Unité 9 – Education et expérience

47 Exercice 1
48 Exercice 6
49 Exercice 7
50 Exercice 8 – 1
51 Exercice 8 – 2
52 Exercice 8 – 3
53 Exercice 10
54 Exercice 12
55 Exercice 15
56 Extra! Exercice 2

Unité 10 – Au travail!

57 Exercice 1
58 Exercice 3 – a
59 Exercice 3 – b

60 Exercice 3 – c
61 Exercice 3 – d
62 Exercice 3 – e
63 Exercice 4
64 Exercice 6
65 Exercice 8
66 Exercice 9 – 1
67 Exercice 9 – 2
68 Exercice 11
69 Exercice 13
70 Extra! Exercice 1 – Babette
71 Extra! Exercice 1 – Richard
72 Extra! Exercice 1 – Stéphanie
73 Extra! Exercice 1 – Jean-Marc

Exercices supplémentaires

74 U1 – Exercice 2
75 U1 – Exercice 5
76 U2 – Exercice 1
77 U2 – Exercice 2
78 U2 – Exercice 6
79 U3 – Exercice 1
80 U3 – Exercice 3
81 U4 – Exercice 4
82 U4 – Exercice 5
83 U5 – Exercice 3
84 U5 – Exercice 5
85 U6 – Exercice 1
86 U6 – Exercice 4
87 U6 – Exercice 7
88 U7 – Exercice 2
89 U7 – Exercice 3
90 U7 – Exercice 7
91 U8 – Exercice 6
92 U9 – Exercice 1
93 U9 – Exercice 3 – 1
94 U9 – Exercice 3 – 2
95 U9 – Exercice 3 – 3
96 U9 – Exercice 4
97 U10 – Exercice 2
98 U10 – Exercice 3

Acknowledgements

The following illustration sources are acknowledged:

Helen Bugler p. 53 (left); Ann Carlisle pp. 28, 37, 39, 71, 133, 136, 140; Tim Eaton p. 23, 24; iStock International Inc. pp. 1, 2, 3, 5, 6, 12, 13, 15, 16, 18, 22, 27, 29, 33, 35 (left), 36 (left), 40, 51, 53 (right), 68, 75, 76, 80, 98, 103, 110, 111; Helen Phillips pp. 4, 35 (right), 36 (right), 37, 48, 92, 113; Alison Self pp. 37, 122, 144; Ben Thackeray p. 34; Cécile Tschirhart pp. 21, 37, 62.

The authors would like to thank everyone who helped by posing for photographs.

Every effort has been made to trace all copyright holders, but if any have inadvertently been overlooked the publishers will be pleased to make the necessary arrangements at the first opportunity.

INTRODUCTION

Mainly for the tutor

See also the *Mainly for the student* section which follows …

Foundations French 1 is a course for beginners, principally aimed at students taking a language module on an Institution-Wide Languages Programme (IWLP) or as an option on their degree. In terms of the Common European Framework, it delivers level A2+, with several competences at B1. It forms part of the *Foundations Languages Series*, which is specifically designed for IWLPs and similar provision. Its structure and content are informed by research and consultation within the HE sector and the authors are experienced tutors on IWLP-style university courses. We keep closely in touch with departments using *Foundations Languages* courses and are particularly grateful to the members of the *Foundations French 1* Review Panel for their feedback and ideas, which contributed to this second edition. To find out more about the series, visit the dedicated website at www.palgrave.com/modernlanguages

Structure

The course is designed to fit the typical university teaching year and assumes two or three hours of class contact per week. Intensive courses with more contact hours will take commensurately less time. For such courses *Foundations French 2* is the ideal follow-up. There are ten units, structured in the same way. Extension work, pairwork pages and a private study strand provide flexibility. Grammar and vocabulary are fully supported within each unit as well as in the reference pages. The standard format for each unit is as follows.

Element	Pages	Function	Skills*
Core	6/8	Introduces, practises new material	LSRW
Extra!	1	Extension work (e.g. longer dialogues, more demanding reading)	LR
Grammaire	2	One page exposition, one page exercises	
Vocabulaire	1	French–English, listed by topic	
Travail à deux	2	Consolidation	S
Exercices supplémentaires	2	Consolidation, private study	LSWR

*Skills – L = Listening, S= Speaking, R= Reading, W= Writing

Methodology

The introduction of new material is carefully prepared and dosed. Typically, it builds upon a listening item, most often combined with reading-based exercises on the text of the dialogue, sometimes with questions, wordsearch or matching exercises. Once the input is introduced, follow-up exercises apply and develop it.

To facilitate the use of French in the classroom, the exercises in the unit cores are marked with an icon indicating the linguistic activity or activities involved. They are listed and explained on page xvi.

Recorded material

There are two CDs to accompany the course. Digital licences are also available. Visit http://www.palgrave.com/modernlanguages/license.asp#Digital for more information.

Mainly for the student

1. Structure

There are ten **units.** All have the same clear, consistent structure, which you will soon get used to.

The **core** section is six (sometimes eight) pages in which new material is introduced, then practised and used in various ways. Each unit is divided into numbered items. Two CDs accompany the textbook.

The core is followed by a page headed **Extra!** This material, while on the same topics as the core, makes extra demands and is a little more challenging. Two pages are then devoted to the **grammatical structures** you have met in the unit, with exercises to practise them. The next page is the **new vocabulary** from the unit. Then come two pages of **partnerwork**, communication exercises where you are given prompts for half a conversation (Partner A page) and your partner has the prompts for the other half (Partner B page).

Beginning on page 125 there are **supplementary exercises** for each unit. These are for work outside the classroom. Your tutor may sometimes set work from these pages or you can use them as and when it suits you to consolidate what you have done from the unit core.

For reference there are a **guide to grammatical terms**, an overall **grammar summary** and a **vocabulary list**. Also at the end of the book, you will find **answers** to all the exercises.

2. Using the book

Each unit focuses on one or more themes or situations in which the language is used. The short **summary** at the start of the unit tells you what the themes are and describes what you will be able to do with the language once you have completed the unit. That's a key word (*do*): while language learning requires and develops knowledge and understanding, above all it means developing the capability of using the language in given circumstances.

The **core** contains the input (new language) for the unit as well as a range of tasks designed to help you master it and make it your own. The key inputs come in various forms such as: <u>presentation</u>, when you are given, for example, the numbers or the system for telling the time; <u>listening exercises</u>, especially involving gap-filling; <u>matching exercises</u>, where you are introduced to new words or structures by matching up a word or phrase with a picture, a person with an activity or questions and answers in a dialogue; <u>reading exercises</u>, where you may, for example, be asked to re-arrange the order of a dialogue or narrative; <u>using a model</u>, the best example of which is working on your pronunciation and intonation using the audio.

Whatever the form of input, it is absolutely vital to spend time and effort mastering this material. Be guided by your tutor. He or she will introduce it in class or ask you to prepare it in advance. If there's a word or phrase you're unsure of, turn to the vocabulary page for the unit and check. If a grammatical point puzzles you, refer to the unit grammar pages or the Grammar summary on pages 148–157. If you wonder what a grammatical term means, look it up in the Guide to grammatical terms on pages 146–147.

The material introduced in an input exercise flows into exercises in the section(s) immediately following, enabling you to practise, use and master this language. The exercises practising and applying the input material are carefully devised to enable you to progress and consolidate in manageable steps. They are very varied, as the following examples show. They include above all many <u>speaking exercises</u>, typically involving you working with a partner. Here, you are communicating in a controlled situation using the language introduced in the input sections; there are also <u>listening and reading exercises</u> involving gap-filling, answering questions and re-ordering information or correcting errors, etc.

<u>Grammar exercises</u> develop your ability to deduce rules from examples as well as to recognise and use the structures of French correctly. Grammatical points are highlighted in boxes throughout the core pages of each unit. As to <u>writing</u>, work in the unit core is mostly carefully controlled.

After you have done these exercises in your class (or gone over them there, having prepared them in advance) make sure you revise the input material and key structures in your private study time.

The **Extra!** page in each unit gives you the opportunity of further developing your French, taking in particular listening and reading skills beyond the confines of the core input material while staying on related topics. The listening material is lively and natural and you have to extract specific information from it. In such exercises, it's important to avoid the temptation to fret over every word: check what information you are being asked for and listen with that in mind.

The **grammar** pages follow. In each unit, the first page gives you a clear overview of the grammar content of the unit, and the second provides a set of short exercises so that you can test yourself (answers at the back of the book). Don't skip these pages: they simply clarify and check off grammatical structures you have met and used in the course of the unit. This is how you become aware of the language as a system.

The **vocabulary** page gives the new words occurring in the unit by topic. Learn them as you go along and revise them regularly.

The **partnerwork** material can be used in or out of the classroom to develop communication skills. The scenarios are always based on the material in the unit core, so you are securely in a known context. The challenge is to use the language you have learnt to communicate information your partner needs and to respond to what he or she says.

The **supplementary exercises** give further practice on a unit-by-unit basis and are designed to be used in private study. Answers are given at the back of the book. As the section *Learning a language* stresses, work outside the classroom, both that set by the tutor and that done on your own initiative to meet your own priorities, is an essential part of a taught language course.

Now you have a clear idea of how the book is designed to be used, read the section on *Learning a language* which follows. It gives detailed practical advice which will help you to get maximum benefit from your course.

LEARNING A LANGUAGE

A language-learning programme is essentially workshop-based rather than lecture-based. It involves active classroom sessions and a variety of social interactions, including working with a partner, small-group activity and role-play, as well as answering questions and working through exercises. Feeding into the classroom sessions and flowing from them is what is called directed study, set by your tutor but allowing you a lot of flexibility in organising your work in ways that suit you. Beyond that there is private study, where you determine the priorities.

Increasing attention is now paid to **transferable skills**, that is skills which are acquired in one context but which can be used in others. Apart from competence in the language itself, successful language learning is also recognised to be rich in skills particularly valued by employers, such as communication skills and self-management.

How can you make sure you get maximum benefit from your language course?

1. A practical point first. Check the course or module guide and/or syllabus to see exactly what is required of you by your university or college. In particular, find out how the course or module is assessed. The course guide and assessment information will probably be expressed in terms of the four language skills of listening, speaking, reading and writing. The relative importance of these skills can vary between institutions.

2. Remember this is a taught course – you're not on your own. **Your tutor** is there to guide you. Using the material in the book, he or she will introduce new structures, ensure you practise them in class and then enable you to produce similar language until you develop the capacity to work autonomously. The first rule of a taught language course, then, is to follow your guide.

3. Of course a guide can't go there for you. While your tutor will show you the way, **only you can do the learning**. This means hard work both in the classroom and outside the timetabled hours.

4. **Regular attendance** at the language class is vital. This isn't like a lecture-based course, where you can miss one session and then catch up from a friend's notes or even live with the fact that there is going to be a gap in your knowledge. A language class is a workshop. You do things. Or to put it more formally, you take part in structured activities designed to develop your linguistic competence.

5. But mere attendance isn't enough. Being there isn't the same thing as learning. You have to **participate**. This means being an active member of the class, listening carefully, working through the exercises, answering questions, taking part in dialogues, contributing to group work, taking the risk of speaking without the certainty of being right. It also means preparing before classes and following up afterwards …

6. … because what you do **outside the classroom** is vital, too. While new topics will normally be introduced in class, your tutor will also set tasks which feed in to what you will be doing in the next session. If you don't do the preparation, you can't benefit from the classroom activity or the tutor will have to spend valuable time going over the preparation in class for the benefit of those who haven't done it in advance. Classroom contact time is precious, normally no more than two or three hours a week, and it's essential to use that time to the best effect. Similarly, the tutor will sometimes ask you to follow up work done in class with tasks designed to consolidate or develop what you have done.

7. You should also take time to **review** and reflect on what you have been doing, regularly going over what you have done in class, checking your learning. This will also enable you to decide your priorities for private study, working on areas you find difficult or which are particular priorities for you (see point 9 below).

8. This assumes that you are **organised**: keep a file or notebook, in which you jot down what you have done and what you plan to do. It's a good idea to work for several shortish bursts a week rather than for a long time once a week.

9. While a lot of out-of-class work will be done at home, your university or college will probably have a Learning Centre, **Language Centre** or similar facility in the library. Check this out and use whatever you can to reinforce and supplement what you are doing in class and from this textbook. Make sure any material you use is suitable for your level: it will probably be classified or labelled using categories such as *Beginners*, *Intermediate* and *Advanced*.

   Possible resources: audio cassettes or CDs, videos, satellite TV, computer-based material, the internet, books (language courses, grammar guides, dictionaries, simple readers), magazines and newspapers, worksheets. Possible activities: listening comprehension, pronunciation practice, reading comprehension, grammar exercises, vocabulary exercises. Computer-based materials and worksheets will usually have keys with answers.

   It is possible your tutor will set specific work to be done in the Language Centre or that you will be expected to spend a certain amount of time there, otherwise you should find times during your week when you can drop in. The course assessment schedule may include a **portfolio** for which you choose coursework items according to guidelines set by the tutor/course.

10. Don't be afraid of **grammar**. This is simply the term for how we describe the way a language works. Learn it and revise it as you go along. There are boxes with grammar points throughout each of the units in this book, a grammar summary for each unit and a grammar overview for the whole book. You probably feel hesitant about grammatical terms such as *direct object* or *definite article* but they are useful labels and easily learned. There is a guide to such terms towards the end of the book.

11. In addition to listening-based work in class, you should regularly work in your own time on the accompanying audio material. Try to reproduce the **pronunciation and intonation** of the native speakers on the recording. It's easier if you work at this from the start and establish good habits than if you approximate to the sounds of the language and have to correct them later. It's important that you repeat and speak out loud rather than in your head. Why not work with a friend?

12. Always bear in mind that, in learning a foreign language, you can normally understand (listening and reading) more than you can express (speaking and writing). Above all, relax when listening or reading, remember **you don't have to be sure of every word** to get the message and you don't need to translate into your native language.

13. Regular **practice** is the key. Remember *fluency* comes from the Latin for 'to flow': it means speaking 'flowingly', not necessarily getting everything perfectly right. It is also a good idea to dip back into earlier units in the book to test yourself.

14. Universities and colleges are increasingly international and you will almost certainly be able to make contact with **native speakers** of French. Try out your language, get them to correct your pronunciation, find out about their country and culture.

   And cheap flights mean that you can afford to go there …!

15. And finally, **enjoy** your language learning!

Tom Carty, *Series Editor*

La langue utilisée en classe/
THE LANGUAGE OF THE CLASSROOM

These symbols appear next to the rubric of most exercises and indicate the type of skill or activity required.

Ecoutez	Listen	
Parlez	Speak	
Lisez	Read	
Ecrivez	Write	

Travail à deux	Pair work	
En groupe	Group work	
Trouvez le mot	Wordsearch	

L'abécédaire

Lettre	Prononciation de la lettre	Exemple	Lettre	Prononciation de la lettre	Exemple
A a	a	**A**lgérie	O o	o	**O**man
B b	bé	**B**elgique	P p	pé	**P**ays de Galles
C c	cé	**C**anada	Q q	cu	**Q**uébec
D d	dé	**D**anemark	R r	èr	**R**oyaume-Uni
E e	euh	Angl**e**terre	S s	ès	**S**énégal
F f	èf	**F**rance	T t	té	République **t**chèque
G g	gé	**G**rande-Bretagne	U u	u	Lit**u**anie
H h	ach	**H**ongrie	V v	vé	Nor**v**ège
I i	i	**I**talie	W w	double vé	Ko**w**eit
J j	ji	**J**amaïque	X x	ix	Luxembourg
K k	ka	Ira**k**	Y y	i grec	Ch**y**pre
L l	èl	**L**aos	Z z	zèd	Nouvelle-**Z**élande
M m	èm	**M**aroc			
N n	èn	**N**ouvelle-Calédonie			

1 Toi et moi

When you have completed this unit you will be able to greet someone, introduce yourself, talk about yourself, ask/answer questions about yourself and others, and count up to seventy.

1 Bonjour!

a Ecoutez les dialogues. Notez les différences et la prononciation. Listen to the dialogues and notice the different greetings and the pronunciation.

Juliette	Salut Bernard!
Bernard	Salut! Ça va?
Juliette	Oui, ça va?

Bernard	Bonjour Madame!
Shopkeeper	Bonjour Monsieur!

Juliette	Bonsoir Monsieur!
Neighbour	Bonsoir!

b Listen to three other exchanges and decide which conversation matches with which picture.

| a | b | c |

Salut!   Bonsoir!   Salut Bernard!   Bonsoir Monsieur!   Ça va?   Au revoir!
Bonjour!   Au revoir Monsieur!   Bonjour Madame!   Bonne nuit!

2 Salut! Bonsoir!

Moving around the room, take on the role of different characters, at different times of the day, and greet each other, paying particular attention to your pronunciation and intonation.

1 ≣

3 Je suis …

Ecoutez les deux dialogues et soulignez les expressions pour se présenter. In the transcripts below, underline three different expressions to introduce oneself.

– Bonjour, je suis Hélène Dupuis. Et vous?
– Moi, je m'appelle Anne Petit.
– Je m'appelle Antoine Lebœuf.
– Moi, je m'appelle Jean-Marc Latour.

– Salut! Je m'appelle Alain, et toi?
– Moi, c'est Sabine.

Je m'appelle … / Je suis … / Moi, c'est …   Et vous?/Et toi?

4 Nationalités et professions

A deux, traduisez en anglais les nationalités et professions. With a partner, translate into English the following nationalities and occupations.

espagnol(e)
français(e)
irlandais(e)
africain(e)
italien(ne)
indien(ne)
sénégalais(e)
écossais(e)
grec(que)
allemand(e)
gallois(e)

secrétaire
infirmier (infirmière)
médecin
professeur
directeur (directrice)
étudiant(e)
avocat(e)
journaliste
serveur (serveuse)
technicien(ne)
vendeur (vendeuse)

grammaire

masculine	feminine	masculine or feminine
français	française	belge
italien	italienne	suisse
étudiant	étudiante	journaliste
infirmier	infirmière	secrétaire

5 Quelle nationalité?

Ecoutez 6 personnes. Using the list above, tick the nationalities and occupations that you hear.

6 Je suis anglais

Présentez-vous. Donnez votre nom, votre nationalité et votre profession. Moving around the room, introduce yourself, giving your name, nationality and occupation.

7 Masculin ou féminin?

Ecoutez les nationalités et professions et complétez les mots. Listen to a list of nationalities and occupations and write the end of the words.

a améric_____; **b** ind_____; **c** écoss_____; **d** belg_____; **e** allem_____;

f secrét_____; **g** étud_____; **h** technic_____; **i** vend_____; **j** infirm_____.

8 Je m'appelle ...

a Ecoutez Muriel et 6 autres personnes et remplissez les cases. Listen to Muriel and six other people and complete the grid below.

Muriel:

> Bonjour. Je m'appelle Muriel. Je suis française. Je suis vendeuse. Je suis de Bordeaux mais j'habite à Paris.

		nationalité	profession	origine	domicile
a	Electra			Rhodes	
b	Ravi		médecin		
c	Mesenge				Nice
d	Matthias		réceptionniste		
e	Silva			Barcelone	
f	Steve	gallois			

b Présentez-vous à la classe: nom, nationalité, profession, origine et domicile.

9 Compter

a Ecoutez la prononciation des nombres.

1 un	6 six	11 onze	16 seize	21 vingt et un
2 deux	7 sept	12 douze	17 dix-sept	22 vingt-deux
3 trois	8 huit	13 treize	18 dix-huit	23 vingt-trois
4 quatre	9 neuf	14 quatorze	19 dix-neuf	24 vingt-quatre
5 cinq	10 dix	15 quinze	20 vingt	25 vingt-cinq

30 trente   40 quarante   50 cinquante   60 soixante   70 soixante-dix

b Cochez les nombres. Tick the numbers.

☐ 1   ☐ 2   ☐ 3   ☐ 4   ☐ 6   ☐ 7   ☐ 8   ☐ 9
☐ 10   ☐ 12   ☐ 13   ☐ 14   ☐ 15   ☐ 18   ☐ 22   ☐ 25
☐ 27   ☐ 30   ☐ 31   ☐ 40   ☐ 42   ☐ 44   ☐ 55   ☐ 60

10 Vous êtes …?

Un colloque international: écoutez et complétez le dialogue.

– Bonjour, je m'_____**(a)** David Brown. Et vous (*looking at her badge*), vous êtes Stéphania Gardon?

– Oui, c'est _____**(b)**. Bonjour. Vous êtes anglais?

– Oui, et vous, vous êtes française?

– Non, je _____**(c)** sénégalaise. J'habite _____**(d)** Paris mais je _____**(e)** de Dakar. Et vous, vous êtes d'où?

– Je suis _____**(f)** Manchester. Je suis _____**(g)** de Funn Holly. Et vous, qu'est-ce que vous faites?

– Moi, je suis _____**(h)**.

grammaire

I	you (informal)	you (formal)
Je <u>suis</u> Stéphania.	Tu <u>es</u> Malika?	Vous <u>êtes</u> français?
Je m'appell<u>e</u> David.	Tu t'appell<u>es</u> Stéphane?	Vous vous appel<u>ez</u> Hélène?
Je travaill<u>e</u> dans un magasin.	Tu travaill<u>es</u>?	Vous travaill<u>ez</u> dans un magasin?
Je <u>fais</u> …	Qu'est-ce que tu <u>fais</u>?	Qu'est-ce que vous <u>faites</u>?
J'habit<u>e</u> à …	Tu habit<u>es</u> où?	Où habit<u>ez</u>-vous?

11 Questions

Imaginez que vous êtes Stéphania. Répondez aux questions et écrivez les réponses. A deux, lisez le dialogue, puis changez de rôle. Imagine that you are Stéphania (in the dialogue above). Take turns with a partner to answer the following questions orally and then write down the answers.

a Vous êtes Stéphania Gardon? _____

b Vous êtes de quelle nationalité? _____

c Vous êtes d'où? _____

d Qu'est-ce que vous faites? _____

12 Quelle est la question?

Joseph est au téléphone. Imaginez les questions. You hear your friend Joseph answering questions on the phone. Can you guess what questions are being asked?

a Oui, je m'appelle Joseph Toure.

b Non, je suis sénégalais.

c Je suis de Dakar.

d Je suis infirmier.

13 Je ne suis pas …

A deux, mettez les phrases dans l'ordre pour faire un dialogue. Re-order the sentences to make a dialogue. Then listen to the recording to check your answers.

a Je suis technicienne en informatique … Tu es algérien?

b Non, j'habite à Angers. Et toi, tu habites où?

c A Paris. Je suis étudiant à la Sorbonne. Et toi, qu'est-ce que tu fais?

d Mehdi. Tu habites ici?

e Non, je ne suis pas algérien, je suis marocain.

f Salut. Moi c'est Juliette. Comment tu t'appelles?

g Oui, je suis serveur dans un café.

h Et … tu travailles?

grammaire

Negative form

Tu es algérien?	Non, je <u>ne</u> suis <u>pas</u> algérien.
Tu habites à Paris?	Non, je <u>n'</u>habite <u>pas</u> à Paris.

14 Tu travailles?

Imaginez les questions. Utilisez "tu".

a Salut, moi c'est Janet.

b Je suis étudiante en maths, et toi?

c Oui, je suis anglaise.

d Je suis de Liverpool.

e J'habite à Newcastle.

f Non, je ne travaille pas.

15 Qu'est-ce que tu fais?

Posez des questions à 3 personnes de votre classe. Utilisez "tu" ou "vous".

	Personne 1 (tu)	Personne 2 (vous)	Personne 3 (tu)
Nom			
Profession			
Nationalité			
Domicile			
Origine			

16 Il est …/Elle est …

Lisez les fiches d'identité et complétez les phrases.

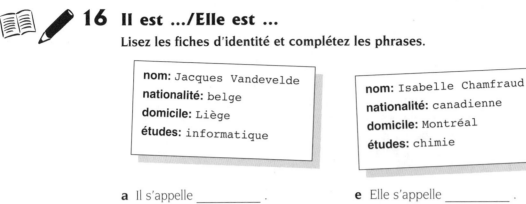

nom: Jacques Vandevelde
nationalité: belge
domicile: Liège
études: informatique

nom: Isabelle Chamfraud
nationalité: canadienne
domicile: Montréal
études: chimie

a Il s'appelle _____ .
b Il est _____ .
c Il habite _____ .
d Il est _____ en informatique.

e Elle s'appelle _____ .
f Elle est _____ .
g Elle habite _____ .
h Elle est _____ en chimie.

17 Il/Elle s'appelle …

A deux, lisez les fiches d'identité et présentez les personnes.

nom: Boris Neumann
nationalité: allemande
domicile: Berlin
études: histoire de l'art

nom: Nicos Micaleas
nationalité: grecque
domicile: Athènes
études: philosophie

nom: Rosa Fernandez
nationalité: espagnole
domicile: Alicante
études: géographie

nom: Pritti Patel
nationalité: indienne
domicile: Calcutta
études: droit

18 Il est étudiant

Ecoutez 4 personnes. Notez les informations et comparez à deux.

Extra!

 ## 1 Vous travaillez?

Une secrétaire pose des questions à 6 étudiants. Ecrivez les réponses (answers).
(NB: **Vous étudiez quoi?** = What are you studying?; **les études** = course)

	Nom	Nationalité	Domicile	Etudes	Travail
a					
b					
c					
d					
e					
f					

2 Un e-mail

> **A: rebec264@univ-tlse2.fr**
> **Objet: Salut!**
>
> Salut Rebecca,
>
> Comment ça va? Moi, ça va. Pour le moment, j'habite à Paris avec Bertrand, Lucille
> et leur bébé. Je suis étudiante en droit à la Sorbonne, c'est super! Je travaille aussi à
> mi-temps dans un bar comme serveuse. C'est un travail fatigant, mais c'est bien payé.
> Bertrand travaille à plein temps comme ingénieur. Il travaille à Versailles. Lucille ne
> travaille pas, elle s'occupe du bébé. Voilà. Ecris-moi!
>
> A bientôt,
>
> Stéphanie

a Where does Stéphanie live?

b What is she studying?

c What type of job does she do?

d What does Bertrand do for a living?

e Where does he work?

Grammaire/GRAMMAR

~ Gender

Each noun in French has a gender, either masculine (m) or feminine (f).

E.g. **le droit** (m)   **la chimie** (f)

Most words used to refer to people have a masculine and a feminine form.

E.g. **un étudiant** (m)   **une étudiante** (f)

The most common endings for nationalities and occupations are as follows:

ais (m) – aise (f)   (e.g. angl<u>ais</u>, angl<u>aise</u>)
ain (m) – aine (f)   (e.g. améric<u>ain</u>, améric<u>aine</u>)
ien (m) – ienne (f)   (e.g. ital<u>ien</u>, ital<u>ienne</u>)
ier (m) – ière (f)   (e.g. infirm<u>ier</u>, infirm<u>ière</u>)
eur (m) – euse (f)   (e.g. vend<u>eur</u>, vend<u>euse</u>)
teur (m) – trice (f)   (e.g. ac<u>teur</u>, ac<u>trice</u>)

~ Verbs

So far you have seen the verbs **être** (to be), **faire** (to do) and the **-er** verbs **habiter** (to live), **travailler** (to work) and **s'appeler** (to be called). You have been using the pronouns **je** (I), **tu** (you, informal), **il/elle** (he/she) and **vous** (you, formal). Notice the regular pattern of endings in verbs ending in **-er**:

je <u>suis</u>	je <u>fais</u>	j'habit<u>e</u>	je travaill<u>e</u>	je m'appell<u>e</u>
tu <u>es</u>	tu <u>fais</u>	tu habit<u>es</u>	tu travaill<u>es</u>	tu t'appell<u>es</u>
vous <u>êtes</u>	vous <u>faites</u>	vous habit<u>ez</u>	vous travaill<u>ez</u>	vous vous appel<u>ez</u>
il/elle <u>est</u>	il/elle <u>fait</u>	il/elle habit<u>e</u>	il/elle travaill<u>e</u>	il/elle s'appell<u>e</u>

~ Negatives

In order to make a sentence negative you need to add two words: **ne** before the verb and **pas** after the verb: e.g. **Je <u>ne</u> suis <u>pas</u> serveuse.** (Note: **ne** in front of a vowel or an **h** becomes **n'**.) When people speak fast, they tend to omit the **ne**: e.g. **je suis <u>pas</u> française.**

~ Asking questions

There are three ways of asking questions in French:

– in informal speech, just raising the intonation at the end of the sentence.

E.g. **Ça va? / Tu es anglais? / Vous êtes de Paris? / Il travaille dans un magasin?**

– in all situations, informal or formal, using **est-ce que** to signal that a question is being asked.

E.g. <u>**Est-ce que**</u> **tu es espagnole? /** <u>**Est-ce que**</u> **vous êtes vendeur? /** <u>**Est-ce qu'**</u>**elle habite à Londres?**

– in formal speech and in writing, inverting the verb and the subject pronoun.

E.g. **Êtes-vous de Bruxelles?**

Note the position of the question word in the following questions:

Tu habites <u>où</u>?	<u>Où</u> habitez-vous?
Tu es <u>d'où</u>?	<u>D'où</u> êtes-vous?
Tu t'appelles <u>comment</u>?	<u>Comment</u> vous appelez-vous?
	<u>Qu'est-ce que</u> tu fais/vous faites?

Exercices de grammaire

Gender

1 Look at the following list of nationalities and occupations. Fill in the masculine and feminine alternatives as appropriate.

Masculine (m)	Feminine (f)	Masculine (m)	Feminine (f)
a _____	espagnole	h infirmier	_____
b irlandais	_____	i _____	réceptionniste
c _____	sénégalaise	j secrétaire	_____
d gallois	_____	k _____	directrice
e _____	suisse	l vendeur	_____
f belge	_____	m _____	professeur
g _____	grecque	n étudiant	_____

Negatives

2 Use the information below to write a paragraph about each person described.

(–) false   (+) true

E.g. (–) Jean (+) français = Il ne s'appelle pas Jean. Il est français.

a (–) Mary (+) étudiante (–) américaine (+) Rome (–) bureau
b (+) Laurent (–) infirmier (+) français (–) Toulouse (+) café

Asking questions

3 Find the appropriate question(s) for the following answers, then, with a partner, imagine the possible context(s).

a Non, moi c'est Michèle.
b Je viens de Lyon. Et toi?
c Elle est avocate.
d Non, il ne travaille pas.
e J'habite à Edimbourg.
f Oui, je suis américaine.
g J'étudie l'anglais.
h Elle s'appelle Alice.

4 The words in the following sentences have been jumbled up: put them back in the right order to make questions.

a à / habite / elle / Marseille?
b il / qu' / fait / est-ce qu'?
c Londres / es / étudiant / tu / à?
d Rome / est-ce que / de / êtes / vous?
e t' / tu / comment / appelles?
f un / travaille / il / café / dans?
g vous / où / d' / êtes?
h pas / n' / anglaise / est / elle?

1 Toi et moi

Vocabulaire

~ Salutations — Greetings

Salut!	Hi!/Goodbye! (informal)
Bonjour!	Hello!
Bonsoir!	Good evening!
Bonne nuit!	Goodnight!
Au revoir!	Goodbye!
Ça va?/Ça va.	How are you?/I am fine.
madame	madam
monsieur	sir

~ Nationalités — Nationalities

français(e)	French
anglais(e)	English
écossais(e)	Scottish
irlandais(e)	Irish
sénégalais(e)	Senegalese
polonais(e)	Polish
gallois(e)	Welsh
danois(e)	Danish
suédois(e)	Swedish
américain(e)	American
marocain(e)	Moroccan
italien(ne)	Italian
indien(ne)	Indian
algérien(ne)	Algerian
canadien(ne)	Canadian
estonien(ne)	Estonian
norvégien(ne)	Norwegian
letton(ne)	Latvian
espagnol(e)	Spanish
allemand(e)	German
grec(que)	Greek
belge	Belgian
suisse	Swiss
russe	Russian
tchèque	Czech

~ Professions — Occupations

vendeur(euse)	sales assistant
serveur(euse)	waiter/tress
directeur(trice)	director
acteur(trice)	actor/tress
infirmier(ière)	nurse
technicien(ne)	technician
étudiant(e)	student
avocat(e)	lawyer
secrétaire	secretary
réceptionniste	receptionist
journaliste	journalist
médecin	doctor
chauffeur	driver
professeur	teacher
ingénieur	engineer

~ Études — Courses

l'informatique (f)	computing
la physique	physics
les mathématiques (f)	maths
la chimie	chemistry
la géographie	geography
la philosophie	philosophy
le droit	law
l'histoire (f) de l'art (m)	history of art

~ Lieux de travail — Work places

le magasin	shop
le bureau	office
le café	pub/café
le supermarché	supermarket
à mi-temps	part-time
à plein temps	full-time
les études (f)	studies
le domicile	residence

~ Pronoms — Pronouns

je	I
tu	you (informal)
vous	you (formal)
il	he
elle	she
moi	me
ce	it

~ Questions — Questions

Où?	Where?
Comment?	How?
Qu'est-ce que ...?	What ...?
oui / non	yes / no

~ Verbes — Verbs

être	to be
s'appeler	to be called
habiter	to live
travailler	to work
s'occuper (de)	to look after
faire	to do/to make
lire	to read
écrire	to write
écouter	to listen (to)
à/dans	in/at/to
de	from
avec	with
mais	but

Travail à deux

1 Se présenter

Introduce yourself to your partner. After greeting him/her, tell him/her:

your name
the town or city you are from
your nationality
where you live
that you are a student …
… and what you are studying
that you work (if you do) …
… and what your job is

When you have got all the information across, your partner will check it back with you.

Then swap roles.

2 Première rencontre

You meet someone in a bar. Introduce yourself to him/her and then tell him/her about your friend who has just left the bar, using the information below.

You are Alex Andrews. You are English and you come from Liverpool, but you live and work in New York as an engineer.

Your friend is Carmen Bradley. She is a manager and she works in Ireland. She has dual nationality (Irish and Spanish). She comes from Bilbao and lives in Dublin.

Your partner will then introduce himself/herself and tell you about his/her friend who has gone to the bathroom! In order to make sure that you have understood what your partner has said, fill in the following grid. Ask for repetition if necessary.

	your partner	**his/her friend**
Nom:		
Nationalité:		
Travail:		
Lieu de travail:		
Ville d'origine:		

Travail à deux

1 Se présenter

Greet your partner in French, then listen carefully to what s/he tells you, jotting down key words when it helps. You can ask for any items of information that you want again but you must request it in French.

Check with your partner that you have understood everything by repeating some of the information, e.g. **Tu es français**, **Tu ne travailles pas**, etc.

Then swap roles.

2 Première rencontre

You meet someone in a bar. S/he introduces him/herself and tells you about his/her friend who has just left the bar. In order to make sure that you have understood what your partner has said, fill in the following grid. Ask for repetition if necessary.

	your partner	his/her friend
Nom:		
Nationalité:		
Travail:		
Lieu de travail:		
Ville d'origine:		

Now introduce yourself and tell your partner about your friend who has gone to the bathroom!

Your name is Bernie Lyons. You are a taxi driver in Glasgow. You work part-time. You live in Paisley and originally come from Motherwell.
Your friend is Christos Panalopoulou. He is Greek. He is a teacher. He comes from Athens and he lives in Edinburgh. He is also studying literature.

Les autres

When you have completed this unit, you will be able to give and understand information about your friends and your family, ask and answer questions about age, and order drinks and snacks.

 1 Quel âge as-tu?

Ecoutez Maria et Pierre devant une boîte de nuit.
Listen to a dialogue outside a nightclub.

Maria	Tu as quel âge?
Pierre	J'ai 19 ans. Et toi?
Maria	Moi, j'ai 18 ans.
Bouncer	Quel âge avez-vous, mademoiselle?
Maria	J'ai 18 ans. Et il a 19 ans.

Tu <u>as</u> quel âge? / Vous <u>avez</u> quel âge?	J'<u>ai</u> 18 ans.
Quel âge <u>as</u>-tu? / Quel âge <u>avez</u>-vous?	
Elle/Il <u>a</u> quel âge?	Elle/Il <u>a</u> 19 ans.
Quel âge <u>a</u>-t-elle/il?	

2 Et toi, tu as quel âge?

Posez des questions à 5 personnes de votre classe. Utilisez "tu" ou "vous".

3 J'ai un copain ...

Ecoutez le dialogue au bar de l'université et cochez les mots que vous entendez.
Tick the words that you hear in the conversation.

salut!	bonjour!	tu travailles	j'ai un copain	congolais	j'ai vingt ans
français	tu as quel âge?	une copine			

Tu as des amis?   J'ai un copain/une copine.   Je n'ai pas de copain.

4 Ah! La famille!

a Ecoutez le dialogue et traduisez les mots ci-dessous. Translate the words below.

marié(e)	divorcé(e)	un fils	une fille
une femme	un mari	des enfants	

b Pourquoi la deuxième personne dit: "C'est compliqué!"? Why does she say "C'est compliqué!"?

5 Photos de famille

Nadia montre des photos de vacances à son ami Marc. Ecoutez et répondez aux questions. Listen to Nadia showing some holiday pictures to her friend Marc and answer the following questions:

a Who is next to her friend Anne in the first picture?

b Who are the other two people in the picture with Nadia?

c What job does Nadia's boyfriend do?

d How old is his daughter?

> C'est <u>ma</u> copine, avec <u>son</u> fils.   C'est <u>mon</u> copain, avec <u>sa</u> fille.   C'est <u>ton</u> copain?

grammaire

Possessive adjectives

<u>je</u>	<u>tu</u>	<u>il/elle</u>	<u>vous</u>
<u>mon</u> fils	<u>ton</u> fils	<u>son</u> fils	<u>votre</u> fils
<u>ma</u> fille	<u>ta</u> fille	<u>sa</u> fille	<u>votre</u> fille

Note the use of the possessive with **ami(e)** or **copain/copine** when referring to close relationships.
E.g. **C'est un copain** (a friend)
     C'est <u>mon</u> copain (my boyfriend)

6 C'est ma copine

Lisez et complétez le dialogue. Ensuite, écoutez la conversation et vérifiez vos réponses. Fill in the gaps with the appropriate word and then listen to check your answers.

– Elle s'appelle comment, _____ **(a)** copine?
– Elodie.
– Elle a _____ **(b)** âge?
– Dix-neuf _____ **(c)**.
– Et, _____ **(d)** est-ce qu'elle habite?
– Ici, _____ **(e)** Paris, mais elle _____ **(f)** de Marseille.
– Elle est _____ **(g)**?
– Oui, en biologie. Et elle _____ **(h)** le soir dans un supermarché.

7 Tu es marié(e)?

A deux, posez des questions. Find out as much as you can about each other's partner or friend. Write a short piece about that person and swap notes to check both the content and the language.

 8 La famille d'Hervé

Observez l'arbre généalogique de la famille d'Hervé et dites si les phrases ci-dessous sont vraies (true) ou fausses (false).

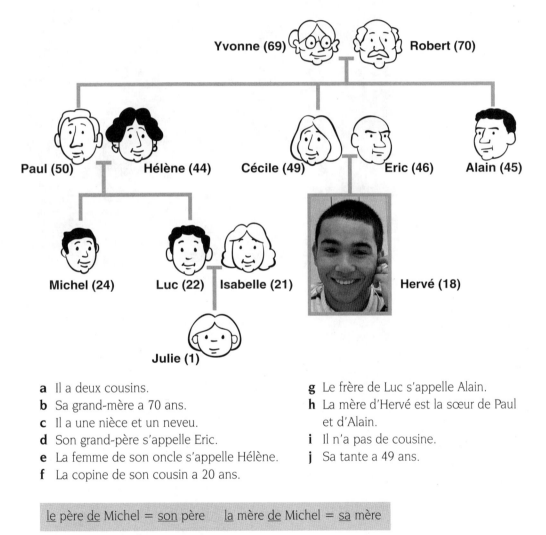

a Il a deux cousins.
b Sa grand-mère a 70 ans.
c Il a une nièce et un neveu.
d Son grand-père s'appelle Eric.
e La femme de son oncle s'appelle Hélène.
f La copine de son cousin a 20 ans.
g Le frère de Luc s'appelle Alain.
h La mère d'Hervé est la sœur de Paul et d'Alain.
i Il n'a pas de cousine.
j Sa tante a 49 ans.

le père de Michel = son père   la mère de Michel = sa mère

9 Mes copines et mes cousines ...

Mettez les phrases dans l'ordre pour faire un dialogue. Ensuite, écoutez la conversation pour vérifier vos réponses.

a Non, ce sont mes copines!

b Hélène, Rachel et Corinne.

c Elles habitent avec Didier?

d Ce sont tes cousines?

e Oui, ce sont ses sœurs!

f Comment s'appellent les trois filles, au bar?

grammaire		
Singular		Plural
C'est <u>ma/ta/sa</u> copine		Ce sont <u>mes/tes/ses</u> copines
C'est <u>mon/ton/son</u> copain		Ce sont <u>mes/tes/ses</u> copains
elle/il <u>s'appelle/habite</u>		elles/ils <u>s'appellent/habitent</u>
elle/il <u>a</u>		elles/ils <u>ont</u>
elle/il <u>est</u>		elles/ils <u>sont</u>

10 Ce sont ...

Mettez les phrases au pluriel.

E.g. **C'est mon frère.** > *Ce sont mes frères.*

a C'est ma copine.

b Il travaille à Londres.

c Il habite à Paris.

d C'est ton copain?

e Il a treize ans.

f Mon amie est étudiante.

11 Nos enfants ...

Nadia montre des photos à son ami Marc. Ecoutez et dites si les phrases sont vraies (V) ou fausses (F).

a Her daughter is three years old.

b Michel is a cousin of hers.

c Michel's children are not in the picture.

d The two couples' children are friends.

e The cousins have jobs.

f They live in Paris.

> C'est <u>votre</u> fille, à Michel et à toi?   Oui, c'est <u>notre</u> fille.
> <u>Nous habitons</u> dans la même rue.   Ce sont mes cousins et <u>leurs</u> amis.

12 Tu veux un café?

Lisez les dialogues et choisissez l'image correspondante. Ecoutez les 3 conversations.

1

2

3

a – Bonjour monsieur, vous voulez une bière?
   – Oui, merci.
   – Vous voulez un croque-monsieur ou un sandwich peut-être?
   – Non merci, juste une bière.

b – Salut Béatrice, ça va?
   – Oui, ça va bien merci.
   – Tu veux un café?
   – Ah, oui, merci.
   – Et un croissant?
   – Non, merci.

c – Salut Josette, ça va?
   – Bien, merci.
   – C'est ta fille?
   – Oui, c'est ma fille Manon.
   – Manon, tu veux une glace?
   – Oui, merci.

> Tu veux un thé?   Tu veux une limonade?
> Vous voulez un sandwich?   Vous voulez une bière?
> Tu veux quelque chose à boire?   Vous voulez quelque chose à manger?

13 Pas pour moi, merci

Lisez la conversation entre 3 amies et complétez les phrases. Ecoutez le dialogue et vérifiez vos réponses.

Marie	Salut Bettina, _____ **(a)** va?
Bettina	Oui, très bien merci.
Marie	Bettina, je te présente Juliette, _____ **(b)** sœur.
Bettina	Bonjour Juliette.
Juliette	Bonjour Bettina.
Marie	Tu _____ **(c)** un café ou un thé peut-être?
Bettina	Oui, _____ **(d)** café s'il te plaît.
Marie	Et toi Juliette?
Juliette	_____ **(e)** chocolat chaud pour moi.
Marie	Bettina, tu veux quelque chose à _____ **(f)** aussi?
Bettina	Ah non, pas pour moi _____ **(g)**.
Marie	Et toi, Juliette?
Juliette	Oui, _____ **(h)** croissant, s'il te plaît.

un café	un coca	un sandwich	une glace
un thé	une limonade	un croque-monsieur	une pâtisserie
un chocolat chaud	un citron pressé	un croissant	un gâteau

un sandwich	une glace
au jambon	au chocolat
au fromage	à la vanille
au saucisson	à la fraise

14 Un thé, peut-être?

A deux, proposez-vous l'un(e) à l'autre quelque chose à boire et à manger.

Extra!

 ## 1 La famille et les amis

Listen to three students who are talking about their friends and their family. Make some notes in the grid below before writing a short summary in English.

	Family	Friends	Places mentioned
François			
Anne-Marie			
Gabriella			

 ## 2 Un mail à une amie

Jane, who is learning French, writes an email to her new friend in France, Monique.

> **A: m.jolly@hotmail.fr**
> **Objet: Bonjour d'Angleterre**
>
> Chère Monique,
>
> C'est moi, Jane, ta copine anglaise. J'ai vingt et un ans. Je suis de Southport, mais j'habite à Liverpool parce que je suis étudiante en histoire à l'université. J'habite dans un appartement avec deux amies et leurs copains. Moi, je n'ai pas de copain, mais j'ai beaucoup d'amis. Je travaille à mi-temps dans un cinéma. Le reste de ma famille habite à Southport: mes parents et mes quatre sœurs! Une sœur est mariée (j'ai un petit neveu qui a deux ans!) et les trois autres sont toujours à la maison. Et toi? Quel âge as-tu? Est-ce que tu as un copain?
>
> A bientôt,
>
> Jane

a How old is Jane?
b Why does she live in Liverpool?
c With how many people does she live?
d Does she have a boyfriend?
e How many brothers and sisters does she have?
f Where do they live?

Grammaire

~ Verbs

You will notice that a number of the verbs that you have used so far end in **er**.

E.g.   **travaill<u>er</u>** = to work   **habit<u>er</u>** = to live

Here are the plural endings for **-er** verbs (used when talking about more than one person)

nous travaill<u>ons</u>	nous habit<u>ons</u>	we
vous travaill<u>ez</u>	vous habit<u>ez</u>	you
ils/elles travaill<u>ent</u>	ils/elles habit<u>ent</u>	they

Vous is used formally for one or more people, informally only for more than one.

Avoir means 'to have'. Note that in French **avoir** is used to talk about age.
E.g.   **Tu as quel âge?   J'ai 20 ans.**
This verb does not follow a regular pattern.

J'<u>ai</u> un ami	Nous <u>avons</u> une copine.
Tu <u>as</u> une amie?	Vous <u>avez</u> un ami.
Il/elle <u>a</u> un copain.	Ils/elles <u>ont</u> un ami.

~ Possessive adjectives (my, your, his/her, our, their)

<u>je</u>	<u>tu</u>	<u>il/elle</u>	<u>nous</u>	<u>vous</u>	<u>ils/elles</u>
<u>mon</u> père	<u>ton</u> père	<u>son</u> père	<u>notre</u> père	<u>votre</u> père	<u>leur</u> père
<u>ma</u> mère	<u>ta</u> mère	<u>sa</u> mère	<u>notre</u> mère	<u>votre</u> mère	<u>leur</u> mère
<u>mes</u> parents	<u>tes</u> parents	<u>ses</u> parents	<u>nos</u> parents	<u>vos</u> parents	<u>leurs</u> parents

Possessive adjectives agree in gender (masculine or feminine) and number (singular or plural) with the thing or person that is 'possessed'. So, depending on what follows, 'my' will be translated by either **mon**, **ma** or **mes**. Similarly, 'his' or 'her' (no matter which one) will be translated by **son**, **sa** or **ses**, etc.

~ un, le or mon?

So far, you have seen three types of words which can go before a noun: (i) **un/une/des**, (ii) **le** (or **l'**)/**la** (or **l'**)/**les** and (iii) the possessive adjectives (see above).

(i) **un**, etc. is used when the person or thing referred to is not specified (e.g. **Il travaille dans un magasin.**): we don't know which shop.

(ii) **le**, etc. is used to refer to a specific person or thing which can be identified by the person you are talking to (e.g. **C'est <u>la</u> copine de Paul.**): not just a friend of Paul's but his girlfriend.

(iii) possessives are used when the person or thing referred to is specified as 'belonging' to someone (e.g. **Il est dans <u>mon</u> groupe.** : my group / **C'est <u>ma</u> copine.** : my girlfriend).

Exercices de grammaire

Verbs

1 Read the following text and replace the infinitive verbs in italics with the appropriate form.

E.g. **Elle *travailler* à Lyon.** > *Elle travaille à Lyon.*

La famille Lemire (*habiter*) **a** à Paris. Luc et Marie-Claude Lemire (*avoir*) **b** un fils et un chien. Leur fils (*s'appeler*) **c** Marcel et il (*avoir*) **d** vingt-deux ans. Il (*être*) **e** étudiant en histoire de l'art. Marcel (*travailler*) **f** aussi dans un supermarché. Son chien (*s'appeler*) **g** Toby. Marcel (*avoir*) **h** une copine, Gabriella. Elle (*être*) **i** italienne. Elle (*être*) **j** de Rome mais elle (*habiter*) **k** à Paris. Elle (*travailler*) **l** comme vendeuse dans un magasin. Elle (*avoir*) **m** dix-neuf ans.

Possessive adjectives

2 Read the following dialogue and fill in the blanks with an appropriate possessive adjective.

Isabelle, who lives with her sister, tells her new friend Josée about the rest of the family:

Isabelle: _____ **(a)** sœur et moi, nous habitons à Paris, mais _____ **(b)** parents habitent en Normandie. _____ **(c)** père est agriculteur. Nous avons un frère qui est marié. _____ **(d)** femme s'appelle Raymonde, elle est présentatrice de télévision. Ils habitent aussi à Paris, avec _____ **(e)** deux enfants.

Josée: Et _____ **(f)** copain, il habite avec vous?

Isabelle: Non, il habite avec _____ **(g)** cousin qui est aussi étudiant.

un, le or mon?

3 Read the following sentences and select the appropriate form(s). (There may be more than one).

a Comment s'appelle une/la/ta copine?
b Nous habitons avec une/la/notre sœur.
c Tu as des/les/tes enfants?
d Elle travaille dans un/le/son supermarché.
e Un/Le/Mon professeur est de Genève.
f Un/Le/Son copain est étudiant en chimie.
g C'est un/le/son frère de Jacqueline.
h J'habite avec un/le/mon ami.
i C'est un/le/votre mari?
j Tu veux un/le/ton café?

2 Les autres

Vocabulaire

L'âge

L'âge	Age
quel âge ...?	how old ...?
sept ans	seven years old
mademoiselle	miss

La famille

La famille	The family
le mari	husband
la femme	wife
le copain, l'ami	boyfriend, friend (m)
la copine, l'amie	girlfriend, friend (f)
les parents	parents
le père	father
la mère	mother
les enfants	children
le fils	son
la fille	daughter/girl
le frère	brother
la sœur	sister
le beau-père	stepfather/father-in-law
la belle-mère	stepmother/mother-in-law
le demi-frère	half-brother
la demi-sœur	half-sister
les grands-parents	grandparents
le grand-père	grandfather
la grand-mère	grandmother
l'oncle	uncle
la tante	aunt
le cousin	cousin (m)
la cousine	cousin (f)
le neveu	nephew
la nièce	niece

Au café

Au café	At the snack bar
le café	coffee
le thé	tea
le chocolat chaud	hot chocolate
la bière	beer
la limonade	lemonade
le coca	Coke
le citron pressé	fresh lemon juice
le croque-monsieur	toasted ham and cheese sandwich
le gâteau	cake
le biscuit	biscuit
la pâtisserie	pastry
le croissant	croissant
le sandwich	sandwich
le jambon	ham
le fromage	cheese
le saucisson	salami, cured meat
le chocolat	chocolate
la glace	ice cream
la vanille	vanilla
la fraise	strawberry
l'orange pressée (f)	fresh orange juice
merci	thank you
s'il te/vous plaît	please
boire	to drink
manger	to eat
vouloir	to want
quelque chose	something
aussi	also, too

Le travail et la maison

Le travail et la maison	Home and work
le soir	in the evening
le supermarché	supermarket
l'appartement	flat
la maison	house
la boîte (de nuit)	(night)club

22

Travail à deux

1 Mon frère

Your friend is asking you questions about your brother. Answer them using the following information.

He is 27 years old.
He is a student of biology.
He lives in Manchester.
He works in a café.
He is divorced.
He has two children, a five-year-old daughter and a three-year-old son.
The children live in Bolton with their mother.
He has a girlfriend. She is a teacher.

2 Un(e) vieil(le) ami(e)

In a café, you are meeting a friend you have not seen for a long time. Use the following prompts. You start the conversation.

– Say: 'Hello!'
– Ask: 'How are you?'
– Ask: 'Do you want something to drink?'
– Ask: 'Where do you live?'
– Say: 'I live in Limoges too.'
– Say: 'No, I work in an office.' Ask: 'Are you married?'
– Ask: 'How old is your son?'
– Ask: 'Do you want something to eat?'

3 Au bar

You are in a bar with a friend. Ask each other what snacks and drinks you would like. Your partner will start the conversation.

La carte déjeuner

Sandwiches baguettes
jambon beurre
fromage
saucisson
thon mayonnaise

Glaces
vanille
chocolat
fraise
café

Boissons
café
thé
eau minérale

Travail à deux

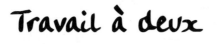

1 Mon frère

You are asking your friend questions about her/his brother. Find out the following information. You will start the conversation.

How old is he?
What does he do?
Where does he live?
Is he working?
Is he married?
Has he got children?
Where do the children live?
Does he have a girlfriend?

You can use the questions below to guide you if you wish:

Est-ce qu'il a une copine?   Où habitent les enfants?   Est-ce qu'il travaille?
Quel âge a-t-il?   Qu'est-ce qu'il fait?   Où habite-t-il?
Est-ce qu'il a des enfants?   Est-ce qu'il est marié?

2 Un(e) vieil(le) ami(e)

In a café, you are meeting a friend you have not seen for a long time. Use the following prompts. Your partner will start the conversation.

– Say: 'Hello.'
– Say: 'I am very well.'
– Say: 'I would like a Coke.'
– Say: 'I live in Limoges.'
– Ask: 'Are you a student?'
– Say: 'No, I am not married but I have a son.'
– Say: 'He is two years old.'
– Say: 'I would like a sandwich.'

3 Au bar

You are in a bar with a friend. Ask each other what snacks and drinks you would like. You start the conversation.

La carte déjeuner

Sandwiches baguettes
jambon beurre
fromage
saucisson
thon mayonnaise

Glaces
vanille
chocolat
fraise
café

Boissons
café
thé
eau minérale

3 La routine

When you have completed this unit, you will be able to talk about everyday activities; ask for/give the time; explain when you do things; say what you like/dislike doing and what you have to do.

1 Qu'est-ce que tu fais?

Regardez les images et observez les expressions en français.

Ils regardent la télévision.   Elles écoutent un CD.   Il mange un sandwich.

Elle fait des courses.   Il lit un livre.   Elle écrit une lettre.

2 Je fais la cuisine

Ecoutez 6 conversations au téléphone et écrivez les activités mentionnées.
(NB: **une dissertation** = an essay)

Qu'est-ce que tu fais/vous faites?	Je regarde la télé.
	Je lis un livre.
	Je fais une dissertation.
	Rien de spécial.

grammaire

regarder (to watch)	lire (to read)	écrire (to write)	faire (to do/to make)
je regarde	je lis	j'écris	je fais
tu regardes	tu lis	tu écris	tu fais
il/elle regarde	il/elle lit	il/elle écrit	il/elle fait
nous regardons	nous lisons	nous écrivons	nous faisons
vous regardez	vous lisez	vous écrivez	vous faites
ils/elles regardent	ils/elles lisent	ils/elles écrivent	ils/elles font

3 Tu parles!

A deux, mimez des activités.
(Exemple: – Qu'est-ce que je fais? – Tu écris une lettre.)

 4 Faire le ménage ou une promenade?

Trouvez l'expression en anglais qui correspond à l'expression en français.

1 faire le ménage	**a** to go sailing
2 faire une promenade	**b** to play the piano
3 faire du sport	**c** to go swimming/to go to the swimming pool
4 faire du vélo	**d** to play sport
5 faire de la voile	**e** to do the housework
6 jouer au football	**f** to go to the cinema
7 jouer du piano	**g** to go for a walk
8 aller au cinéma	**h** to go cycling
9 aller à la piscine	**i** to go to a nightclub/to go clubbing
10 aller en boîte	**j** to play football

5 Qu'est-ce que tu fais ce week-end?

Ecoutez Gabrielle et Bertrand qui parlent de leur week-end et répondez aux questions. (NB: **aujourd'hui** = today; **demain** = tomorrow)

a Whose turn is it to do the housework?
b Where is Bertrand going with his friend Michel?
c What is he doing afterwards?
d What is Gabrielle doing tonight?
e Who is going with her?
f What is she doing tomorrow after her piano lesson?

 grammaire

Je vais <u>au</u> cinéma.	Je joue <u>au</u> football.	Je joue <u>du</u> piano
Je vais <u>à la</u> piscine.	Je joue <u>à la</u> balle.	Je joue <u>de la</u> guitare.

 6 Ce soir, je vais au restaurant

A deux, demandez et expliquez ce que vous faites ce soir (tonight) et ce week-end.

7 Il est quelle heure?

Regardez les horloges (clocks) et lisez les expressions pour dire l'heure.

a Il est midi/douze heures.   **b** Il est quatre heures.   **c** Il est onze heures dix.

d Il est neuf heures moins vingt/huit heures quarante.   **e** Il est une heure et demie/une heure trente.   **f** Il est minuit et quart/zéro heure quinze.

Il est	une heure	cinq/dix/vingt/ …
	deux heures	et quart
	trois heures	et demie
	…	moins cinq/dix/vingt/ …
	midi/minuit	moins le quart

8 Il est minuit

a Ecoutez 6 conversations et écrivez l'heure.

a _____	b _____	c _____
d _____	e _____	f _____

b Ecoutez encore une fois les conversations et écrivez les différentes questions pour demander l'heure.

9 Tu as l'heure?

Working with a partner, draw six blank clock faces each and secretly write down six different times each. Take turns to ask each other what the time is and fill in the answers on your blank clocks. Check to see if your answers are correct.

3 La routine

 **10 Les jours de la semaine**

Put the days of the week in the correct order. **Ecoutez et vérifiez vos réponses.**

mercredi – lundi – dimanche – mardi – jeudi – samedi – vendredi

 11 Fermé le dimanche

A deux, traduisez en anglais les heures d'ouverture et de fermeture (opening and closing times**).**

a Ouvert de 9h à 13h, du lundi au vendredi.

b Fermé le week-end.

c Ouvert de midi à 16h, le mardi et le jeudi.

d Fermé le dimanche après-midi de 13h à 15h.

e Ouvert le soir de 18h à 21h.

Heures d'ouverture de votre boutique SNCF
du **lundi** au **vendredi** de 9h00 à 19h45
le **samedi** de 9h00 à 18h15
Ventes et informations SNCF
Grandes Lignes

ouvert	fermé	le matin	l'après-midi
le soir	le week-end	le lundi	de midi à 14 heures

12 La routine

a Ecoutez Nicolas qui décrit sa journée (day) à l'université. Cochez (✓) les verbes que vous entendez.

je mange	je prends	je travaille	j'habite
j'étudie	je pars	je termine	j'ai
j'arrive	je finis	je vais	je suis
je regarde	je commence		

b Ecoutez encore une fois et dites si les phrases sont vraies ou fausses. (NB: **petit déjeuner** = breakfast; **déjeuner** = lunch)

i Il prend son petit déjeuner à 8h.
ii Les cours commencent à midi.
iii Il termine à 14h.
iv Il prend son déjeuner à 13h.
v Il travaille à la bibliothèque jusqu'à 16h.
vi Il va à la piscine entre 16h30 et 18h.
vii Le soir il prend le train.
viii Il arrive à la maison à 19h.

grammaire

Je prends mon petit déjeuner.
Je prends le bus.
Je commence les cours à 9 heures et je termine à 5 heures.
Je finis mon travail.
J'arrive à la maison à 6 heures. Je pars à 5 heures.

je prends
tu prends
il/elle prend
nous prenons
vous prenez
ils/elles prennent

13 A quelle heure …?

A deux, posez-vous les questions ci-dessous.

A quelle heure …

a … est-ce que tu prends ton petit déjeuner?

b … est-ce que tu commences tes cours?

c … est-ce que tu finis?

d … est-ce que tu vas à la bibliothèque?

e … est-ce que tu arrives à la maison?

14 Qu'est-ce que tu aimes faire?

Ecoutez 4 personnes qui expliquent ce qu'elles aiment (like) faire. <u>Soulignez</u> les erreurs dans les phrases ci-dessous.

a J'aime le sport. J'aime l'athlétisme.

b J'aime le ski et je n'aime pas la planche à voile.

c J'aime beaucoup le football et je déteste le rugby.

d J'aime bien le cinéma mais je n'aime pas le théâtre.

J'aime bien (+)	J'aime (++)	J'aime beaucoup (+++)
Je n'aime pas beaucoup (–)	Je n'aime pas (– –)	Je déteste (– – –)

15 J'aime bien le sport

Lisez et complétez le texte. Ecoutez pour vérifier vos réponses.

J'aime bien le sport. J'aime _____**(a)** à la piscine et j'aime _____**(b)** au tennis. J'aime aussi _____**(c)** au ping-pong et au volley-ball. J'aime beaucoup _____**(d)** de l'athlétisme, surtout de la course. Je n'aime pas beaucoup _____**(e)** du ski et je déteste _____**(f)** aux fléchettes.

3 La routine

16 Je déteste la gym!

Ecoutez 4 dialogues. Put a tick by the things that the speakers like doing and a cross by the ones that they dislike doing.

a Archie	going swimming	☐	**c** Electra	going to the gym	☐
	playing football	☐		going shopping	☐
	playing rugby	☐		listening to music	☐
	going to the cinema	☐		going to the theatre	☐
b Thomas	going dancing	☐	**d** Claudia	watching television	☐
	playing sport	☐		playing cards	☐
	going cycling	☐		doing yoga	☐
	going windsurfing	☐		cooking	☐

grammaire

J'aime <u>jouer</u> au tennis.   J'aime beaucoup <u>faire</u> du sport.   Je n'aime pas <u>lire</u>.

17 Tu dois travailler!

Quel est le problème de Catherine? Lisez le dialogue pour répondre à la question. Ensuite, écoutez la prononciation.

Catherine	Pierre, qu'est-ce que je dois faire?
Pierre	Tu as un problème?
Catherine	Oui, c'est dimanche soir et je n'ai pas fini ma dissertation et je dois finir ce soir.
Pierre	Il est huit heures, tu as le temps!
Catherine	Mais je voudrais regarder la télé!
Pierre	Ecoute Catherine, tu dois travailler!

Qu'est-ce que je <u>dois</u> faire?   Tu <u>dois</u> travailler.   Vous <u>devez</u> travailler.

18 Qu'est-ce que je dois faire?

A deux, donnez des conseils (advice). Utilisez le verbe "devoir".
(Exemple: – Je suis trés fatigué(e). – Tu dois aller au lit.)

a Je n'ai pas d'argent.

b Nous n'avons pas de lait.

c Zut! La bibliothèque est fermée.

d Oh là là! Il est 3 heures.

e Je n'ai pas fini ma dissertation.

f Le bus n'arrive pas.

Extra!

🎧 1 Le week-end

Listen to three people describing their weekend and list three activities below.

Ricardo _____

_____

_____

_____

Anne _____

_____

_____

_____

Daniela _____

_____

_____

_____

2 J'aime rester au lit

Read through a description of Madeleine's weekend and answer the questions below.

Le week-end je suis toujours très occupée. Le samedi j'aime beaucoup faire des courses avec mes amis. D'habitude nous prenons le petit déjeuner ensemble à neuf heures et puis nous allons au centre-ville. Nous faisons le tour des magasins et puis nous déjeunons ensemble vers une heure. Le samedi après-midi je vais à la gym ou à la piscine avec ma copine Hélène. Le samedi soir j'aime sortir avec mes amis aussi. Souvent, nous allons au restaurant et puis nous regardons un film ou bien nous allons dans un bar ou en boîte. Le dimanche, par contre, j'aime faire la grasse matinée, j'aime rester au lit jusqu'à midi.

a What does Madeleine like doing on Saturday mornings?

b At what time does she have breakfast?

c What does she often do at about one o'clock?

d Name two things she might do on a Saturday afternoon.

e Describe a typical Saturday evening.

f What time does Madeleine get up on Sundays?

Grammaire

~ à and de followed by le or les

Some verbs can be constructed with a preposition (**à** or **de**), for example **aller à**, **jouer à** (+ game), **jouer de** (+ musical instrument). When **à** and **de** are followed by the articles **le** or **les**, they always merge as follows:

à + le > <u>au</u>	de + le > <u>du</u>	E.g. **Je vais <u>au</u> parc. / Nous allons <u>à la</u> piscine.**
à + la = à la	de + la = de la	
à + l' = à l'	de + l' = de l'	**Ils jouent <u>au</u> football. / Elle joue <u>de la</u> guitare.**
à + les > <u>aux</u>	de + les > <u>des</u>	

~ aller

The very useful verb **aller** (to go) is the only **-er** verb which does not follow the regular pattern: **je v<u>ais</u>, tu v<u>as</u>, il/elle v<u>a</u>, nous all<u>ons</u>, vous all<u>ez</u>, ils/elles v<u>ont</u>**

~ Verbs ending in -ir and -re

Most verbs ending in **-ir** and **-re** follow a regular pattern when conjugated.
There are two types of verb ending in **-ir**, the **partir** and **sortir** type and the **finir** type.

pren<u>dre</u>	**part<u>ir</u>** (to leave)	**fin<u>ir</u>** (to finish)
pren<u>ds</u>	je par<u>s</u>	je fin<u>is</u>
pren<u>ds</u>	tu par<u>s</u>	tu fin<u>is</u>
pren<u>d</u>	il/elle par<u>t</u>	il/elle fin<u>it</u>
pren<u>ons</u>	nous part<u>ons</u>	nous fin<u>issons</u>
pren<u>ez</u>	vous part<u>ez</u>	vous fin<u>issez</u>
pren<u>nent</u>	ils/elles part<u>ent</u>	ils/elles fin<u>issent</u>

The present tense in French can express both something that you do and something that you are doing. E.g. **Je vais au parc.** = 'I go to the park' or 'I am going to the park'.

~ aimer and devoir

If you want to say that you or someone likes something, you need to use the <u>article</u> **le/la/les/l'**. E.g. **J'aime le football. / Elles aiment la danse. / Il aime les fléchettes.**

If you want to say that you like doing something, e.g. 'I like playing golf', you need to use the infinitive after the verb. E.g. **Il aime regarder la télévision. / Nous aimons jouer au tennis. / Elles aiment faire de la natation.**

The verb **devoir** is used to indicate that you must do something. Note again that the infinitive is used after the verb. E.g.

Je dois aller à la banque.　　　**Il/elle doit rester au lit.**
Vous dev<u>ez</u> arrêter de fumer.　　**Nous dev<u>ons</u> faire du sport.**

Exercices de grammaire

à and de followed by le or les

1 Complete the following sentences with the correct pronoun (**je**, **tu**, **il**, **elle**, **nous**, **vous**, **ils**, **elles**) and the appropriate preposition (**à** or **de**) combined with the article (e.g. **au**, **à la**, **à l'**, **aux**, **du**, **de la**, **de l'**, **des**). E.g. **Je joue au football**.

a _____ jouons _____ piano.   **d** _____ allez _____ université?

b _____ joues _____ tennis.   **e** _____ jouent _____ cartes.

c _____ vais _____ cinéma.   **f** _____ vas _____ piscine?

aimer and devoir

2 Read the following text and put the verb in italics in the appropriate form.

Je suis très active et je **a** *aimer* faire du sport. Deux fois par semaine je **b** *aller* à la piscine et j'aime aussi **c** *faire* du yoga. Je **d** *n'aimer pas* lire. Le weekend je **e** *sortir* avec mes amis. Nous **f** *aller* au cinéma ou au théâtre et après nous **g** *aimer* aller au café ou au bar ensemble. Mon copain **h** *n'être* pas très sportif. Il **i** *préférer* faire des choses plus tranquilles, par exemple il **j** *aimer* aller à la pêche et surtout il **k** *adorer* regarder la télévision.

3 How would you say the following in French?
   a Do you (*formal*) like playing sport?   **d** He does not like going to the cinema.
   b She does not like swimming.   **e** I like watching television.
   c We really like playing cards.

4 Re-order the following jumbled sentences.
   a à/dimanche/l'église/matin/il/aller/le/doit   **d** quelque/tu/boire/chose/dois
   b soir/ce/je/sortir/dois   **e** après-midi/devons/cet/travailler/nous
   c lit/au/doivent/ils/aller   **f** faire/vous/du/sport/devez

3 La routine

Vocabulaire

~ Les jours de la semaine — Days of the week
lundi	Monday
mardi	Tuesday
mercredi	Wednesday
jeudi	Thursday
vendredi	Friday
samedi	Saturday
dimanche	Sunday
fermé	shut
ouvert	open

~ Les repas — Meals
le petit déjeuner	breakfast
le déjeuner	lunch
le dîner	evening meal
prendre	to take
manger	to eat

~ Quand? — When?
avant	before
après	after
quand?	when?
à quelle heure?	what time?
à 1 heure	at 1 o'clock
de 3 heures à 5 heures	from 3 o'clock to 5 o'clock
les cours (m)	lectures, lessons
toujours	always
le matin	in the morning
l'après-midi (m) or (f)	in the afternoon
le soir	in the evening
le week-end	at the weekend
aujourd'hui	today
demain	tomorrow
à la maison	at home
devoir	to have to

~ Les loisirs — Leisure activities
regarder la télévision	to watch television
écouter de la musique	to listen to music
lire un livre	to read a book
aller à la gym/piscine	to go to the gym/ swimming pool
aller au cinéma/ théâtre	to go to the cinema/ theatre
aller en boîte	to go to a nightclub/ to go clubbing
écrire une lettre	to write a letter
écouter un CD	to listen to a CD
jouer du piano/violon	to play the piano/violin
jouer de la guitare	to play the guitar
jouer au tennis/aux fléchettes/au football	to play tennis/darts/ football
jouer à la balle/ pétanque	to play ball/boules
faire une dissertation	to write an essay
faire le ménage	to do the housework
ne rien faire de spécial	to do nothing special
faire de l'aérobic/ l'athlétisme	to do aerobics/to do athletics
faire du sport	to do sport
faire du vélo/yoga/ footing	to cycle/to do yoga/ to go jogging
faire du rugby/volleyball	to play rugby/volleyball
faire du ping-pong	to play table tennis
faire de la marche/ danse/photographie	to go walking/to do dancing/to do photography
faire de la planche à voile/la voile	to go windsurfing/to go sailing
faire des courses	to do the shopping
faire la cuisine	to cook
aimer bien/beaucoup	to like/like a lot
préférer/détester	to prefer/detest

Travail à deux

1 Tu aimes …?

Working with a partner, use the prompts below to ask about the different types of things s/he likes and dislikes doing. You start.

– Do you like to play sport?

– What different types of sport do you like doing?

– What different types of sport do you not like doing?

– What do you like to do at the weekend?

2 Prendre rendez-vous

You are trying to organise a meeting with your partner. Look at your diary below and ask your partner whether he or she is free at the times of the day you are available. S/he will try to find out when you are available. E.g. – **Tu es libre mardi matin? – Non, je ne suis pas libre, je …**

lundi	10h00 – 12h00 anglais / 2h00 – 5h00 séminaire
mardi	rendez-vous chez le dentiste 10h15
mercredi	9h00 – 10h30 chimie / 6h00 match de foot
jeudi	2h00 bibliothèque / 7h00 piscine
vendredi	9h30 – 12h30 maths / 2h00 – 4h00 biologie
samedi	2h30 rendez-vous avec Richard / 8h00 cinéma
dimanche	12h00 déjeuner chez grand-mère

Travail à deux

1 Tu aimes ...?

Working with a partner, use the prompts below to answer questions about the different types of things you like and dislike doing. Your partner will start.

– You like playing sport a lot.

– You like swimming, jogging and cycling. You also like watching football.

– You do not like watching or playing rugby. You hate golf!

– At the weekend you like to go shopping on Saturdays and in the evenings you often go out with friends to the cinema or to a bar. On Sundays you go swimming or you go to the gym.

2 Prendre rendez-vous

You are trying to organise a meeting with your partner. Look at your diary below and ask your partner whether he or she is free at the times of the day you are available. S/he will try to find out when you are available. E.g. **– Tu es libre mardi matin? – Non, je ne suis pas libre, je ...**

lundi	0h30 – 1h00 linguistique / 6h00 supermarché
mardi	10h00 – 12h30 espagnol / 2h00 – 4h00 littérature / 6h00 supermarché
mercredi	2h00 – 4h30 séminaire / 6h00 supermarché
jeudi	3h00 – 5h00 poésie / 6h00 supermarché
vendredi	10h00 – 12h30 espagnol / 6h00 supermarché
samedi	8h30 anniversaire Jacqueline
dimanche	2h00 tennis

4 En ville

When you have completed this unit, you will be able to understand street signs, ask for and give directions, describe locations, shop for clothes and food, count beyond seventy, and express preferences.

 ## 1 Où est la gare?

Observez les photos ci-dessous. Indicate which sign you would need to follow if:

a you wanted to send a postcard;

b you needed to buy medication;

c you wanted to use the underground;

d you had badly hurt yourself;

e you wanted to travel to another town;

f you wanted information about the town;

g you needed to get an official document;

h you were looking for the name of a street.

1 L'Hôtel de ville

2 La rue de la Monnaie

3 La pharmacie

4 La station de métro

5 L'hôpital

6 La poste

7 La gare SNCF

8 L'office du tourisme

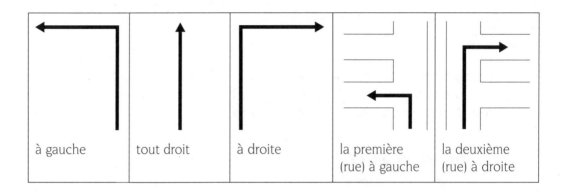

| à gauche | tout droit | à droite | la première (rue) à gauche | la deuxième (rue) à droite |

2 Pardon monsieur!

Ecoutez 4 conversations et complétez les dialogues.

a – Pardon monsieur, où est la gare, s'il vous plaît?
  – C'est là, tout _____.
  – Ah! Merci.

b – Pardon madame, vous savez où est l'Hôtel de ville, s'il vous plaît?
  – Alors, vous allez tout droit, et c'est … la deuxième à _____.
  – Merci beaucoup.
  – Je vous en prie.

c – Pardon, il y a une station de métro près d'ici?
  – Oui. Prenez la _____ rue à droite, et c'est sur la place.
  – Merci.
  – De rien.

d – Pardon, où est la poste, s'il vous plaît?
  – C'est là, tout droit, à _____, après les feux.
  – Merci!

Pardon monsieur/madame, (vous savez) <u>où est</u> l'Hôtel de ville, <u>s'il vous plaît</u>?
  <u>il y a</u> une station de métro <u>près d'ici</u>?

C'est tout droit.	(Vous) prenez	la première (rue)	à gauche.
(Vous) allez …		la deuxième (rue)	à droite.
(Vous) continuez …		la troisième (rue)	

| C'est ici / là / là-bas. | (Vous) tournez | | à gauche / à droite. |
| | (Vous) traversez | | la rue / la place / le carrefour. |

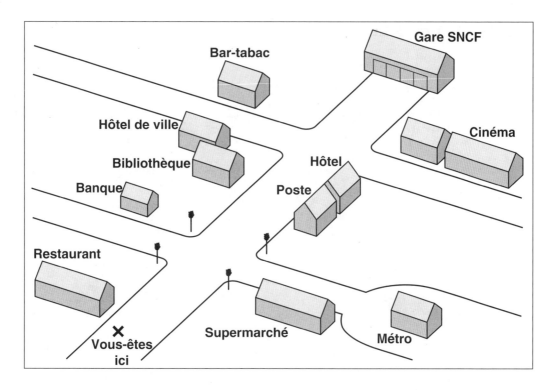

3 Où vont-ils?

a Lisez les instructions et trouvez les 3 endroits (places) sur le plan.
- C'est là, tout droit, à gauche après les feux.
- Alors, vous prenez la première rue à droite, et c'est là, à droite.
- Allez tout droit et prenez la deuxième à gauche. C'est à droite.

b Ecrivez les instructions pour aller au cinéma et à la banque.

c A deux, imaginez deux conversations similaires.

🎧 4 Plan de Lille

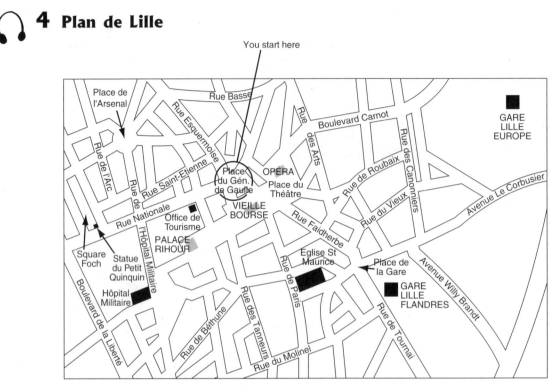

You start here

Ecoutez 4 conversations et indiquez les endroits sur le plan. Start <u>each time</u> from Place du Général de Gaulle.

C'est	à	gauche/droite.	– C'est près/loin d'ici?
	sur la		– Non, c'est à 200 m / 1 km (d'ici).
	sur votre		5 min. / ½h
Prenez la rue Nationale, puis la deuxième à gauche.			

👥 5 C'est à 5 minutes

Vous êtes à Lille, place du Général de Gaulle. A deux, demandez et indiquez le chemin (way) pour aller à:

– l'opéra;
– la gare de Lille-Flandres;
– l'office du tourisme;
– la place de l'Arsenal.

Lille

6 La boulangerie est en face

Ecoutez la conversation dans un office du tourisme et traduisez les mots
ci-dessous. Utilisez le plan pour vous aider.

a à côté de   **b** entre   **c** en face de   **d** devant   **e** au coin de   **f** derrière

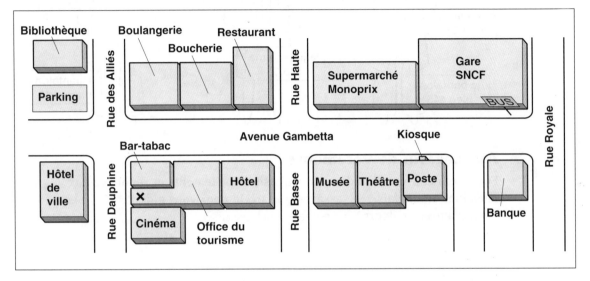

7 Devant ou derrière?

Regardez le plan et dites si les phrases ci-dessous sont vraies ou fausses.
Ensuite, corrigez les phrases qui sont fausses.

a Le restaurant est derrière la boucherie.

b La bibliothèque est dans l'avenue Gambetta.

c Entre la poste et le musée, il y a une pharmacie.

d Le supermarché est à côté de la gare SNCF.

e L'office du tourisme est au coin de la rue Dauphine et de l'avenue Gambetta.

f La boucherie est à côté du restaurant.

g La boulangerie est en face du bar-tabac.

h Il y a un arrêt d'autobus devant la poste.

8 C'est quoi?

Travaillez à deux. Choisissez un endroit sur le plan. Indiquez le chemin pour y
aller et demandez à votre partenaire de le trouver. (Exemple: – C'est au coin
de la rue Haute et de l'avenue Gambetta, à côté de la boucherie. – C'est le
restaurant.)

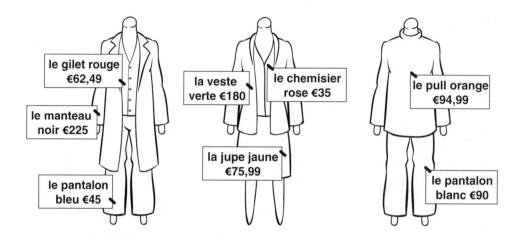

le gilet rouge €62,49

le manteau noir €225

le pantalon bleu €45

la veste verte €180

le chemisier rose €35

la jupe jaune €75,99

le pull orange €94,99

le pantalon blanc €90

9 Au magasin de vêtements

Ecoutez la conversation dans un magasin de vêtements et répondez aux questions en anglais. (NB: **essayer** = to try; **Je peux vous aider?** = Can I help you? **Il y a d'autres couleurs?** = Are there other colours?)

a What does David want to try on?

b What else does he want?

c What is wrong with the item he has tried on?

d What colours are available?

e What does he eventually buy?

grammaire

Vous prenez le manteau? Oui, je <u>le</u> prends.
Vous prenez la chemise? Oui, je <u>la</u> prends.
Vous prenez les chemises? Oui, je <u>les</u> prends.

le manteau noir   la chemise noir<u>e</u>
les pulls noir<u>s</u>   les jupes noir<u>es</u>

Il/Elle coûte combien? Il/Elle coûte €40.

70 soixante-dix	80 quatre-vingts
71 soixante et onze	81, 82, 83 quatre-vingt-un, -deux, -trois, etc.
72 soixante-douze	
73 soixante-treize	90 quatre-vingt-dix
74 soixante-quatorze	91, 92, 93 quatre-vingt-onze, -douze, -treize, etc.
75 soixante-quinze	
76 soixante-seize	100 cent
77 soixante-dix-sept	101, 102 cent un, cent deux, etc.
78 soixante-dix-huit	200 deux cents
79 soixante-dix-neuf	1000 mille, 10 000 dix mille, 100 000 cent mille
	1 000 000 un million

10 C'est combien?

Ecoutez 2 autres conversations dans un magasin de vêtements et remplissez les cases.

	a	b	c	d	e	f	g	h
vêtement	jupe		gilet vert		veste			pantalon
prix		60 euros		100 euros		55 euros	55 euros	

11 Tu aimes cette jupe?

Ecoutez la conversation entre deux amies devant un magasin et corrigez les erreurs dans la transcription (il y a 8 erreurs).

– Je voudrais ce pull rose.
– Il coûte combien?
– 80 euros.
– Moi, je voudrais cette veste bleue et ces deux tee-shirts jaunes.

– Et ce pantalon?
– (Jokingly) Non merci, il est rose!
– Et tu n'aimes pas la jupe verte là?
– Non, je n'aime pas beaucoup les jupes.
– Oh là là!, elle coûte 220 euros!

grammaire

Demonstrative adjectives (this/that/these/those)

un/le pull > ce pull   une/la veste > cette veste   des/les tee-shirts > ces tee-shirts

12 Tu préfères le rouge?

a Ecoutez la conversation et répondez aux 2 questions en anglais. (NB: **des chaussures** = shoes; **les deux** = both.)

i What does Jacques need to buy?
ii What does he finally purchase? Give all the details.

b Ecoutez encore une fois et traduisez les phrases en français.

i Do you like these trousers?
ii Me too.
iii I like both of them.
iv I prefer the black ones.
v Do you want to try them on?

Tu aimes ce pull marron?	Non, je ne l'aime pas, je préfère le bleu.
Tu aimes cette jupe verte?	Non, je ne l'aime pas, je préfère la rouge.
Tu aimes ces chaussures noires?	Non, je ne les aime pas, je préfère les grises.

13 Je prends la bleue

A deux, inventez un dialogue au magasin de vêtements.

14 Au marché

Qu'est-ce que vous pouvez acheter au marché? Cochez les cases.

du papier ☐

du poisson ☐

des timbres ☐

du fromage ☐

de la charcuterie ☐

des fruits ☐

du saucisson ☐

de l'alcool ☐

du pain ☐

des médicaments ☐

des journaux ☐

des légumes ☐

des cigarettes ☐

de l'huile ☐

de la viande ☐

des épices ☐

grammaire

The article 'du' (some)

du pain   de l'eau
de la viande   des fruits

15 Les magasins

a Ecoutez la conversation et cochez les noms de magasins que vous entendez.

la boucherie	l'épicerie	le marchand de journaux
la boulangerie	la poissonnerie	la librairie-papeterie
la pâtisserie	le marchand de fruits et légumes	la pharmacie
la crèmerie	la charcuterie	la quincaillerie

b A deux, traduisez en anglais les noms des magasins.

16 Où est-ce qu'on achète ...?

A deux, faites la liste des produits qu'on peut acheter dans chaque magasin.

Extra!

1 Voyage à Londres

Alain is going to visit his English friend Dennis in London for the first time. He has just received an email from him, with directions on how to get to his place. Read the email and indicate whether the following statements are true (T) or false (F).

a Dennis loves London.

b Dennis's brother will be staying with them as well.

c When Alain comes out of the station, he has to turn right.

d Dennis lives in the second street on the right after the supermarket.

e The house is opposite a library.

f It is a long walk from the tube station.

A: alaingodet@orange.fr
Objet: Voyage à Londres

Cher Alain,

Comment ça va? Je suis impatient de te voir ici, à Londres. J'adore cette ville! Il y a beaucoup de choses à faire: promenades, musées, shopping, cinéma, sorties en boîte, etc., etc.! Mon frère est là aussi en ce moment, ce sera sympa!

Alors, pour aller à l'appartement de la station de métro de Holloway Road (sur la ligne Piccadilly), tu tournes à gauche et tu continues tout droit dans Holloway Road. Au carrefour, tu tournes à droite, puis tu prends la première rue à gauche (derrière un supermarché) et puis la deuxième à droite. C'est là, au numéro 25a. C'est à côté d'une petite bibliothèque.

Voilà. Ce n'est pas très loin, à dix minutes environ. Bon voyage!

A très bientôt,

Dennis
PS: mon numéro de portable est le 06 87 12 43 62.

---

2 Combien coûte la jupe?

Listen to a conversation between Sarah and Alex in a clothes shop and answer the questions below in English.

a What item of clothing does Alex try on?

b What items of clothing does Sarah try on?

c How much is the skirt?

d What does Alex eventually buy?

4 En ville

Grammaire

~ Verbs: imperative form

When giving instructions or telling someone to do something, the imperative form can be used: e.g. **Attendez!** (= Wait!) / **Faites attention!** (= Be careful!). It is generally constructed like the present indicative (the form you have been using up until now, e.g. **vous faites …**), but without the pronoun **vous**. Similarly, in informal style the pronoun **tu** is left out.

E.g. **Tournez à droite. / Prenez la deuxième à gauche.
Prends la Rue Dauphine. / Continue tout droit.** (Note that with **-er** verbs, the final **-s** is dropped.)

However, because the imperative form is very direct, the **vous/tu** of the present indicative form is generally preferred, especially when giving instructions (e.g. **Vous tournez à droite. / Tu prends la Rue Basse.**).

~ Prepositions of location

When you are describing where something is in relation to something else, you need to use a preposition. Some prepositions of location are constructed with **de** (e.g. **en face de la banque**), others not (e.g. **la boulangerie est derrière le parking**). Remember that when **de** is followed by **le** or **les** it merges to become **du/des**.

E.g. **La banque est près du bar-tabac. / Il y a un téléphone près des toilettes.**

~ le/la/l'/les

The direct object pronouns **le/la/les** are used to avoid repetition of the object in a sentence.

E.g. – **Vous prenez la jupe bleue? – Oui, je la prends.**

When the object is masculine it is replaced with **le** (or **l'**), when it is feminine with **la**

(or **l'**), and when it is plural with **les**. Note that these pronouns come before the verb.

~ ce/cet/cette/ces

The demonstrative adjectives **ce/cet/cette** ('this' or 'that') and **ces** ('these' or 'those') are used when referring to an object or a person by pointing at them. E.g. **Ce manteau, dans le magasin.** When the noun that follows is masculine, **ce** and **cet** (+vowel) are used. If it is feminine **cette** is used and if it is plural **ces** is used. E.g. **Je prends cette jupe, cet imperméable, ce pull et ces chemises.**

~ Adjectives

Adjectives are usually placed directly after the noun and agree in gender (**la chemise grise**) and number (**les chemises grises**). With a masculine noun, the adjective does not change. With a feminine noun, an **-e** is added to the ending: e.g. **la veste verte**. However, there are some exceptions: e.g. **le pull blanc/la veste blanche**. Adjectives which already end with an **-e** do not change with a feminine noun: e.g. **le pull rouge/la veste rouge**. With a plural noun, an **-s** is added to the ending: e.g. **les jupes bleues**, unless the adjective already ends in **-s**.

~ du/de la/de l'/des

The article **du** is used to refer to an unspecified quantity:

du pain (masculine)
de la crème (feminine)
de l'eau (word starting with a vowel)
des fruits (plural)

Exercices de grammaire

Verbs: imperative form

1 Fill in the gaps in the text below with the imperative form of the verb in brackets:

Vous voulez aller au Musée d'Art Ancien? Eh bien, (*prendre*) _____ **(a)** cette rue, (*aller*) _____ **(b)** tout droit et (*tourner*) _____ **(c)** à gauche aux feux. Vous arrivez à une place; (*traverser*) _____ **(d)** la place et (*prendre*) _____ **(e)** la rue entre la poste et le cinéma. (*Continuer*) _____ **(f)** toujours tout droit et c'est là, en face de vous.

Prepositions of location

2 Fill in the gaps in the following sentences.

La bibliothèque est dans _____ **(a)** rue de Nancy au coin _____ **(b)** rue de Guise et _____ **(c)** avenue Charles de Gaulle. C'est en face _____ **(d)** théâtre et à côté _____ **(e)** Hôtel de ville.

La gare SNCF n'est pas loin. C'est près _____ **(f)** supermarché Océan. Il y a une pharmacie juste en face.

L'office du tourisme est sur _____ **(g)** place Gambetta. C'est entre _____ **(h)** boucherie et _____ **(i)** bar-tabac.

le/la/l'/les

3 Read the following sentences and fill in the gap with the appropriate object pronoun.

– Je voudrais le manteau blanc. – Vous voulez _____ **(a)** essayer?

– J'aime bien la jupe rouge. – Tu _____ **(b)** prends? – Oui, je _____ **(c)** prends.

– Vous prenez les deux pantalons verts? – Oui, je _____ **(d)** prends.

– Elle aime la chemise rose? – Oui, elle _____ **(e)** aime beaucoup.

ce/cet/cette/ces

4 Replace the underlined article with the appropriate demonstrative adjective.

E.g. **Prenez <u>la</u> rue à droite, ici.** > *Prenez <u>cette</u> rue à droite, ici.*

a <u>La</u> boulangerie est excellente.

b Tournez à gauche après <u>les</u> feux.

c C'est tout droit après <u>le</u> carrefour.

d <u>La</u> jupe rouge est magnifique!

e Vous prenez <u>les</u> pantalons?

f Je voudrais essayer <u>l'</u>imperméable.

Adjectives

5 Change the following sentences to the plural form.

E.g. **le pull vert** > *les pulls verts*

a la chemise rose >

b le tee-shirt blanc >

c le pantalon rouge >

d la jupe bleue >

e le gilet gris >

f la robe jaune >

4 En ville

Vocabulaire

~ Trouver le chemin — Finding the way

aller	to go
continuer	to carry on / continue
prendre	to take
tourner	to turn
traverser	to cross
savoir	to know
la rue	street
l'avenue (f)	avenue
le boulevard	boulevard
la place	square
le carrefour	crossroads
les feux (m)	traffic lights
puis	then
avant	before
là-bas	over there
après	after
tout droit	straight on
à gauche	on the left
à droite	on the right
près (de)	near
loin (de)	far (from)
sur	on
entre	between
devant	in front (of)
derrière	behind
à côté (de)	beside
en face (de)	opposite
au coin (de)	on the corner (of)
ici	here
là	there

~ Les bâtiments et magasins — Buildings and shops

l'Hôtel (m) de ville	town hall
la bibliothèque	library
l'office (m) du tourisme	tourist office
le musée	museum
la gare	train station
la station de métro	underground station
l'arrêt (m) d'autobus	bus stop
l'épicerie (f)	grocer's
l'hôtel (m)	hotel
le restaurant	restaurant
la poste	post office
l'hôpital (m)	hospital
le théâtre	theatre
la boulangerie	baker's
la boucherie	butcher's
la pharmacie	chemist's
le tabac	tobacconist's
le parking	car park
le plan	street map

la pâtisserie	cake shop
la crèmerie	dairy shop
la charcuterie	delicatessen
la poissonnerie	fishmonger's
le marchand de fruits et légumes	greengrocer
le marchand de journaux	newsagent
la librairie-papeterie	stationer's and bookshop
la quincaillerie	hardware shop

~ Les vêtements — Clothing

la veste	jacket
l'imperméable (m)	rain coat
le manteau	coat
la robe	dress
la jupe	skirt
le pantalon	trousers
le pull	jumper
le gilet	cardigan
la chemise	shirt
le chemisier	blouse
le tee-shirt	tee-shirt
les chaussures (f)	shoes
la cabine d'essayage	changing room
aider	to help
essayer	to try
la caisse	till, checkout

~ Les couleurs — Colours

blanc(he)	white
bleu(e)	blue
marron	brown
noir(e)	black
rouge	red
orange	orange
jaune	yellow
vert(e)	green
rose	pink
beige	beige
gris(e)	grey

Travail à deux

1 Demander son chemin

a Find out from your partner where the following places are on the map and mark them on: the nearest underground station, the 'Hôtel du Centre', the restaurant 'Chez Marcel' and the library.

b Answer your partner's questions about where certain buildings are.

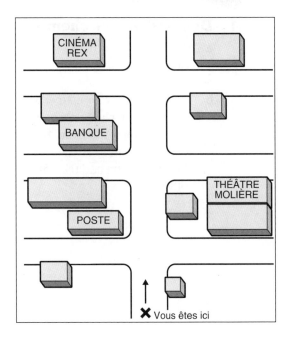

2 Au magasin de vêtements

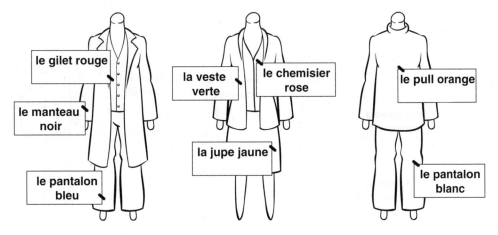

le gilet rouge
le manteau noir
le pantalon bleu
la veste verte
le chemisier rose
la jupe jaune
le pull orange
le pantalon blanc

You are shopping for clothes and you have a budget of €350.
Ask the shop assistant for the price of each item you are interested in and work out what you are going to buy.

Travail à deux

B

1 Demander son chemin

a Answer your partner's questions about where certain buildings are.

b Find out from your partner where the following places are on the map and mark them on: the Rex cinema, the nearest bank, the Molière theatre and the post office.

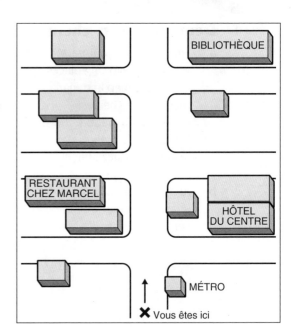

2 Au magasin de vêtements

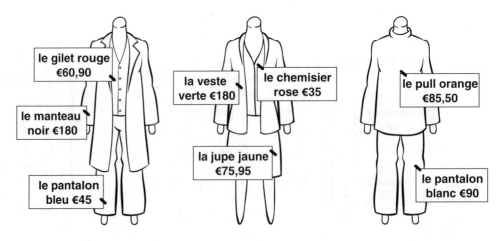

A customer who has a specific amount of money to spend is enquiring about the price of different items of clothing. Tell him/her the prices and ask if s/he would like to try and/or buy the said items.

En train

When you have completed this unit, you will be able to locate places on a map and state what you are going to do; request and give information about travelling by train and other means of transport; deal with timetables.

1 Je vais en France!

Ecoutez un dialogue entre trois étudiants et cochez sur la carte à la page 52 les villes et pays mentionnés.

la France > aller en France	l'Angleterre > aller en Angleterre
le Portugal > aller au Portugal	les Pays-Bas > aller aux Pays-Bas
Rome > aller à Rome	Paris > aller à Paris

2 Tu vas où?

Voici un résumé du dialogue. Trouvez les prépositions qui manquent.

Je vais aller _____ (a) Porto _____ (b) Portugal.

Je vais commencer par aller _____ (c) Suisse puis _____ (d) Italie.

Tu vas aller _____ (e) Grèce?

Non, je vais partir _____ (f) Pays-Bas.

Mon copain va travailler _____ (g) Madrid _____ (h) Espagne.

La Seine, Paris

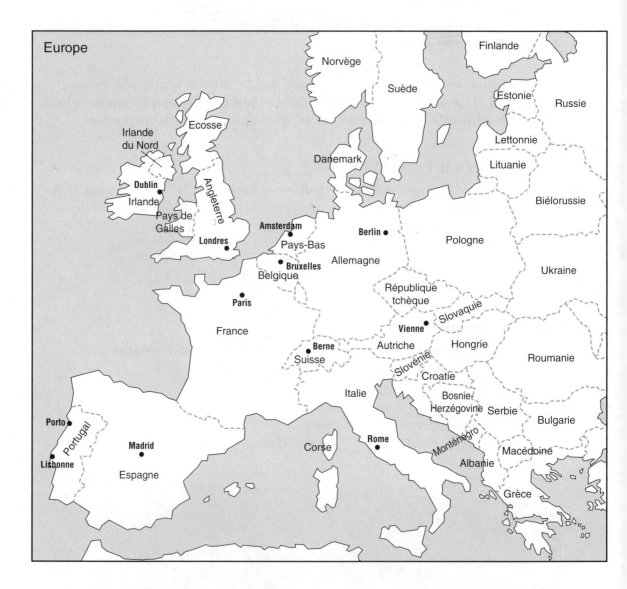

Europe

Norvège

Finlande

Suède

Estonie

Russie

Ecosse

Irlande
du Nord

Lettonnie

Danemark

Lituanie

Dublin

Biélorussie

Irlande

Angleterre

Pays de
Galles

Amsterdam

Berlin

Pologne

Londres

Pays-Bas

Bruxelles

Allemagne

Ukraine

Belgique

République
tchèque

Paris

Slovaquie

France

Vienne

Berne

Autriche

Hongrie

Roumanie

Suisse

Slovénie

Italie

Croatie

Bosnie-
Herzégovine

Serbie

Bulgarie

Porto

Portugal

Rome

Monténégro

Macédoine

Madrid

Corse

Albanie

Lisbonne

Espagne

Grèce

grammaire

Qu'est-ce que vous <u>allez faire</u> pendant les vacances?   Je <u>vais aller</u> à Madrid.
Où est-ce que tu <u>vas aller</u>?   Elle <u>va partir</u> aux Pays-Bas.

3 Tu vas travailler?

Réfléchissez! Qu'est-ce que vous allez faire pendant les vacances? A deux, parlez de vos projets de vacances. Utilisez "aller" + infinitif. (Ex: – Je vais travailler en France.)

L'Arc-de Triomphe

Sacré-Cœur, Montmartre

4 Un aller-retour ...

Ecoutez et lisez le dialogue au guichet de la gare de Lille-Flandres et répondez aux questions ci-dessous.

– A quelle heure part le prochain train pour Arras?
– Euh, attendez ... à dix heures onze.
– Bien. Trois aller-retour, s'il vous plaît.
– Seconde classe?
– Oui, oui.
– Voilà. Ça fait vingt-quatre euros.
– Voilà. Le train arrive à quelle heure à Arras?
– Alors, il arrive à Arras à ... dix heures cinquante-deux.
– Merci. C'est quel quai?
– Quai deux, mademoiselle.
– Bon. Merci beaucoup!

A quelle heure part le prochain train pour Arras?	Un (billet)	aller-retour, SVP.
premier		aller simple
dernier		
Il arrive à quelle heure?		première/seconde classe
C'est quel quai?		

a What time does the next train for Arras leave?
b How many tickets does Marie need? First or second class?
c What time does the train arrive in Arras?
d Which platform does Marie have to go to?

grammaire

un quai > <u>quel</u> quai?	des quais > <u>quels</u> quais?
une heure > <u>quelle</u> heure?	des heures > <u>quelles</u> heures?

5 Première classe, s'il vous plaît!

A deux, posez ces questions en français et répondez.

– What time does the next train for Calais leave?
– What time does the last train for Paris leave and what time does it arrive in Paris?
– Two single tickets to Paris, please.
– One return ticket to Arras, second class, please.
– What platform is it?

6 L'Eurostar

Ecoutez et complétez le dialogue à la gare de Lille Europe. (NB: TGV – train à grande vitesse)

Le client veut une _____ **(a)** pour _____ **(b)** personnes.
Le client veut aller _____ **(c)** Bruges en Belgique.
Le client veut _____ **(d)** le matin, vers _____ **(e)**.
Il faut changer à Bruxelles. Il y a une _____ **(f)** à 10h36.
Le train _____ **(g)** à Bruges à 11h26.
Les billets coûtent _____ **(h)** euros.
Il n'y a pas de _____ **(i)** pour le train de Bruxelles à Bruges.
Il ne faut pas _____ **(j)** les billets Eurostar.

> Je peux faire une réservation?
> Je voudrais partir/arriver le matin/l'après-midi/le soir/vers 9h.
> Départ de Lille Europe à 9h47, arrivée à Bruxelles Midi à 10h25.
> Une place côté couloir/fenêtre.
> Vous avez un horaire, SVP?
> Il faut changer à Bruxelles. Il y a une correspondance à 21h02.
> Il faut composter les billets?

grammaire

Je <u>peux réserver</u>? / Vous <u>voulez aller</u> à Bruges? / <u>Il faut changer</u> à Bruxelles.

7 Quelle heure est-il?

A deux, entraînez-vous à dire l'heure. Utilisez le système de 24 heures. (Ex: 07:15 = sept heures quinze; 20:32 = vingt heures trente-deux.) Puis écoutez la prononciation.

a 01:45 **b** 19:51 **c** 12:24 **d** 15:30 **e** 23:16 **f** 10:05

8 Je voudrais aller à ...

Travaillez à deux, et faites le jeu de rôle suivant.

– One of you wants to travel with two friends from Paris (Gare de Lyon station) to Lyon (Perrache station) by TGV. You want to leave on Friday afternoon and travel second class. You want to return on Sunday evening and be in Paris before 22:00.
– One of you works at the ticket desk and has to supply the relevant information for the journey (approx. journey time from Paris to Lyon is two hours and ten minutes).

9 Les horaires

Lisez les horaires de train ci-dessous. Trouvez les mots et expressions anglais qui correspondent aux abréviations françaises.

1 les mar, mer et jeu
2 TGV
3 tous les jours
4 sauf
5 fêtes
6 les sam, dim
7 jusqu'au

a until
b every day
c bank holidays
d on Tuesdays, Wednesdays and Thursdays
e high speed train
f on Saturdays and Sundays
g except

numéro de train		7207	7007	73291	73293	73295	73301	7211	7015	7021	73311	7229	73313	7033	73333	7235	7043	73353
notes à consulter		3	4	5	6	7	8	9	10		8					9		
		TGV	TGV					TGV	TGV	TGV		TGV		TGV		TGV	TGV	
		♿	♿		🚲	🚲		♿	♿	♿		♿		♿	🚲	♿	♿	
Paris-Nord.	Dep	07.28	07.28					07.58	08.28	08.58		09.58		10.58		11.58	12.58	
Lille Flandres	Arr			07.35	08.00	08.09	08.29	08.59	09.29	09.59	09.35		10.09	11.59	12.08	12.59	13.59	14.08
Lille Europe	Arr	08.27	08.27									10.56						
Croix Wasquehal	Arr			07.43	08.07	08.17	08.37	09.17			09.43		10.16		12.15	13.17		14.15
Roubaix	Arr			07.48	08.10	08.20	08.42	09.22			09.47		10.20		12.20	13.22		14.20
Tourcoing	Arr			07.52	08.14	08.23	08.47	09.28			09.52		10.23		12.23	13.28		14.23

JOURS DE CIRCULATION ET SERVICES DISPONIBLES

3. tous les jours sauf les sam, dim et fêtes ; circule le 1er nov.
4. Les 30 mai et 2 juin ; du 6 juin au 11 juil et à partir du 29 août : les mar, mer et jeu sauf les 13 juin et 1 er nov.
5. jusqu'au 30 juin et à partir du 28 août : tous les jours sauf les dim et fêtes.
6. tous les jours sauf les sam, dim et fêtes.
7. les sam sauf le 11 nov.
8. jusqu'au 30 juin et à partir du 28 août : tous les jours sauf les sam, dim et fêtes.
9. tous les jours sauf les 11 et 12 juin.
10. jusqu'au 15 juil et à partir du 28 août : tous les jours sauf les dim et sauf le 12 juin.

🚲 Vélo : transport gratuit

♿ Place(s) handicapés

TGV Réservation obligatoire

10 Quel train?

Consultez les horaires et trouvez un train qui correspond aux besoins des voyageurs.

a Anne et son mari veulent un train qui arrive à Lille Flandres, le lundi, vers neuf heures du matin. Ils préfèrent prendre un train rapide.

b Lorraine habite à Lille. Elle a un vélo et elle ne veut pas prendre le TGV (c'est plus cher) pour aller à Tourcoing. Elle voudrait partir avant 9 heures.

c C'est samedi matin, et Pierre et son amie veulent aller à Lille pour le congrès des personnes handicapées qui commence à dix heures. Pierre voyage en chaise roulante et désire prendre un train rapide.

11 A la gare

Trouvez le dialogue qui correspond à chaque exemple de l'exercice 10.

12 J'y vais à pied

Ecoutez le dialogue et remplissez les blancs. (NB: **la circulation** = traffic, **moins cher** = cheaper, **l'aéroport** (m) = airport)

– Georges, tu _____ **(a)** aller en Ecosse la semaine prochaine?

– Oui, je vais _____ **(b)** vendredi soir.

– Tu y vas en _____ **(c)**?

– Non, pas cette fois, c'est trop _____ **(d)**. Je vais y aller en avion.

– En avion?

– Oui, c'est beaucoup moins cher le _____ **(e)** soir. Un aller-retour Londres-Edimbourg coûte _____ **(f)** euros. En plus le trajet ne dure qu'une heure. Pas mal, hein?

– C'est super. Tu vas à l'_____ **(g)** en voiture?

– Non, en train, c'est plus simple. Il y a toujours _____ **(h)** de circulation le vendredi soir.

| en bus | en voiture | en taxi | en moto |
| en vélo | en avion | en bateau | à pied |

grammaire

Est-ce tu vas <u>à</u> Paris ce week-end?	Oui, j'<u>y</u> vais.
Comment est-ce qu'elle va <u>à</u> l'université?	Elle <u>y</u> va à pied.
Est-ce qu'elle va aller <u>à</u> Londres la semaine prochaine?	Oui, elle va <u>y</u> aller.
Comment vont-ils aller <u>au</u> cinéma?	Ils vont <u>y</u> aller à pied.

13 J'y vais en vélo

A deux, parlez des moyens de transport que vous utilisez tous les jours et répondez aux questions suivantes.

a Comment allez-vous à l'université tous les jours?

b Après une soirée au café, comment est-ce que vous rentrez chez vous?

c Comment est-ce que vous allez d'Angleterre en Irlande?

d Vous voulez aller en France. Comment est-ce que vous y allez?

14 Pendant les vacances ...

Ecrivez un résumé de vos projets pour les vacances en utilisant les informations suivantes:

a Where you are going to go, with whom.

b Details of how you are going to get there.

c A few things that you are going to do.

15 La voiture est en panne!

Voici une liste de problèmes possibles. A deux, trouvez les équivalents en anglais.

La voiture est en panne. > The car has broken down.

a Il y a une grève.

b Je n'ai plus d'essence.

c Mon vélo a un pneu crevé.

d Le train est annulé.

e Je suis en retard.

f Il y a beaucoup de circulation.

1 The train is cancelled.

2 I am late.

3 There is a strike.

4 There is a lot of traffic.

5 My bicycle has a flat tyre.

6 I have run out of petrol.

être en avance / être à l'heure / être en retard

16 Je suis en retard ...

Mettez les phrases dans l'ordre et écoutez le dialogue pour vérifier la réponse.

a Ce n'est pas possible!

b Il est à la gare. Je vais le chercher demain.

c Ah! Bonjour Yelena! Tu es en retard ...

d Il est où ton vélo?

e Parce qu'il y a une grève demain!

f Pourquoi?

g Oui, je suis désolée – mon vélo a un pneu crevé.

17 Les problèmes de voyage

Ecoutez les quatre dialogues. Notez chaque problème mentionné.

a ...

b ...

c ...

d ...

Extra!

1 Les annonces

Listen to some announcements that you might hear in a train station in France, and fill in the grid below with the relevant information (you will notice that not all the boxes need to be filled in!). (Note: **Le train 917 <u>en provenance de</u> Paris, <u>à destination de</u> Lyon** = Train 917 <u>from</u> Paris <u>to</u> Lyon; **la voie** = track.)

	Train number	From	To	Platform	Track	Delay
a		Nantes		2		
b			Marseille		8	
c	289					
d			Avignon			
e	472					
f		Mâcon				15 mins
g	591					

2 Le métro

Read the travel information about the Paris métro below and answer the following questions in English.

Quatre kiosques d'information sont à votre disposition. Vous pouvez obtenir tous les documents d'information sur les lignes de bus et de métro. Vous pouvez également y acheter vos cartes d'abonnement et vos billets de transport.

Renseignements: Du lundi au vendredi: 8h30 à 12h.   Le samedi: 9h à 17h.
Horaires Métro: Du lundi au samedi:
Ligne 1   Premier métro: 5h12   Dernier métro: 0h12
Ligne 2   Premier métro: 6h24   Dernier métro: 0h30

Notez bien!
Un métro passe environ chaque minute aux heures d'affluence et toutes les 4 à 6 minutes aux heures creuses. La station est fermée le dimanche.

---

a How many information desks are there?

b What different types of information can you get from these desks?

c What time are the desks open at the weekend?

d At what time does the last train leave on Line 1?

e How frequent are the trains during the rush hour?

Grammaire

～ Prepositions before countries and towns

Names of countries can be feminine, masculine or plural. When talking about where you are or where you are going to go, the following prepositions are used:

Before feminine countries (the majority) and countries starting with a vowel: **en** (e.g. **Je vais en France. J'habite en Irak.**)

Before singular masculine countries: **au** (e.g. **Je pars au Portugal.**)

Before plural countries: **aux** (e.g. **Je vais aux Pays-Bas.**)

Remember before cities the preposition **à** is used. (e.g. **J'habite à Paris.**)

～ aller + infinitive verb

One way to talk about the near future is to use the verb **aller** and to add the infinitive form of the verb describing what you are going to do. E.g. **Je vais prendre le train. / Tu vas aller où? / Nous allons partir en Afrique. / Vous allez faire des courses?**

Note: You can also use the present tense to talk about the near future. E.g. **Demain, je prends le train**.

～ pouvoir, vouloir and il faut

pouvoir + infinitive	**vouloir** + infinitive	**il faut** + infinitive
(can/be able)	(want/wish)	(have to)
je peux	je veux	'impersonal' verb
tu peux	tu veux	(only **il** form)
il/elle peut	il/elle veut	
nous pouvons	nous voulons	
vous pouvez	vous voulez	
ils/elles peuvent	ils/elles veulent	

～ The pronoun y

The basic meaning of the pronoun **y** is 'there'. It replaces a word or an idea introduced by **à**. E.g.

Est-ce que tu vas à Montpellier?	**Oui, j'y vais.**
Are you going to Montpellier?	Yes, I'm going there.

Note: When using the immediate future, **y** changes place and comes before the infinitive verb.

Est-ce qu'elles vont aller à Lyon?	**Oui, elles vont y aller.**
Are they going to go to Lyon?	Yes, they are going to go there.

Exercices de grammaire

Prepositions before countries and towns

1 Indicate which preposition you would use before the following countries and continents (using **aller** or **habiter**). E.g. **l'Allemagne** > *Je vais aller en Allemagne.*

   a le Portugal   **e** le Royaume-Uni   **i** l'Irak   **m** l'Irlande
   b les Antilles   **f** la Suède   **j** l'Afrique   **n** l'Ouganda
   c la Belgique   **g** le Danemark   **k** l'Egypte
   d l'Ecosse   **h** les Etats-Unis   **l** le Liban

aller + infinitive verb

2 Make up complete sentences out of the information below using **aller** + infinitive verb.

  E.g. **Je/aller/vacances/Italie** > *Je vais aller en vacances en Italie.*

   a Je/prendre/train/pour Milan   **d** Elle/prendre le bateau/pour la Corse

   b Nous/prendre l'avion/pour Rome   **e** Tu/visiter la ville/pour acheter/souvenirs?

   c Ils/partir/pour Naples   **f** Vous/sortir/avec Pierre/ce soir?

pouvoir, vouloir and il faut

3 Complete the following sentences with **faut** or the appropriate form of **pouvoir** or **vouloir**.

Ils _____**(a)** voyager en 1ère classe: c'est plus confortable.
Elle ne _____**(b)** pas prendre l'avion: il y a une grève!
Dans les gares françaises, il _____**(c)** composter son billet.
Vous _____**(d)** le plein d'essence?
Il _____**(e)** aller en France pour voir sa copine.
Nous ne _____**(f)** pas partir à 23h00: le dernier train est à 22h35!
Il _____**(g)** changer à Paris; il y a une correspondance à 11h34.
Elles _____**(h)** réserver leur billet ici?

The pronoun y

4 Translate the following questions and answers. Be careful - the word "there" is not always needed in English but the French **y** is always included. It replaces a word introduced by **à**.

   a How are you getting to Bordeaux?   **d** How do you get to work?
     I am going there by car.   We get there on foot.

   b Are they going to France on Tuesday?   **e** Are you going to Paris by plane?
     No, they are going on Monday.   No, I'm going by Eurostar.

   c Does she go to the supermarket every day?
     Yes, she goes there every day.

Vocabulaire

~ **Voyager en train** — Travelling by train
le train — train
le TGV — high speed train
réserver — to book
la réservation — booking
prochain(e) — next
dernier(ière) — last
vers 1h — at around 1.00
le billet — ticket
l'aller simple (m) — single ticket
l'aller-retour (m) — return ticket
en première classe — first class
en seconde classe — second class
circuler — to run (trains)
tous les jours — every day
sauf — except
le système de 24 heures — the 24-hour clock
les jours fériés/les fêtes — public holidays
la place — seat
le côté fenêtre — window seat
le côté couloir — aisle seat
changer — to change
la correspondance — connection
le quai — platform
composter — to validate
l'arrivée (f) — arrival
le départ — departure
l'horaire (m) — timetable
cher — expensive
jusqu'au — until
une chaise roulante — wheelchair
personnes handicapées — disabled people

~ **Pays et régions** — Countries and regions
l'Afrique du Sud (f) — South Africa
l'Allemagne (f) — Germany
l'Angleterre (f) — England
les Antilles (f) — West Indies
la Belgique — Belgium
la Corse — Corsica
le Danemark — Denmark
l'Ecosse (f) — Scotland
l'Espagne (f) — Spain
l'Estonie (f) — Estonia
les Etats-Unis (m) — United States
la France — France
la Grèce — Greece
l'Irak (m) — Irak
l'Irlande (f) — Ireland
l'Italie (f) — Italy
la Lettonie — Latvia
la Lituanie — Lithuania

la Norvège — Norway
l'Ouganda (m) — Uganda
les Pays-Bas (m) — Netherlands
le pays de Galles — Wales
la Pologne — Poland
le Portugal — Portugal
la République tchèque — Czech Republic
la Suède — Sweden
la Suisse — Switzerland
le nord — north
le sud — south
See the vocabulary list on pages 158–170 for more countries and for the nationalities to go with these.

~ **Autres moyens de transport** — Other means of transport
la voiture — car
le taxi — taxi
le vélo — bike
la moto — motorbike
le bus — bus
l'essence (f) — petrol
la station-service — petrol station
la grève — strike
la circulation — traffic
fermé — closed
annulé — cancelled
être en avance — to be early
être à l'heure — to be on time
être en retard — to be late
le car — coach
le bateau/ferry — boat/ferry
l'avion (m) — airplane
à pied — on foot
le garage — garage
l'aéroport (m) — airport
la gare routière — coach station
en panne — broken down/out of order
le pneu crevé — a flat tyre

Travail à deux

1 Arrivées et départs

Find out from your partner the missing information about arrivals in and departures from the Gare Montparnasse in Paris, and complete the grid below.

Arrivées				Départs			
Provenance	Train	Heure	Quai	Destination	Train	Heure	Quai
Rennes		08:05	5	Quimper	763		
Brest	644			Rennes		10:40	
Le Mans		12:46	3	Le Mans		11:15	6
Nantes	595		1	Brest	770		
Saint-Nazaire	904			Nantes		13:55	2
Poitiers		21:28		Saint-Nazaire	814		8
Tours			7	Bordeaux		17:12	
Limoges	319	23:05		Toulouse	558		2

2 Réservations

You are in Paris and would like to go to Nancy for the weekend. You intend to travel by train and need to make the necessary travel arrangements. Create a dialogue with a partner (the ticket assistant) using the information below.

Two return tickets to Nancy.
Second class.
You would like to leave on Friday morning at around 11:00 and return on Sunday evening, leaving Paris at around 19:00. You would prefer a direct train.

Find out:

a From which station the train leaves.

b The train times – you may be given a choice of trains.

c Whether you need to reserve.

d The price.

Travail à deux

1 Arrivées et départs

Find out from your partner the missing information about arrivals in and departures from the Gare Montparnasse in Paris, and complete the grid below.

Arrivées				Départs			
Provenance	Train	Heure	Quai	Destination	Train	Heure	Quai
Rennes	259		7	Quimper		07:38	8
Brest		09:15	5	Rennes	438		4
Le Mans	622			Le Mans	251		
Nantes		13:32		Brest		13:30	4
Saint-Nazaire		16:50	3	Nantes	486		
Poitiers	230		9	Saint-Nazaire		14:12	
Tours	546	21:47		Bordeaux	671		6
Limoges			5	Toulouse		20:42	

2 Réservations

You work for SNCF behind the ticket desk. A customer would like to make some travel arrangements. Create a dialogue with a partner (the customer) using the information below.

The customer will tell you what s/he requires. Remember to find out the destination, the type of ticket and the class.

Les trains pour Nancy partent de Paris Gare de l'Est.

Vendredi
Paris Est 10:50   Nancy Ville 12:49 (direct)   Réservation obligatoire
Paris Est 12:49   Nancy Ville 15:50 (direct)   Réservation obligatoire

Dimanche
Nancy Ville 18:53   Paris Est 22:07 (direct)   Réservation obligatoire
Nancy Ville 19:25   Paris Est 22:20 (direct)   Réservation recommandée

Aller simple 16 euros
Aller-retour 33 euros

6 A l'hôtel

When you have completed this unit, you will be able to make a hotel booking, make complaints, understand holiday brochures and describe accommodation.

Je voudrais une chambre …

pour deux personnes …

pour deux nuits.

1 Je voudrais une chambre

Ecoutez Nadia et complétez le dialogue.

– Bonsoir, je _____ **(a)** une chambre, s'il _____ **(b)** plaît.
– Oui, pour _____ **(c)** de personnes?
– Pour _____ **(d)** personnes. Pour _____ **(e)** nuit seulement.
– Bon, ça _____ **(f)** €110.

2 Combien de nuits?

Ecoutez les 3 dialogues et remplissez les cases.

	chambres?	personnes?	nuits?	prix?
Conversation 1				
Conversation 2				
Conversation 3				

3 Une réservation

A deux, utilisez l'exemple de l'exercice 1 et réservez une chambre d'hôtel.

4 Comment ça s'écrit?

Ecoutez l'alphabet et notez le nom des trois clients.

5 C'est à quel nom?

Reliez les expressions françaises à leur équivalent anglais, puis écoutez et notez l'ordre des expressions.

1 au premier étage
2 à quel nom?
3 au nom de …
4 télévision par satellite
5 salle de bains
6 ascenseur

a in the name of …
b lift
c satellite television
d bathroom
e under what name?
f on the first floor

6 C'est à quel étage?

Les phrases suivantes sont mélangées. Remettez-les dans l'ordre pour faire des phrases complètes, puis écoutez le dialogue pour vérifier vos réponses.

a Bonjour, je voudrais
b Pour combien
c Pour deux nuits,
d Je voudrais une
e Voilà, ça fait
f C'est très bien. Je
g Voilà, une chambre avec un lit
h C'est la chambre numéro 526 au

1 chambre avec salle de bains.
2 cinquième étage.
3 la prends.
4 une chambre pour trois personnes.
5 s'il vous plaît.
6 de nuits?
7 €98.
8 double et un lit simple.

Une chambre avec un lit <u>double/simple</u>. Une chambre avec <u>douche</u> au premier <u>étage</u>.

7 Il y a un problème…

Ecoutez et notez les problèmes et les solutions en anglais. (NB: **un interrupteur/ bouton** = switch; **appuyer** = press; **une armoire** = wardrobe)

8 Ça ne marche pas!

A deux, traduisez les phrases suivantes. (NB: **le chauffage** = heating; **une couverture** = blanket; **assez de** = enough)

The shower is not working. / There is no hot water. / The heating does not work. / There are not enough towels. / There are not any blankets.

Il se réveille …   Il se lève …   Il se rase …   Il ne se douche pas!

grammaire

Reflexive verbs have an extra pronoun in front of them.

E.g.	<u>se</u> réveiller (to wake up)	<u>se</u> plaindre (to complain)
	je <u>me</u> réveille	nous <u>nous</u> réveillons
	je <u>me</u> plains	nous <u>nous</u> plaignons
	tu <u>te</u> réveilles	vous <u>vous</u> réveillez
	tu <u>te</u> plains	vous <u>vous</u> plaignez
	il <u>se</u> réveille	ils <u>se</u> réveillent
	elle <u>se</u> plaint	elles <u>se</u> plaignent

9 Un séjour à Paris

Suzanne est à Paris. Utilisez le vocabulaire pour décrire sa journée. (Ex: se réveiller tard/téléphone/hôtel/cassé > Elle se réveille tard parce que le téléphone de l'hôtel est cassé.**)** (NB: **se promener** = to go for a walk; **s'amuser** = to have fun; **tard** = late; **rentrer** = to come/go back; **se coucher** = to go to bed; **parce que** = because)

a se lever/se laver/problème douche

b aller réception/se plaindre

c se promener/Tour Eiffel/Notre-Dame

d s'amuser beaucoup

e rentrer/hôtel/se coucher tard

 **10** **Le petit déjeuner dans la chambre**

Ecoutez un client de l'hôtel et répondez aux questions en français. (NB: **la veille** = the day before; **le prix** = the price)

a A quelle heure est-ce qu'il peut prendre le petit déjeuner?
b Où peut-il le prendre?
c Quel est le prix du petit déjeuner?

> Dans la salle de restaurant, c'est une formule buffet à volonté.
> Il faut commander la veille.

 11 **Nos services**

Lisez les informations suivantes et avec votre partenaire traduisez les expressions soulignées. Vous pouvez consulter un dictionnaire.

Hôtel Les Mimosas

a Un réveil automatique est à votre disposition dans toutes les chambres.

b La piscine est ouverte de 8 heures à 21 heures et le sauna de 10 heures à 20 heures.

c L'hôtel accepte les cartes suivantes: Carte bleue, MasterCard, American Express.

d Les chèques de voyage et les devises peuvent être changés à la réception.

e Le parking est ouvert 24h/24.

f Le petit déjeuner est servi entre 7 heures et 9 heures.

g La télévision par satellite est disponible dans toutes les chambres et dans le bar.

h La direction n'est pas responsable des objets de valeur placés dans les chambres.

le printemps   l'été   l'automne   l'hiver

janvier–février–mars–avril–mai–juin–juillet–août–septembre–octobre–novembre–décembre

12 C'est ouvert?

Lisez les informations et dites si les phrases ci-dessous sont vraies ou fausses.

Hôtel Catalan

Haute saison:	Du 4 juillet au 29 août.
Demi-saison:	Vacances d'hiver et vacances de printemps.
Vacances de Noël:	Du 19 décembre au 2 janvier.
Basse saison:	Autres périodes.

a Spring holidays are in the low season.
b The high season starts on 4 July.
c Christmas holidays, which end in January, are in the mid-season.

haute/demi-basse saison   du 19 décembre au 2 janvier

13 L'hôtel de la Ruche

Ecoutez et complétez le message sur le répondeur de l'hôtel.

Bonjour, l'Hôtel de la Ruche est _____**(a)** toute l'année sauf le 25 _____**(b)** et le premier _____**(c)**. Notre restaurant est ouvert _____**(d)** mardi _____**(e)** dimanche midi et soir, sauf en _____**(f)** saison du 25 _____**(g)** au 30 _____**(h)**.

14 A vous de jouer!

A deux, pratiquez les situations suivantes.

1 Book two bedrooms with bathroom, one with single bed, one with double bed for two nights from 12 June until 14 June.
2 Complain at reception that your television set does not work and that you have not got any towels (**serviettes**) for the bathroom.
3 Ask for information about facilities in the hotel, e.g. car park, swimming pool, etc.

15 Une maison à la campagne

Ecoutez Jean-Marc et Stéphanie comparer deux gîtes, puis corrigez la transcription ci-dessous. (NB: **un gîte** = holiday cottage)

Jean-Marc	Il y a deux gîtes dans le livre, ils sont très bien tous les deux.
Stéphanie	Quelle est la différence entre les deux?
Jean-Marc	Tu vois, le premier est plus petit, il fait 80 m².
Stéphanie	Oui, mais celui-ci est plus beau, il est à la campagne.
Jean-Marc	Le deuxième est moins intéressant que celui-ci mais il est moins cher.
Stéphanie	Lequel est-ce que tu préfères? Celui-ci ou celui-là?
Jean-Marc	Celui-ci est aussi beau mais je préfère celui-là.

> Il est <u>plus petit</u>.   Il est <u>moins cher que</u> le deuxième.   Il est <u>aussi</u> beau.
> <u>Lequel</u> est-ce que tu préfères? <u>Celui-ci</u> ou <u>celui-là</u>?

16 Votre maison idéale!

a **Lisez la description d'un gîte en France et regardez le plan. Ecoutez le propriétaire décrire la maison et faites une liste de toutes les rénovations.**

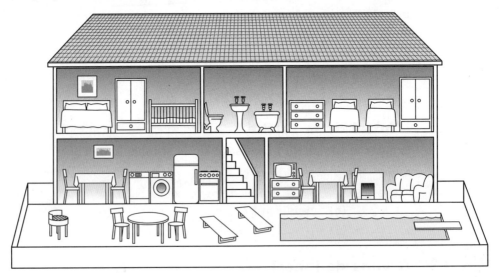

Maison indépendante rénovée en 1998, située en campagne.
Rez-de-chaussée: salle de séjour avec canapé-lit, cheminée, meuble et télévision couleur.
Cuisine avec lave-linge et lave-vaisselle, cuisinière, réfrigérateur.
Première chambre: lit double, armoire et lit d'enfant.
Deuxième chambre: deux lits, commode et armoire.
Salle de bains: baignoire, lavabo et toilettes.
Extérieur: piscine dans jardin clos, salon de jardin, relax, barbecue.

b **A deux, comparez cette maison avec votre maison idéale.**

Extra!

 1 Votre choix d'hôtel

Read the descriptions of facilities in three hotels and decide which hotel would best suit your needs.

1 You want a quiet hotel by the sea.
2 You are looking for a peaceful holiday and walks in the country.
3 You are interested in wines and enjoy good food.
4 Your priority is being able to play tennis every day and go for a swim.
5 You want a small hotel. You do not mind being in the country as long as you can park your car safely.
6 You want to go between 6 November and 8 November.

Hôtel Beau site

Fermeture annuelle: du 5 novembre au 30 novembre
75 chambres de 65 € à 102 €
Petit déjeuner 9,50 €   Menus: 42 €, 52 €
Dans un cadre de verdure, vous allez découvrir la nature environnante, promenade, étangs et centre équestre. Vous pouvez utiliser les équipements de l'hôtel quand vous voulez: piscine, sauna, ping-pong, jardin etc. Le restaurant vous propose des spécialités régionales et une carte des vins exceptionnelle.

Hôtel Saint Denis

Fermeture annuelle: du 3 janvier au 31 janvier
15 chambres de 70 € à 115 €   Petit déjeuner 8,30 €
Situé dans un site exceptionnel, l'hôtel Saint Denis propose ses chambres tout confort avec douche ou bain, téléphone, wc, vue sur la mer. Merveilleusement situé près de la rivière et de la forêt. Vue panoramique sur le golfe, entouré de montagnes. Le confort et le calme ensoleillé, des véritables vacances, piscine, tennis.

Hôtel-restaurant les Pinsons

Ouvert toute l'année   20 chambres de 60 € à 160 €
Petit déjeuner 7,30 €   Menus 30 €, 35 € et 50 €
Près des volcans d'Auvergne, l'hôtel-restaurant les Pinsons propose dans un cadre calme des chambres confortables et ensoleillées, en face d'un bois. Son restaurant vous propose une cuisine diététique gourmande et régionale. Nos équipements sont nombreux: piscine, mini-golf, grand jardin, parking privé.

2 A la réception

Listen to two people at a hotel reception and note down in English their requirements and/or problems.

Grammaire

~ Reflexive verbs

Reflexive verbs are used with an extra pronoun, e.g. **se laver**, **se promener**, etc.
The pronoun changes with each person.

se laver	se promener
(to get washed/to wash oneself)	(to go for a walk)
je <u>me</u> lave	je <u>me</u> promène
tu <u>te</u> laves	tu <u>te</u> promènes
il <u>se</u> lave	il <u>se</u> promène
nous <u>nous</u> lavons	nous <u>nous</u> promenons
vous <u>vous</u> lavez	vous <u>vous</u> promenez
ils <u>se</u> lavent	ils <u>se</u> promènent

~ Reflexive verbs in a negative sentence

In a negative sentence, the reflexive pronouns (**me**, **te**, **se**, etc.) are placed immediately in front of the verb. E.g. **Je ne <u>me</u> lave pas**.

~ Reflexive verbs with the near future

In the case of the near future (**aller** + infinitive, e.g. **Je vais manger** = I am going to eat), the reflexive pronoun is always placed in front of the verb in the infinitive. E.g. **Je vais <u>me</u> réveiller à 2 heures**. Note that in this case, the pronoun changes depending on the person, e.g. **Tu vas te réveiller à 2 heures**.

Note the negative form: **Je ne vais pas <u>me</u> laver**. The reflexive pronoun is placed before the the verb and after the negation **ne … pas**.

~ Comparatives (adjectives)

To make a comparison, you can use **plus** (more), **moins** (less) or **aussi** (as) before the adjective in a sentence. E.g. **Cet hôtel est plus beau, il est moins grand et il est aussi cher que l'autre hôtel.**
When you want to compare two things you use **que** to introduce the second element. E.g. **Mon appartement est <u>plus</u> beau <u>que</u> ta maison.**

~ il n'y a pas de …

When using **il y a** (there is/there are), e.g. **Il y a <u>une</u> piscine dans l'hôtel**, in a negative sentence, **un/une/des** becomes **de**. E.g. **Il n'y a pas <u>de</u> piscine dans l'hôtel.**

Exercices de grammaire

Reflexive verbs

1 Fill in the gaps in the text with the appropriate pronoun. (Note: **se baigner** = to swim/ bathe, **se fatiguer** = to get tired, **se coucher** = to go to bed.)

En vacances, je _____ **(a)** lève à dix heures du matin. Je _____ **(b)** lave avant de prendre mon petit déjeuner. Je vais à la piscine avec mon frère et nous _____ **(c)** baignons pendant une heure. Ensuite nous _____ **(d)** promenons près de la plage. En général, nous _____ **(e)** amusons bien. Ici le soleil _____ **(f)** couche tard et les gens _____ **(g)** promènent jusqu'à minuit! Mon frère _____ **(h)** fatigue rapidement alors nous rentrons tôt à l'hôtel et nous _____ **(i)** couchons tout de suite.

2 Put the words in the following sentences in the appropriate order.

a nous/réveillons/ne/pas/avant/nous/dix heures.
b aujourd'hui/lèves/tôt/tu/te!
c ne/vous/habillez/pas/vous?
d promènent/se/elles/dans/le jardin.
e ne/elle/se/pas/douche/tous/les/matins.
f tôt/je/vais/réveiller/me/demain.

Comparatives

3 You have been looking at two houses in a holiday brochure and have made a few notes. Using the grid below, compare the two houses and write your answer in a full sentence. Note: + indicates **plus**, – indicates **moins**, = indicates **aussi**.

	maison 1	maison 2
E.g. **petit salon**	=	=

Dans la première maison, le salon est aussi petit que dans la deuxième maison.

		maison 1	maison 2
a	agréable		+
b	cuisine spacieuse	–	
c	salle de bains moderne	=	=
d	jardin pratique	+	
e	tranquille		–
f	grandes chambres		+

il n'y a pas de ...

4 Fill in the gaps.

Dans ma maison, il y a _____ **(a)** petite chambre mais il n'y a pas _____ **(b)** salon. Dans la cuisine il y a _____ **(c)** grande table. Dans le bureau de mon frère il n'y a pas _____ **(d)** table. A l'extérieur, il n'y a pas _____ **(e)** jardin mais il y a _____ **(f)** piscine.

Vocabulaire

~ L'hôtel — Hotels

l'armoire (f)	wardrobe
l'ascenseur (m)	lift
à votre disposition	available
la carte	card
cassé	broken
la chambre	bedroom
le chauffage	heating
le chèque de voyage	traveller's cheque
commander	to order
la couverture	blanket
la devise	currency
la direction	management
la douche	shower
l'eau (f) chaude	hot water
l'étage (m)	floor
la fenêtre	window
l'interrupteur (m)	switch
le lit	bed
la nuit	night
l'objet (m) de valeur	valuable
l'oreiller (m)	pillow
le parking	car park
la réservation	booking
le réveil automatique	early morning call
la salle de bains	bathroom
la serviette	towel
le téléphone	telephone
la télévision par satellite	satellite television
la veille	the day before

~ Verbes pronominaux — Reflexive verbs

s'amuser	to have fun
se baigner	to bathe, swim
se coucher	to go to bed
se doucher	to shower
se fatiguer	to get tired
se lever	to get up
se laver	to get washed
se réveiller	to wake up
se promener	to go for a walk
se plaindre	to complain
se raser	to shave

~ Mois et saisons — Months and seasons

la haute saison	high season
la demi-saison	mid-season
la basse saison	low season
l'automne (m)	autumn
l'été (m)	summer
l'hiver (m)	winter
le printemps (m)	spring
janvier	January
février	February
mars	March
avril	April
mai	May
juin	June
juillet	July
août	August
septembre	September
octobre	October
novembre	November
décembre	December

~ La maison — Home

la baignoire	bath
beau/belle	beautiful
la campagne	countryside
le canapé-lit	sofa bed
celui-ci/celui-là	this one/that one
la cheminée	fireplace
la commode	chest of drawers
la cuisine	kitchen
la cuisinière	cooker
l'évier (m)	sink
la fermeture annuelle	annual closure
le gîte (m)	holiday cottage
idéal	ideal
intéressant	interesting
le jardin	garden
le lavabo	washbasin
le lave-linge	washing machine
le lave-vaisselle	dishwasher
lequel?/laquelle?	which one?
le meuble	cabinet
petit	small
plus/moins/aussi	more/less/as
le réfrigérateur	fridge
le relax	garden lounger
le rez-de-chaussée	ground floor
la salle de séjour	living room
le salon de jardin	garden table/chairs
les toilettes	toilet

Travail à deux

1 Une réservation

You are booking a hotel room for your family. Create a dialogue with your partner using the prompts below. You begin.

– Say that you would like to book a room for two people and a baby (**un bébé**).
– Say that you want it for two nights.
– Explain that you would like a room with a double bed and a cot (**lit enfant**) and ask if there is a room with a bathroom.
– Ask how much it is.
– Say that you'll take it.
– Spell your name and ask if there is a car park in the hotel.
– Repeat the instructions to check that you have understood.
– Ask if breakfast is served in your room and at what time.
– Say thank you.

2 Se plaindre

The owner of the **gîte** where you are staying on holiday has just popped in to see if all is well. Unfortunately, you have had a few problems. Tell him/her about them using the list below and listen to his/her excuses.

(Note: **une erreur** = mistake, **brancher** = plug in, **couvertures** = covers/blankets, **changer** = change, **désolé** = sorry.)

a The swimming pool is smaller than the swimming pool in the brochure!

b The television does not work, there is no satellite!

c The heating does not work and there are no blankets in the bedrooms!

d The window in the kitchen is broken.

e You would like to change **gîte**.

Nice, France

Travail à deux

1 Une réservation

You are the hotel receptionist and a client is making a booking. Use the prompts below to create a dialogue with your partner. Your partner will begin.

- Ask for how many nights.
- Ask if they want double or single beds. (cot = **lit enfant**)
- Say that you have a room with shower.
- Say that it costs €80 per night.
- Ask what name the booking is under.
- Say that the car park is on the left behind the hotel.
- Explain that breakfast is served in the restaurant between 8 a.m. and 10 a.m.
- Finish the conversation saying 'you are welcome'.

2 Se plaindre

You are the owner of a **gîte**. You have just popped in to see if your new tenants are happy. Unfortunately, they have had a few problems. Listen to their complaints and use the following instructions to reassure them.

(Note: **une erreur** = mistake; **brancher** = plug in; **couvertures** = covers/blankets; **changer** = change; **désolé** = sorry; **réservé** = booked).

Start by apologising

a There is a mistake in the brochure.

b You need to plug in the satellite.

c The blankets are in the wardrobe in the third bedroom on the second floor. There is no heating in the **gîte** in the summer.

d Explain that you are going to look at the window.

e Sorry, it is not possible. All the **gîtes** are booked.

Nice, France

7 Au restaurant

When you have completed this unit, you will be able to get through to someone on the telephone, arrange to meet someone, describe physical appearances and order a meal.

1 Janella est là?

Ecoutez les conversations téléphoniques, puis reliez les expressions anglaises avec leur équivalent français.

A

– Oui, allô.
– Je voudrais parler à Mohammed, s'il vous plaît.
– Oui, c'est moi.
– Salut Mohammed, c'est Sandeep …

B

– Allô.
– Je pourrais parler à Janella, s'il vous plaît?
– Oui, ne quittez pas, je vous la passe.

C

– Allô.
– Je peux parler à Billy, s'il vous plaît?
– Désolé, il n'est pas là.
– Il pourrait me rappeler? C'est Lucy.
– D'accord, je vais le lui dire.

D

– Allô.
– Pourrais-je parler à Ingrid, s'il vous plaît?
– Désolée, elle n'est pas là. Vous voulez lui laisser un message?
– Non, je vais rappeler plus tard.

a Could I speak to …

b He isn't here.

c I would like to speak to …

d Hold on.

e I'll pass you over to her.

f I'll call back later.

g Would you like to leave her a message?

h Could he call me back?

i Speaking.

j I'll tell him.

1 C'est moi.

2 Vous voulez lui laisser un message?

3 Pourrais-je parler à …

4 Je vais le lui dire.

5 Il pourrait me rappeler?

6 Je vais rappeler plus tard.

7 Ne quittez pas.

8 Je vous la passe.

9 Je voudrais parler à …

10 Il n'est pas là.

Puis-je parler à … /Je pourrais parler à …/Pourrais-je parler à …
à l'appareil   C'est de la part de qui?

2 Ce n'est pas Janine, c'est …

Ecoutez deux conversations téléphoniques et complétez les dialogues.

1 – Allô, oui.
  – Salut Janine, c'est Bernard.
  – Ah non, ce n'est pas Janine, c'est Isabelle!
  – Oh pardon, je _____ **(a)**?
  – Elle n'est pas ici.
  – Je _____ **(b)** un message?
  – Bien sûr.

2 – Allô.
  – _____ **(a)** parler à Etienne, s'il vous plaît? C'est Pierre.
  – Je suis désolé, il _____ **(b)**.
  – Ah bon, il _____ **(c)** rappeler?
  – Oui bien sûr, je vais _____ **(d)** dire.
  – Merci, au revoir.
  – Au revoir.

3 Ça te dirait?

Ecoutez une conversation entre deux amies qui organisent leur soirée, puis répondez aux questions ci-dessous.

a What does Sandrine suggest doing?
b What is her plan?
c How are they going to get in touch with Raphaël and Pierre?
d What arrangements are made? Give three details.

ça te dit/dirait de	j'ai besoin de	j'ai envie de
on pourrait aller	on se retrouve	on se voit

4 A vous de jouer!

A deux, organisez une soirée. Essayez d'utiliser les structures ci-dessus.

grammaire

Vous voulez parler <u>à Bernard</u>?	Oui, je voudrais <u>lui parler</u>.
Vous voulez laisser un message <u>à Pierre et Isabelle?</u>	Oui, je voudrais <u>leur laisser</u> un message.

5 Il porte des lunettes?

Trouvez la signification des descriptions ci-dessous. Vous pouvez consulter un dictionnaire.

a

Il est grand et gros
et il a les cheveux
bruns et courts.
Il a les yeux bleus
et il porte des lunettes.
Il a une barbe
et une moustache.

b

Elle est petite et mince et
elle a les cheveux
blonds et longs.
Elle a les yeux verts
et des taches de
rousseur. Elle porte
des boucles d'oreilles.

6 Il est comment?

Sandrine va rencontrer Raphaël et Pierre mais elle ne les connaît pas. Elle téléphone à Agnès pour avoir une description. Ecoutez leur conversation et notez le plus de détails possible sur les deux hommes.

7 Tu le connais?

Ecoutez et complétez le dialogue entre deux étudiants.

Audrey   Salut Laurent, ça va?
Laurent   Ah, salut Audrey, ça va bien merci. Et toi?
Audrey   Bien, bien aussi. Tu _____ **(a)** un café?
Laurent   Euh … j'ai un _____ **(b)** de math à dix heures.
Audrey   Oh, ça va, il est dix heures moins le _____ **(c)**. Tu as _____ **(d)** un quart d'heure. C'est qui ton prof de maths?
Laurent   Fabien Lecomte. Tu le _____ **(e)**?
Audrey   Non, je ne crois pas. Il est _____ **(f)**?
Laurent   Euh … il est _____ **(g)** et il a les _____ **(h)** noirs et _____ **(i)**. Il a une _____ **(j)** aussi.
Audrey   Et ses _____ **(k)**?
Laurent   Alors ça, je ne sais pas!

8 Il a de beaux yeux!

Travaillez en groupes de trois ou quatre. D'abord, écrivez chacun la description d'une personne dans votre groupe. Puis, échangez vos notes et à tour de rôle lisez-les à voix haute. Devinez à qui correspond la description.

7 Au restaurant

La Normandie

9 Qu'est-ce que tu prends?

a Regardez le menu, puis écoutez et notez en anglais ce que les clients commandent.

b Notez comment on dit "dish of the day".

c Ecoutez encore une fois et notez ci-dessous le choix de viande [cow], de poisson [fish], et de légumes [carrot] .

Formule « express » €18,00

Entrée du jour *ou*
12 escargots *ou*
Assiette de crudités

Plat du jour *ou*
Plat végétarien *ou*
Truite aux amandes

Fromage *ou*
Corbeille de fruits *ou*
Coupe glacée (3 boules)

comme entrée/plat principal/dessert
un steak saignant/à point/bien cuit
Qu'est-ce que c'est, le plat du jour?

[cow]	[fish]	[carrot]

10 Tu en veux?

Ecoutez un dialogue dans un restaurant et dites si les phrases ci-dessous sont vraies ou fausses. (NB: **surtout** = especially; **copieux** = filling)

a Le steak est délicieux, surtout la sauce.

b Joseph pense que la sauce est bonne.

c Le plat végétarien n'est pas très bon.

d Le plat végétarien est trop copieux.

e Sophie veut commander encore du vin.

f Joseph commande de l'eau minérale.

j'ai faim   j'ai soif

grammaire

J'<u>en</u> prends deux   Tu <u>en</u> veux?   Il n'y <u>en</u> a plus.

11 Avec crème?

Lisez la transcription suivante, puis écoutez et corrigez les erreurs. (Il y en a sept!)

– Monsieur, je peux commander, s'il vous plaît?

– Oui, madame. Qu'est-ce que vous prenez?

– Comme entrée je vais prendre la salade verte et comme plat principal je prends le steak-frites.

– Et votre steak, vous le voulez comment?

– A point, s'il vous plaît.

– Et comme dessert?

– Le gâteau.

– Avec crème?

– Sans crème, s'il vous plaît. Je suis allergique à la crème.

– Très bien, je vais le noter. Et comme boisson?

– Je prends un verre de vin blanc et une bouteille d'eau minérale, s'il vous plaît.

– Et un café?

– Oui, je voudrais bien un café avec mon dessert, s'il vous plaît.

Je suis allergique à la crème.

12 Je ne prends pas de dessert

Reliez les phrases suivantes avec leur équivalent anglais.

a Qu'est-ce que c'est, le plat du jour?

b Pourrais-je avoir le steak saignant?

c On prend encore une bouteille?

d J'en prends deux.

e Je ne prends pas de dessert.

f Tu as faim?

g Vous en voulez?

h Il n'y en a plus.

1 I'll take two.

2 There isn't any left.

3 What is the 'dish of the day'?

4 Shall we have another bottle?

5 Could I have my steak rare?

6 Would you like some?

7 I'm not going to have dessert.

8 Are you hungry?

13 A vous de jouer!

Lisez le menu ci-dessous et avec votre partenaire commandez un repas (l'entrée, le plat principal, le dessert et la boisson). N'oubliez pas de changer de rôle!

Menu Express

servi uniquement à midi, en semaine
€26,00

2 plats au choix + 1 verre de vin + 1 café
(entrée + plat) ou *(plat + dessert)* ou
(entrée + dessert)

Nos entrées

Le tartare de tomates en trois variétés: au basilic, salade d'été, à l'huile d'olive

La tarte fine à la tomate ou *chèvre rôti sur frisée*

Nos plats principaux

Confit de canard avec pommes de terre dauphinoise

Steak frites: sauce au poivre ou *bordelaise*

Pavé de lotte poêlé à l'huile d'olive avec tartiflette

Servi avec un choix de légumes du jour

Nos desserts

Crème caramel
Crème brûlée
Tartelette au citron

Café ou *Thé*

Extra!

 1 Laissez un message, s'il vous plaît

Ecoutez le message sur le répondeur, puis en anglais notez les informations suivantes.

a Who is calling and who the message is being left for.

b The time, venue and location where they will meet.

c Details of the plans for the evening.

2 Quoi de neuf?

Lisez l'e-mail suivant et répondez aux questions ci-dessous. (NB: **ensemble** = together; **se faire bronzer** = to sunbathe)

A: marieclaire1986@yahoo.fr
Objet: Salut toi!

Marie-Claire,

Merci pour ton e-mail ... J'espère que tout va bien et que tu es en forme.

Alors ... quoi de neuf? Moi, j'ai un nouveau copain! Il s'appelle Jacques et il a vingt-huit ans. Il est étudiant mais on travaille ensemble au supermarché le samedi. Je le connais depuis quelques mois mais on sort ensemble depuis deux semaines. Je le trouve très sympa et beau aussi! Il est assez grand, je crois qu'il fait un mètre quatre-vingts. Je suis contente parce que je suis grande aussi! Il a les cheveux noirs et bouclés et les yeux bleus. Il est très sportif, il joue au tennis au moins trois fois par semaine. Comme tu le sais, je ne fais pas trop de sport, mais je vais peut-être commencer!! Si tout va bien, on va partir en vacances ensemble cet été. On voudrait faire du camping dans le sud-ouest de la France. Jacques veut faire de la planche à voile, mais moi, je vais me faire bronzer!

A bientôt j'espère.

Gros bisous

Stéphanie

---

a What news does Stéphanie have to tell Marie-Claire?

b Give a physical description of Jacques. Include at least three points.

c How long have they been together?

d Where are they planning to go for the summer holidays?

e What is each of them planning to do on holiday?

Grammaire

~ The use of the conditional to be more polite

The conditional form of **je peux (je pourrais)** and **je veux (je voudrais)** denotes the meaning 'could/would' and is used to be more polite.

Je <u>veux/peux</u> parler à … > Je <u>voudrais/pourrais</u> parler à …
Il <u>peut</u> me rappeler? > Il <u>pourrait</u> me rappeler?
Vous <u>pouvez</u> lui laisser un message? > Vous <u>pourriez</u> lui laisser un message?

~ Object pronouns lui and leur

The object pronoun **lui** is used to denote both 'to him' and 'to her'. It is used to replace the person who is being referred to and is a generic term for both male and female. It is used when verbs are followed by the preposition **à**, e.g. **dire, parler, téléphoner, laisser, donner.**

– Tu téléphones <u>à Ingrid?</u>   – Oui, je <u>lui</u> téléphone.
– Il va téléphoner <u>à Annie?</u>   – Oui, il va <u>lui</u> téléphoner.

Leur is the plural object pronoun and is used to denote 'to them'. It is a generic term used for both male and female.

– Elle parle <u>à Sophie et Bernadette?</u>   – Oui, elle <u>leur</u> parle.

Notice that **lui** and **leur** go in front of the verb in the infinitive when used with the near future tense.

– Vous allez laisser un message <u>à Pierre et Astrid</u>?   – Oui, je vais <u>leur</u> laisser un message.

~ The use of on

On is commonly used in conversation and is used to replace the first person plural **nous**. It is conjugated as the third person singular, i.e. the same form as for **il** and **elle**.

<u>Nous</u> pouvons aller au café. > <u>On</u> peut aller au café.
<u>Nous</u> allons au cinéma? > <u>On</u> va au cinéma?

~ The use of en

En is another pronoun, used to replace a noun when a quantity is mentioned. E.g.
– Vous avez <u>des</u> enfants?   – Oui, j'<u>en</u> ai trois. (but: **– Vous aimez <u>les</u> enfants?**
– Oui, je <u>les</u> aime.)

– Tu veux du pain?   – Oui, j'<u>en</u> veux.
– Il n'y a plus de vin.   – On <u>en</u> prend encore.
– Vous allez prendre des pommes?   – Oui, je vais <u>en</u> prendre trois.
– Je voudrais une cigarette.   – Désolé, il n'y <u>en</u> a plus.

Exercices de grammaire

The use of the conditional to be more polite

1 Make the following requests/suggestions more polite.

E.g. **Je peux parler à Solange?** > *Je pourrais parler à Solange, s'il vous plaît?*

a Je veux parler à Monique.
b On peut aller au cinéma.
c Elle veut un apéritif?
d Il peut venir à la fin de cette semaine.
e Je peux utiliser le téléphone?

Object pronouns lui and leur

2 Insert the object pronoun **lui** or **leur** into the following sentences to replace the nouns that are underlined.

E.g. **Vous parlez à Annie.** > *Vous lui parlez.*

a Tu vas téléphoner à ta mère.
b Ils vont parler à Jacques et Françoise?
c Elle va dire quelque chose à Mélanie.
d Vous donnez de l'argent à Henri?
e Elles vont donner des bonbons aux enfants?

The use of on

3 Make the following text more informal using **on** instead of **nous**. Remember to change the form of the verb.

Le week-end nous aimons sortir. Souvent nous allons au restaurant parce que nous adorons la cuisine française. Après nous allons au cinéma ou en boîte ou bien nous rentrons à la maison pour regarder la télévision. Le dimanche matin nous faisons du sport, nous jouons au tennis ou au ping-pong.

The use of en

4 Answer the following questions using the pronoun **en**, and using the (+) or (–) signs as indicators.

E.g. **Il y a du café? (+)** > *Oui, il y en a.*

a Vous prenez un dessert? (+)
b Ils ont des enfants? (–)
c Elle a des amis français? (+)
d Tu veux du chocolat? (–)
e Il mange de la viande? (+)
f Il y a du vin? (–)

7 Au restaurant

Vocabulaire

～ Parler à quelqu'un au téléphone — Getting through to someone on the telephone

Je voudrais parler à …	I'd like to speak to …
Pourrais-je parler à …	Could I speak to …
Etienne est là?	Is Etienne there?
C'est moi.	Speaking.
Ne quittez pas.	Hold on.
Je vous le/la passe.	I'll pass you over.
Désolé, il/elle n'est pas là.	Sorry, s/he isn't here.
Pourrais-je lui laisser un message?	Could you leave him/her a message?
Je vais rappeler plus tard.	I'll ring back later.
Il/elle pourrait me rappeler?	Could s/he ring me back?
Je vais le lui dire.	I'll tell him/her.
à l'appareil	on the telephone
C'est de la part de qui?	Who is calling?

～ Sortir — Making arrangements to go out

Ça te dit/dirait de …	Would you like to/do you fancy …
J'ai envie de …	I'd really like to/I fancy …
J'ai besoin de …	I need to …
On se retrouve à …	Let's meet at …
On peut …/On pourrait …	We can …/We could …
On se voit à …	See you at …

～ Décrire une personne — Describing someone

décrire	to describe
les cheveux: noirs/bruns/blonds/roux/longs/courts	black/brown/blond/red/long/short hair
les yeux: verts/bleus/marron	green/blue/brown eyes
des taches (f) de rousseur	freckles
la moustache/la barbe	moustache/beard
des lunettes/des boucles d'oreilles	glasses/earrings
grand(e)/petit(e)/mince/gros(se)	tall/short/slim/fat

～ Sortir au restaurant — Eating out

le menu/la carte	set menu/menu
comme entrée/plat principal/dessert	for starter/main course/dessert
commander	to order
l'entrée/le plat du jour	starter/dish of the day
la viande/le poulet/le steak/les escargots (m)	meat/chicken/steak/snails
le lapin/le canard	rabbit/duck
le poisson/la truite/la lotte	fish/trout/monkfish
végétarien	vegetarian
le (fromage de) chèvre	goat's cheese
les noix (f)/les champignons (m)/les crudités (m)	walnuts/mushrooms/raw vegetables
l'huile (f)/la tartiflette	oil/potato gratin
poêlé(e)/fumé(e)	pan fried/smoked
une (boule de) glace à la vanille/au chocolat	a (scoop of) vanilla/chocolate ice cream
saignant/à point/bien cuit	rare/medium/well done (steak)
le choix	selection/choice
thé nature/à la menthe/au citron	black/mint/lemon tea
Qu'est-ce que c'est?	What is it?
je suis allergique à	I am allergic to
l'addition (f)	the bill
avoir faim/soif	to be hungry/thirsty
encore	more

Travail à deux

1 On sort ce soir?

You are trying to arrange a night out. Phone a friend and use the following information in the dialogue. Your friend will speak first.

– Say hello and ask to speak to X. Introduce yourself.
– Ask how s/he is.
– Ask if s/he wants to go out at the weekend.
– Ask if s/he is free on Saturday evening.
– Suggest meeting outside the station at 7:30 p.m.
– Finish the conversation appropriately.

2 Au restaurant

Use the information below to order a meal in a restaurant. Your partner is the waiter/waitress and will start the conversation.

– Ask for the menu.
– When asked, order a starter. Find out if there is a dish of the day.
– Say OK. Choose the steak.
– Say that you will have the pepper sauce.
– Say you would like the steak well done.
– Order a glass of red wine.
– (Finish your main course.) Order a chocolate mousse.
– When asked, you would like a coffee after your dessert.

Formule « express »
€18,00

Les entrées
Salade de tomates et mozzarella
Terrine de lapin
Gratinée de Coquilles St Jacques

Les plats principaux
Lit de ratatouille fraîche
Salade maison: tomates, jambon fumé, noix, toast de chèvre chaud
Confit de canard avec pommes de terre dauphinoises
Steak frites avec sauce bordelaise, au poivre *ou* au roquefort

Les desserts
Mousse au chocolat
Sorbet pamplemousse, fraise *ou* vanille
Café
Thé nature, à la menthe *ou* au citron

Travail à deux

B

1 On sort ce soir?

You receive a phone call. Use the following information in the dialogue. You start.

– The phone rings. Say hello.
– It is a friend. Greet him/her.
– Say you are fine.
– S/he suggests a night out. Say it is a good idea and that you would like to see a film.
– Say you are free on Saturday evening. Ask what time and where.
– Confirm the time and place.
– Finish the conversation appropriately.

2 Au restaurant

You are a restaurant waiter. Use the information below to create a dialogue with your partner who is the customer. You start the dialogue.

– Say good evening to the customer.
– Ask which starter the customer would like.
– Say that there is no dish of the day.
– Ask which sauce the customer would like: wine, pepper or roquefort cheese.
– Find out how the customer would like the steak cooked.
– Ask if s/he would like some wine.
– (The customer finishes the main course.) Ask if s/he would like a dessert.
– Ask if s/he would like coffee with the dessert.

Formule « express » €18,00

Les entrées
Salade de tomates et mozzarella
Terrine de lapin
Gratinée de Coquilles St Jacques

Les plats principaux
Lit de ratatouille fraîche
Salade maison: tomates, jambon fumé, noix, toast de chèvre chaud
Confit de canard avec pommes de terre dauphinoises
Steak frites avec sauce bordelaise, au poivre *ou* au roquefort

Les desserts
Mousse au chocolat
Sorbet pamplemousse, fraise *ou* vanille

Café
Thé nature, à la menthe *ou* au citron

8 Vacances et loisirs

When you have completed this unit, you will be able to: talk about what you did at the weekend, explain why you are late, discuss your holidays, and describe places and the weather.

1 Tu as passé un bon week-end?

a Ecoutez la conversation et dites (en anglais) pourquoi Sylvie a passé un excellent week-end, et Jeanne un mauvais week-end. (NB: **sympa** = nice, friendly; **le portefeuille** = wallet)

b Lisez le dialogue et soulignez les 16 verbes au passé composé (perfect tense).

Jeanne   Tu <u>as passé</u> un bon week-end?

Sylvie   Oui, super! Samedi soir, j'ai vu Pierre; on a mangé dans un restaurant sympa et on a dansé toute la nuit. Dimanche, j'ai dormi tard, j'ai pris un bain et j'ai lu un bon livre: un week-end très relaxant, quoi!

Jeanne   Ah oui, c'est sympa!

Sylvie   Et toi, qu'est-ce que tu as fait?

Jeanne   Oh, moi ... Samedi j'ai fait des courses, mais j'ai perdu mon portefeuille, j'ai dû aller à la police ...

Sylvie   Non! Est-ce qu'ils l'ont retrouvé?

Jeanne   Non, malheureusement ... Et dimanche, j'ai passé la journée chez mes parents; ils ont acheté une nouvelle voiture et ...

Sylvie   Vous avez fait un tour à la campagne?

Jeanne   Non, ils ont préféré rester à la maison; nous avons regardé la télévision, c'est tout.

Sylvie   Ah bon.

c A deux, retrouvez l'infinitif des verbes que vous avez soulignés.
(Ex: **as passé** > *passer*)

Passé composé (perfect tense) avec "avoir"

			Regular verbs:		Irregular verbs:	
j'	ai	passé	passer>	passé	faire >	fait
tu	as	passé	dormir >	dormi	prendre >	pris
il/elle/on	a	passé	perdre>	perdu	lire >	lu
nous	avons	passé			voir >	vu
vous	avez	passé			devoir >	dû
ils/elles	ont	passé				

2 Un week-end culturel

a Ecoutez la conversation et répondez aux questions en anglais. (NB: **plein de** = lots of; **épicé(e)** = spicy, hot)

    1 With whom did Elise spend the weekend?
    2 What kind of 'cultural things' did they do together?
    3 Why didn't Jean-Marc play tennis on Saturday?
    4 Why did he sleep all day on Sunday?

b Ecoutez la conversation encore une fois et complétez le résumé.

Elise   J'_____**(a)** plein de choses avec ma copine anglaise; on _____**(b)** des musées, on _____**(c)** une pièce de théâtre et un film. ,

Jean-Marc J'_____**(d)** ma dissertation samedi. Le soir, j'_____**(e)** des amis à dîner. Ma copine Isabelle _____**(f)** un plat indien très épicé. On _____**(g)** plein de bière et on _____**(h)** toute la journée dimanche.

– Tu <u>as joué</u> au tennis?   – Non, je **n'**<u>ai</u> **pas** <u>joué</u> au tennis.
– Tu <u>as pris</u> un bain?   – Non, je **n'**<u>ai</u> **pas** <u>pris</u> **de** bain.

3 La copine anglaise

Ecrivez le résumé ci-dessus à la 3ème personne. (Ex: <u>Elise a fait</u> plein de choses avec sa copine anglaise, <u>elles ont visité</u> ...**)**

 4 Qu'est-ce que tu as fait?

A deux, posez-vous des questions sur vos activités du week-end dernier.
(Ex: – Tu as mangé au restaurant? – Oui, j'ai mangé au restaurant. / Non, je n'ai pas mangé au restaurant.)

a	manger au restaurant	**e**	faire des courses
b	danser	**f**	faire du sport
c	regarder la télé	**g**	voir une pièce de théâtre ou un film
d	travailler	**h**	lire un livre

5 Désolé, je suis en retard ...

Ecoutez 5 personnes qui sont en retard. Trouvez l'excuse de chaque personne dans la liste ci-dessous.

a Problem with car.

b Bus was late.

c Lost track of time.

d Lost the address.

e Unfinished work.

> Qu'est-ce qui s'est passé?
> Pardon / Je suis désolé(e), j'ai perdu …
> j'ai eu un problème avec …
> je n'ai pas fini …
> je n'ai pas vu …
> j'ai dû retourner …
> Ce n'est pas grave. / Ça ne fait rien.

6 Qu'est-ce qui s'est passé?

a Remettez les phrases dans l'ordre pour faire un dialogue. (NB: je n'ai pas pu = I couldn't; les flics = police (coll.))

a Ah bon! C'est grave?

b Je suis vraiment désolé, je n'ai pas pu venir hier soir parce que j'ai eu plein de problèmes!

c Allô?

d Ah, Daniel! Eh bien, qu'est-ce qui s'est passé, mon vieux?

e Eh bien, j'ai pris la voiture de mes parents et … j'ai eu un accident.

f Oh, la voiture … mon père est furieux!

g Non, mais j'ai dû aller chez les flics; j'ai oublié de te téléphoner, excuse-moi!

h Ah bon, qu'est-ce qui s'est passé?

i Salut Luc, c'est Daniel.

j Je comprends … et la voiture?

b Ecoutez le dialogue pour vérifier vos réponses.

7 J'ai eu un problème

Ecoutez le dialogue et notez toutes les excuses données.

8 Quelle excuse!

Traduisez les phrases suivantes.

a I couldn't come to the party (**la soirée**); **b** because I met (**rencontrer**) a friend in the street; **c** he suggested (**proposer de**) going to the pub; **d** we had a lot to drink; **e** I lost track of time; **f** I missed (**rater**) the last bus.

9 Gros bisous de Bretagne

Lisez la carte postale et, à deux, dites si les phrases ci-dessous sont vraies ou fausses.

> Salut Marcel!
> Le Conquet est super! C'est une jolie ville, très animée; il y a plein de cafés et de restos sympas. Axèle connaît bien, elle a de la famille ici. Nous sommes arrivées hier. Ce matin, je suis allée à la plage mais je n'ai pas nagé: l'eau est trop froide!
>
> Gros bisous,
>
> *Laurence*

Marcel Duchêne
16 rue Charcot
75013 Paris

a Laurence is holidaying on her own.

b She has just started her holiday.

c She likes Le Conquet because it is very quiet.

d She has family there.

e She went swimming in the morning.

---

je <u>suis</u> all<u>ée</u>   nous <u>sommes</u> arriv<u>ées</u>

C'est une jolie ville/une ville animée.
Il y a plein de cafés/de restaurants.

---

10 Tu es déjà allé(e) à Paris?

A deux, parlez des villes où vous êtes allé(e)s et décrivez-les. Vous pouvez utiliser les adjectifs suivants:

super, cool, sympa – nul(le) / moderne – ancien(ne), pittoresque / animé(e) – calme, tranquille / (pas) très joli(e), beau (belle) / propre – sale, pollué(e)

11 Et toi, tu es parti?

Ecoutez la conversation et complétez le dialogue. (NB: **pas vraiment** = not really; **rentrer** = to go/come back home)

– Tu es parti, pendant les _____ **(a)** de Pâques?
– Oui, je _____ **(b)** allé en Irlande.
– En Irlande! _____ **(c)**? A Dublin?
– Non, à la campagne, dans le sud-ouest.
– Super! Pendant _____ **(d)** de temps?
– Pendant une _____ **(e)**.
– Il a fait beau?
– Oh, pas vraiment, mais il n'a pas fait froid. On a fait des _____ **(f)** fantastiques! Et toi, tu es parti?
– Oui, je suis _____ **(g)** à la mer, en Bretagne. J'ai _____ **(h)** de la planche à voile pendant deux semaines. Il a fait un temps magnifique!
– Oui, tu es tout bronzé! _____ **(i)** est-ce que tu es rentré?
– Eh bien, dimanche … il y a _____ **(j)** jours.

grammaire

Passé composé avec "être"

je <u>suis</u> parti(<u>e</u>)	nous <u>sommes</u> parti(e)s	<u>Pendant</u> combien de temps?
tu <u>es</u> parti(<u>e</u>)	vous <u>êtes</u> parti(e)s	<u>Pendant</u> une semaine.
il <u>est</u> parti	ils <u>sont</u> partis	Quand? / <u>Il y a</u> combien de temps?
elle <u>est</u> partie	elles <u>sont</u> parties	<u>Il y a</u> trois jours.

les vacances de Noël / de Pâques / d'été   il a fait beau / mauvais
à la mer / à la campagne / à la montagne   il a fait chaud / froid
le nord / le sud / l'est / l'ouest

12 Tu as passé de bonnes vacances?

Ecoutez les 2 conversations et remplissez les cases. (NB: **la plage** = beach)

	Où?	Pendant combien de temps?	Temps? (weather)	Activités?
Benoît				
Sarah et Michel				

13 Nous sommes allés aux Antilles

A deux, posez-vous des questions sur vos dernières vacances (où, quand, pendant combien de temps, quel temps, activités, etc.).

14 Il pleut dans le nord-est

Ecoutez le bulletin météo (weather report) **pour les différentes régions de France et dites à quel dessin correspond chaque expression.**

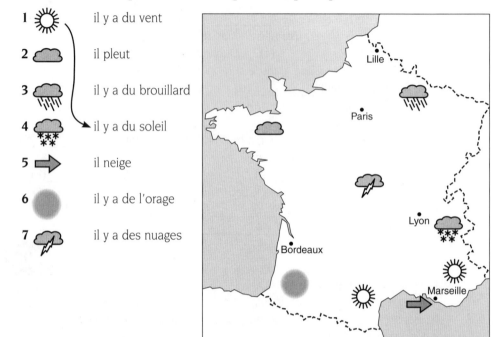

1   il y a du vent

2   il pleut

3   il y a du brouillard

4   il y a du soleil

5   il neige

6   il y a de l'orage

7   il y a des nuages

15 Les saisons au Québec

Ecoutez Pierre qui décrit les saisons au Québec et remplissez les cases.

hiver	printemps	été	automne

16 Quel temps fait-il en hiver?

A deux, décrivez les saisons dans le pays ou la région d'où vous venez. (Ex: En hiver, il ne fait pas froid mais il pleut beaucoup; etc.)

Extra!

1 Le week-end

Listen to four students describing their weekend and write down all the details mentioned.

a Muriel:

b Stéphane:

c Loulou:

d Bernard:

2 Vacances dans les Alpes

Alain has just come back from holiday and is writing an email to his English friend Dennis. Read the email and answer the questions below. (NB: **une balade** = **une promenade**; **l'escalade** = rock climbing)

A: dennismcbride@aol.com
Objet: Salut!

Cher Dennis,

Comment ça va? Tu as passé un bon été? Moi, j'ai passé de super vacances dans les Alpes! Je suis parti pendant trois semaines avec deux copains, Xavier et Eric. On a pris nos vélos et on a fait des balades fantastiques: dures, mais on a vu des paysages magnifiques! En fait, on a plus ou moins suivi la route du Tour de France. (Tu connais le Tour de France? C'est une course cycliste qui se passe chaque année.) En plus, il a fait un temps idéal: beau, mais pas trop chaud, avec quelques nuages … On a pu nager dans des petits lacs et on a même fait un peu d'escalade! On a bien mangé, aussi: on a découvert des petits restos de campagne avec de la cuisine traditionnelle, et vraiment pas chers! Je suis rentré tout à fait en forme. J'ai complètement oublié les cours et les examens! Malheureusement, j'ai dû retourner travailler au bureau de mon père: je n'ai plus d'argent! J'espère que tu es en forme, toi aussi.

A bientôt,

Alain

---

a Where did Alain go? For how long?

b What did he do there? What was it like?

c Why does he mention the 'Tour de France'?

d What was the weather like?

e What was the food like?

f How does he feel now?

g How is he spending the rest of his holiday? Why?

Grammaire

~ Verbs: perfect tense (passé composé)

a Use: the perfect tense is the most common of the past tenses; it is used to report events:
e.g. **Il a perdu son passeport! / Nous sommes partis pendant un mois.**

b Form: as its French name ('passé composé') implies, it is made up of two parts:
the 'auxiliary' verb: **avoir**, or sometimes **être**, in the present tense
+
the 'past participle' of the verb

c Past participle: the past participle of regular verbs is formed as follows:
-er verbs: **-é** (e.g. **regardé**)   **-ir** verbs: **-i** (e.g. **fini**)   **-re** verbs: **-u** (e.g. **vendu**)

There are also many irregular forms. Here are some of them:
faire > fait   avoir > eu
prendre > pris   devoir > dû
lire > lu   pouvoir > pu
voir > vu

d Verbs with **être**: the perfect tense of some verbs is formed with **être**, including:
aller (> allé)   rentrer (> rentré)
arriver (> arrivé)   rester (> resté)
partir (> parti)

When the auxiliary **être** is used, the past participle must agree with the subject:
je (m) suis allé   –   je (f) suis allée
tu (m) es allé   –   tu (f) es allée
il est allé   –   elle est allée
on (m) est allés   –   on (f) est allées
nous (m) sommes allés   –   nous (f) sommes allées
vous (m) êtes allés   –   vous (f) êtes allées
ils sont allés   –   elles sont allées

e Negative: **ne … pas** (or other negatives like **ne … plus**) go on either side of **avoir** or **être**:
e.g. **Il n'a pas fini sa dissertation. / Vous n'êtes pas parties en vacances?**

~ pendant and il y a

– **Pendant** (= for) is used to refer to a specific length of time in the past (but also in the present and in the future).
E.g. **Tu es partie pendant combien de temps? Pendant six mois.**

– **Il y a** (= ago) is used to refer to a moment in the past.
E.g. **Il a fini quand? / Il a fini il y a combien de temps? Il y a deux heures.**

Exercices de grammaire

Verbs: perfect tense (passé composé)

1 Avoir or **être**? Fill in the gaps with the appropriate form of **avoir** or **être**.

  a Nous _____ fini notre travail.
  b Je _____ arrivée hier.
  c Pierre _____ parti au Québec.
  d Ils _____ passé un très bon week-end.
  e Ses parents _____ restés en France.
  f Tu _____ vu ce film?

2 Transform the verbs from the present into the perfect tense. (E.g. **Il _fait_ beau.** > Il _a fait_ beau.)

  a Je fais de la planche à voile.
  b Vous aimez ce film?
  c Elles ne prennent pas l'avion.
  d Mes amis restent ici pendant une semaine.
  e Tu (f) vas en vacances?
  f On doit partir à dix heures.
  g Nous (m) rentrons le 20 juillet.
  h Elle ne part pas aux Etats-Unis.

3 Fill in the gaps in the text by choosing the appropriate verbs from the list below and putting them in the perfect tense. (Note: **louer** = to rent, to hire.)

  louer – voir – parler – décider – passer – adorer – faire – aller – rester

  J'_____ **(a)** à Mira hier, elle _____ **(b)** de super vacances! Elle _____ **(c)** au Maroc avec son copain. Ils _____ **(d)** là pendant un mois. Ils _____ **(e)** une voiture et ils _____ **(f)** le tour du pays: ils _____ **(g)** des endroits magnifiques! Ils _____ **(h)** le pays et les gens, et ils _____ **(i)** d'y retourner l'année prochaine.

pendant and il y a

4 Pendant or **il y a?** Fill in the gaps.

  a Hier, elle a travaillé _____ des heures sur sa dissertation!
  b Ils sont partis de la maison _____ dix minutes.
  c Le film a duré _____ combien de temps?
  d Nous sommes restés en Suisse _____ deux semaines.
  e Il est rentré _____ combien de temps?
  f Quand êtes-vous allés à Nice? _____ un mois.

8 Vacances et loisirs

Vocabulaire

~ Verbes
	Verbs
passer	to spend (time)
rester	to stay
rentrer	to come/go back home
louer	to rent, to hire
rencontrer	to meet
rater	to miss
oublier	to forget
perdre	to lose
attendre	to wait for
connaître	to know
suivre	to follow

~ Les vacances
	Holidays
les vacances (f) de Noël	Christmas holidays
les vacances (f) de Pâques	Easter holidays
les vacances (f) d'été	Summer holidays
la plage	beach
la balade	walk/ride
l'escalade	rock-climbing
la soirée	evening (party)
plein de	lots of
épicé(e)	spicy
les flics (m)	cops, policemen

~ Décrire un endroit
	Describing a place
sympa	nice, friendly
nul(le)	not nice (slang)
moderne	modern
ancien(ne)	old, ancient
pittoresque	picturesque
animé(e)	lively
calme, tranquille	quiet
joli(e)	pretty
propre	clean
sale	dirty
pollué(e)	polluted
la mer	sea, seaside
la montagne	mountain
la campagne	country(side)
le nord	north
le sud	south
l'est (m)	east
l'ouest (m)	west

~ Le temps
	The weather
il fait beau	the weather is nice
mauvais	bad
chaud	hot, warm
froid	cold
il y a du soleil	it is sunny
des nuages (m)	cloudy
du vent	windy
de l'orage (m)	stormy
du brouillard	foggy
il pleut	it rains/it is raining
il neige	it snows/it is snowing
pendant	for, during
il y a	ago (also: there is/are)
(pas) vraiment	(not) really

Travail à deux

1 Lundi matin

It is Monday morning and you are discussing the weekend with a French student. Create a dialogue with your partner using the prompts below. You begin.

– Ask your partner if s/he had a good weekend.
– Find out what s/he did with her/his cousin.
– When asked, explain that you had to work all weekend, that you cleaned the house on Saturday and that you worked on your essay on Sunday.
– Say that you haven't finished your essay, that you still (**encore**) have a lot of work to do.
– Accept the suggestion to go for a coffee.

2 Les vacances

You have incomplete information about your friends' holidays. Find out from your partner the missing details and complete the grid below.

	Ali	**Carla**	**Denis et Francine**
Où? (pays/région/ville)	Tunisie		Provence
Pendant combien de temps?			2 semaines
Avec qui?	famille		
Comment? (moyen(s) de transport)	voiture + bateau	avion	
Où? (logement)		amie	camping
Quoi? (activités)		tourisme, mer	

Travail à deux

1 Lundi matin

It is Monday morning and you are discussing the weekend with a French student. Create a dialogue with your partner using the prompts below. Your partner will begin.

– Explain that you had a good weekend, that your cousin is staying with you at the moment and that you did lots of things.
– Say that your cousin loves sport, and that you saw a football match on TV on Saturday, and played tennis on Sunday. Then, ask your partner what her/his weekend was like.
– Ask your partner if s/he has finished the essay.
– React appropriately and suggest going for a coffee before the lecture.

2 Les vacances

You have incomplete information about your friends' holidays. Find out from your partner the missing details and complete the grid below.

	Ali	Carla	Denis et Francine
Où? (pays/région/ville)		Rome	
Pendant combien de temps?	2 mois	2 semaines	
Avec qui?		seule	2 copains
Comment? (moyen(s) de transport)			train
Où? (logement)	famille + hôtel		
Quoi? (activités)	visites (famille, amis), mer		promenades, escalade

9 Education et expérience

When you have completed this unit, you will be able to talk about your background, your education and your work experience.

 1 Depuis combien de temps ...?

Ecoutez Leila parler de son enfance (childhood) et soulignez les erreurs dans la transcription ci-dessous (il y en a 5).

Je suis née à Alger en 1990. J'ai habité en Algérie pendant quatre ans puis ma mère a obtenu un poste plus intéressant en Italie. Nous avons habité à Rome pendant huit mois et je suis allée à l'école française. Ma mère travaille en Espagne depuis 1999. J'ai déménagé en France pour faire mes études et je travaille à Angers depuis six mois.

> J'ai habité en Algérie <u>pendant</u> trois ans.   J'habite à Angers <u>depuis</u> six mois.

2 Depuis ou pendant?

Complétez les phrases avec "depuis" ou "pendant".

a Elle a étudié l'anglais _____ cinq ans.
b J'apprends l'espagnol _____ dix ans.
c Il a habité à Londres _____ dix ans.
d Nous vivons à Lyon _____ un an.

3 Biographie

Ecrivez une courte biographie de Mustapha en français. Utilisez les informations ci-dessous. (NB: **être à la retraite** = to be retired)

Past
Born / 1975.
Lived / Tunisia / 3 years with parents.
Moved to France / in 1978.
Parents worked / Marseilles / 10 years

Present
Father / retired
Family lives in Toulouse / 4 years.
Mustapha and brother / study English / 3 years.
Brother work / 6 months / computing company

4 Et toi, où est-ce que tu es né(e)?

A deux, parlez et posez-vous des questions sur les événements (events) de votre vie. Utilisez "depuis" et "pendant".

5 Une nouvelle vie

Lisez l'e-mail ci-dessous et répondez aux questions en anglais. (NB: **se sentir à l'aise** = to feel at ease; **s'ennuyer** = to be bored; **s'inscrire (à un cours)** = to enrol (on a course); **se présenter** = to introduce oneself)

a How long has Charlotte been in Liverpool?
b How does she feel about the place?
c What two subjects is she studying?
d When did she see Joseph?

A: stephlem@hotmail.com
Objet: Hello!

Chère Stéphanie,

Me voici donc à Liverpool depuis deux semaines. C'est une ville fascinante, il y a énormément de choses à faire et à voir. Je me suis sentie à l'aise immédiatement ici. Je me suis installée dans ma chambre d'étudiante et je ne me suis pas ennuyée une minute! D'abord, je me suis inscrite en cours d'anglais au collège et j'ai commencé à apprendre le japonais! Il y a tellement de cours intéressants ici. J'ai appris que Joseph Bardou, notre vieux copain, habite ici. Je l'ai vu hier matin mais je ne me suis pas présentée ... Voilà les nouvelles en quelques lignes. Je t'embrasse et à bientôt.

Charlotte

---

 6 Inscription à la fac

a Patrick et Angéline s'inscrivent à l'université (la fac). Ecoutez leur conversation et cochez les verbes que vous entendez. (NB: **un coup de fil** = a phone call)

se présenter	se renseigner	remplir	s'installer
s'inscrire	s'ennuyer	devenir	réussir

b Ecoutez le dialogue encore une fois et répondez aux questions en anglais.

i What course is Angéline interested in?
ii What course has Patrick enrolled on?
iii How long has Angéline been living in her flat?

Passé composé des verbes pronominaux

Je me <u>suis</u> installé(e)
Tu t'<u>es</u> installé(e)
Il s'<u>est</u> installé
Elle s'<u>est</u> installé<u>e</u>

Nous nous <u>sommes</u> installé(e)s
Vous vous <u>êtes</u> installé(e)s
Ils se <u>sont</u> installés
Elles se <u>sont</u> installé<u>es</u>

7 L'année à l'étranger

Lisez l'e-mail ci-dessous et complétez les phrases. Ensuite, écoutez l'enregistrement pour vérifier vos réponses. (NB: **s'amuser** = to enjoy oneself; **pas encore** = not yet; **se sentir** = to feel)

A: j.lamy@wanadoo.fr
Objet: Salut de Bristol

Chère Juliette,

Je suis donc à Bristol _____(a) deux mois mais je ne me _____(b) pas très à l'aise ici! Les étudiants dans mon groupe ne sont pas très sympas! Je me suis _____(c) dans ma chambre mais je _____(d) ennuie. J'ai commencé par visiter la ville et je me suis beaucoup amusée mais je _____(e) ici depuis deux mois et je n'ai pas encore rencontré d'autres étudiants anglais! En plus, je ne comprends pas bien l'anglais. Ils parlent trop vite! Le mois dernier, je me suis _____(f) en cours d'anglais au collège. J'ai vu d'autres étudiants français au café hier soir et je _____(g) suis présentée. Je vais les retrouver ce soir!

Viens me voir bientôt. Je t'embrasse bien fort,

Daniella

Je me suis <u>beaucoup</u> amusée
Je <u>n'ai</u> <u>pas encore</u> rencontré …

8 Etudiant à Londres

a Ecoutez 3 étudiants parler de leur nouvelle vie à Londres et répondez aux questions ci-dessous.
(NB: **s'améliorer** = to improve; **se faire des amis** = to make friends)

   i Depuis combien de temps sont-ils à Londres?
   ii Où habitent-ils? Avec qui?
   iii Que pensent-ils de Londres?

b Ecrivez en français un résumé de leurs impressions.

9 Premiers pas à l'université

A deux, parlez de votre arrivée à l'université:
inscription, logement, amis, vie sociale, etc.

10 Travail et études

Ecoutez Adeline décrire son CV et dites si les phrases ci-dessous sont vraies ou fausses.

a She has been working since 1989.
b She has been living in Paris for three years.
c She studied English for five years.
d Her parents moved to Italy two years ago.
e She goes and visits them every two months.

11 Voici mon CV

Lisez le CV d'Adeline et trouvez l'équivalent des expressions suivantes en français.

a surname **b** place of birth **c** 'A' levels **d** degree **e** MA **f** distinction **g** IT skills
h clerical worker **i** bilingual **j** work placement **k** date of birth **l** company

---

CV

Nom: Dubout
Prénom: Adeline
Adresse: 67 rue Lamarck 75018 Paris
Date de naissance: 24 03 1985
Nationalité: française

Téléphone: 01 42 64 53 03
Lieu de naissance: Londres

Diplômes

2003	Baccalauréat Economie (mention Très Bien)
2005	DEUG Administration Economique et Sociale
2006	Licence Administration Economique et Sociale
2007	Maîtrise Economie et Environnement

Expérience professionnelle

2003	Stage de trois mois à la Société Nestlé, Croydon, Angleterre
2004 – 2006	Employée de bureau. Société d'Import-Export, Toulouse
2006 – à ce jour	Assistante. Conseil Economique et Social, Paris

Langues:
Bilingue français-anglais
Espagnol – parlé, lu et écrit

Connaissances en informatique: Word, Excel, PowerPoint

---

12 Les examens

A deux, remettez dans l'ordre les phrases ci-dessous pour faire un dialogue. Ensuite, écoutez l'enregistrement pour vérifier vos réponses.
(NB: **se débrouiller** = to manage (well); **passer des examens** = to take exams; **réussir** = to pass; **une note** = a mark)

a Mais c'est une très bonne note! Tu as de la chance. Moi, j'ai passé des examens la semaine dernière et je ne sais pas si je les ai réussis.

b Si, mais je ne me suis pas très bien débrouillée. J'ai eu 12 sur 20 seulement.

c Salut Amanda! Ça va?

d Non, je ne l'ai pas vue. Où est-elle?

e Bof! J'ai eu les résultats de mon examen de math ce matin.

f Cinq, la semaine dernière et trois avant.

g Combien d'examens est-ce que tu as passés?

h Est-ce que tu as vu la liste des résultats?

i Tu n'as pas réussi?

j D'accord.

k Dans le hall. On y va?

grammaire

Accord du participe passé

– Tu as réussi <u>tes examens</u>? – Non, je ne sais pas si je <u>les</u> ai réussi<u>s</u>.

– Est-ce que tu as vu <u>la liste des résultats</u>? – Non, je ne <u>l'</u>ai pas vu<u>e</u>.

– Combien d'<u>examens</u> est-ce que tu as passé<u>s</u>?

13 Un bon candidat

Vous travaillez pour une agence qui recherche un professeur d'anglais. Ecrivez en français le résumé de l'expérience de chaque candidat. (NB: **une mention** = distinction; **une formation d'enseignant(e)** = teacher training; **enseigner** = to teach)

Candidat 1

> Julia / from Birmingham / has degree in Italian literature / in 2005 enrolled on a teacher training course / passed with distinction / moved to London six months ago / has taught for two months.

Candidat 2

> John / born in Manchester / got a degree in English literature / spent five years in Europe / worked as waiter and English teacher / worked in London as a teacher for two years.

Candidat 3

> Carmen / bilingual Spanish-English / did a Master's Degree / enrolled on teacher training course last year / passed with distinction / has no teaching experience.

14 J'ai un entretien

Trouvez l'expression en français qui correspond à celle en anglais.

a I have got an interview.

b I did not pass my exam.

c We did a work placement.

d She has already worked in this area.

1 Je n'ai pas réussi mon examen.

2 Nous avons fait un stage.

3 Elle a déjà travaillé dans ce secteur.

4 J'ai un entretien.

15 Bonne chance!

Ecoutez Odile et Samuel parler d'un entretien et complétez les phrases.

NB: **passer un entretien** = to have an interview, **recevoir** = to receive.)

Samuel	Salut Odile, tu vas bien?
Odile	Très bien, merci. J'ai _____**(a)** une lettre ce matin et je vais _____**(b)** un entretien.
Samuel	Super! Pour quelle société?
Odile	C'est pour une société de marketing.
Samuel	Tu as déjà _____**(c)** dans ce secteur?
Odile	Oui. Je travaille à mi-temps _____**(d)** un an aux Galeries Lafayette à Paris. L'année dernière j'ai aussi fait un _____**(e)** de trois mois chez Marks et Spencers à Londres.
Samuel	Tu as passé des examens de marketing?
Odile	Oui. Cet été, j'ai _____**(f)** mon diplôme!
Samuel	Félicitations!
Odile	Merci, et toi? Tu as _____**(g)** tes examens?
Samuel	J'ai _____**(h)** un an à l'université. Je vais finir ma licence l'année prochaine.
Odile	En quoi?
Samuel	En _____**(i)**.
Odile	Et qu'est-ce que tu vas faire après?
Samuel	Je voudrais faire une _____**(j)**.
Odile	Et bien, _____**(k)** chance!
Samuel	Et toi aussi pour ton entretien! Salut!

16 Parlez-moi de vos études

A deux, imaginez une situation d'entretien et posez-vous des questions sur vos études, votre expérience professionnelle et vos qualités personnelles.

Extra!

 1 Lettre de motivation

Read the following covering letter for a job application and answer the questions below.

le 31 juillet 2008

Monsieur,

Suite à votre annonce parue dans le Guardian International du 30 juillet 2008, je me permets de vous proposer ma candidature pour le poste de responsable de marketing. Je pense posséder toutes les qualifications et l'expérience requises.

J'ai quitté l'Université de Warwick en 2005 avec une licence en études commerciales, avec mention très bien. En octobre 2005 j'ai passé un diplôme de marketing et je l'ai obtenu en été 2006. Au cours de mes études supérieures, je me suis spécialisé dans le secteur "études de marchés" et j'ai fait un stage de six mois chez Nestlé à Vevey en Suisse. A l'université j'ai suivi un cours de français intensif pendant un an donc je parle couramment.

Vous trouverez ci-joint mon curriculum vitae.

En attendant une réponse, recevez Monsieur, l'expression de mes salutations distinguées.

Joseph Brown

    a What post is Joseph applying for?
    b Give details of his qualifications.
    c What specialist knowledge does he have?
    d Give details of time spent abroad.
    e What knowledge of foreign languages does he have?

2 CV

Listen to two people talking about their qualifications and work experience and fill in the grid below.

	Diplômes	**Expérience**	**Langues**	**Connaissances en informatique**
Homme				
Femme				

9 Éducation et expérience

Grammaire

~ pendant and depuis

Pendant is used to describe how long something lasted (something which is finished).
E.g. **J'ai habité à Londres pendant 3 ans**. (= I lived in London for three years but do not live there any more.) Note that the perfect tense is used.

Depuis is used to describe something that has lasted and is still occurring.
E.g. **J'habite à Londres depuis 3 ans**. (= I have lived in London for three years and I still live there.) Note that the present tense is used.

~ Reflexive verbs in the perfect tense

All reflexive verbs use **être** as auxiliary in the perfect tense. E.g. **se renseigner = il s'<u>est</u> renseigné.** Note: the past participle agrees with the subject of the verb.

> je me suis renseigné(e)
> tu t'es renseigné(e)
> il/elle s'est renseigné(e)
> nous nous sommes renseigné(e)s
> vous vous êtes renseigné(e)s
> ils/elles se sont renseigné(e)s

Note the word order with:

– the negative:
> Je <u>ne</u> me suis <u>pas</u> inscrit à l'université.
> Elle <u>ne</u> s'est <u>plus</u> ennuyée.
> Nous <u>ne</u> nous sommes <u>jamais</u> sentis à l'aise.

– adverbs:
> Je me suis <u>beaucoup</u> amusé en France.
> Il s'est <u>assez</u> ennuyé à Paris.

~ Object pronouns and the perfect tense

With verbs using **avoir** as auxiliary in the perfect tense, there is no agreement with the subject.
E.g. **j'ai mangé   elle a mangé   nous avons mangé   elles ont mangé**

However, when the direct object is placed before the verb, the past participle must agree with the direct object. This can happen:

– with pronouns (which go before the verb).
E.g. **– Est-ce que tu as vu <u>Paul et Martin</u>?   – Oui, je <u>les</u> ai vu<u>s</u> hier.**
     – Est-ce qu'il a contacté <u>l'entreprise</u>?   – Oui, il <u>l</u>'a contacté<u>e</u> hier.

– with questions, when there is an inversion.
E.g. **– Combien d'<u>examens</u> as-tu passé<u>s</u>?**

Exercices de grammaire

pendant and depuis

1 Translate the following sentences into French:

a I lived in Australia for three years.
b They have been working in England for two months.
c She studied English at school for five years.
d They have been learning French for three months.
e How long did you live there for?

Reflexive verbs in the perfect tense

2 The following outline information describes the lives of Claudia and Aziz when they were students. Use it to write a summary. (Note: **se mettre à** = to begin.)

a Claudia / s'inscrire / université / Paris / 2005.
b Aziz / se renseigner / pour entrer / école de commerce.
c Ils / s'amuser / beaucoup / Paris.
d Claudia / se mettre à / apprendre l'espagnol.
e Aziz / se mettre à / faire de la natation.
f Claudia et Aziz / s'installer / appartement / près de la Sorbonne.

3 Answer the following questions in the negative:

a Est-ce que tu t'es inscrit à l'université?
b Est-ce qu'elle s'est renseignée pour les cours de japonais?
c Est-ce que vous vous êtes installés dans votre nouvelle maison?
d Est-ce qu'elles se sont ennuyées?
e Est-ce que Jacques s'est amusé?
f Est-ce qu'elles se sont senties à l'aise en France?

Object pronouns and the perfect tense

4 Answer the questions by replacing the underlined words with a direct object pronoun. Make sure that the past participle agrees with the pronoun.
E.g. **Est-ce qu'elle a aimé <u>cette ville</u>?** > *Oui, elle l'a aimée.*

a Est-ce que tu as passé <u>ton entretien</u>?
b Est-ce que tu as envoyé <u>ton CV</u>?
c Est-ce qu'elle a obtenu <u>le poste</u>?
d Est-ce qu'il a réussi <u>ses examens</u>?
e Est-ce qu'elles ont contacté <u>l'entreprise</u> pour le poste?
f Est-ce que vous avez rencontré <u>la directrice</u>?

9 Education et expérience

Vocabulaire

~ Verbes pronominaux — Reflexive verbs

s'ennuyer	to be bored
s'installer	to settle
s'inscrire	to enrol
s'amuser	to enjoy oneself
se spécialiser	to specialise
se débrouiller	to cope/manage
se présenter	to introduce oneself/turn up
se sentir à l'aise	to feel at ease
se renseigner	to find out/enquire
se mettre à	to start doing something

~ Examens et qualifications — Exams and qualifications

apprendre	to learn
passer un examen	to sit an exam
réussir	to pass
échouer	to fail
obtenir	to gain/get
le baccalauréat (bac)	'A' levels (equivalent)
la maîtrise	Master's degree
la licence	Bachelor's degree
le doctorat	PhD, doctorate
la fac (coll.)	university
la formation d'enseignant	teacher training
améliorer	to improve
la note	mark
le résultat	result
la mention	distinction
le diplôme	diploma

~ Etudes — Studies

les lettres (f) modernes	humanities
les sciences (f)	sciences
l'ingénierie (f)	engineering
les études (f) commerciales	business studies
la gestion	management
la littérature	literature
l'informatique (f)	computing
le marketing	marketing

~ Le curriculum vitae — CV

la formation	education/training
l'expérience (f) professionnelle	work experience
divers	miscellaneous
le stage	work placement
suivre un cours	to do a course
le cours intensif	intensive course
le séjour à étranger	stay abroad
la langue étrangère	foreign language
parler couramment	to speak fluently
l'outil (m) informatique	computing
le permis de conduire	driving licence
être à la retraite	to be retired
passer un coup de fil	to make a phone call
remplir un formulaire	to fill in a form
fournir	to provide/supply
recevoir	to receive
être obligé(e) de	to have to
déménager	to move
vivre	to live
l'internet (m)	internet
l'entretien (m)	interview
le tour du monde	world trip
bilingue	bilingual
la connaissance	knowledge
depuis	for/since
pendant	for/during
longtemps	a long time
l'assistant(e)	assistant
le chercheur(euse)	researcher
le poste	job/position
la société	company
l'entreprise (f)	firm

Travail à deux

1 Séjour à Paris

You have just moved to Paris for a six-month work placement. You are having a drink with one of your work colleagues. Use the following information in your conversation. Your partner will start.

- You have been living in Paris for two months.
- You are a student and you are going to be working in Paris for six months.
- Your colleague comments on your French. Say you have been learning for two years.
- You are living in a flat near the river. It is very nice and you have settled in well.
- You like Paris and you like the French a lot.
- You have been having fun. You have met lots of people and you go out a lot in the evenings to bars and cafés.

2 Une candidature

You have asked one of your work colleagues to shortlist candidates for an interview. Your partner has selected a CV. Ask the following questions. You start.

- Ask your colleague who s/he has chosen.
- Find out his nationality and age.
- Find out if he has a degree. If so, what subject and when did he finish university.
- Find out if he has a Master's degree.
- Find out if he speaks English.
- Find out if he has IT skills.
- Find out what he is currently doing.
- Find out what other work experience he has.

Travail à deux

1 Séjour à Paris

You are going out for a drink with a colleague from work. S/he is English and has only been at the company for a couple of months. You start.

– Ask how long s/he has been in Paris.
– Ask how long s/he is staying.
– Say that s/he speaks very good French. Ask how long s/he has been learning.
– Find out where s/he lives and ask if s/he likes the flat.
– Ask if s/he likes Paris.
– Ask if s/he has been having a good time and ask what s/he does in the evenings.

2 Une candidature

You have been asked to compile a shortlist for an interview panel. You have selected the following CV as you think it is appropriate. Your partner is your manager and wants to know more information about the candidate. Use the CV below to answer any questions you are asked. Your partner will start.

Nom: Lucas Rocher
Adresse: 12 rue de la Craffe, 56000 Nancy
Nationalité: française
Date de naissance: 15/10/86 à Nancy

Formation:
Diplôme d'ingénieur, obtenu juillet 2006, Ecole Nationale de Paris
Licence en biochimie 2002–2005, La Sorbonne, Paris
Baccalauréat scientifique (mention bien), obtenu en juillet 2001, Lycée Georges Pompidou, Nancy

Expérience professionnelle:
Depuis septembre 2008: Ingénieur chez SOFICAM, Nancy
Janvier–juillet 2006: Stage de six mois chez BELLCANADA, Calgary, Canada
Mai–septembre 2002: Caissier à l'hypermarché de Vandœuvre, Nancy

Divers:
Bonne connaissance de l'outil informatique (Word/Excel)
Anglais parlé courant: séjour au Canada

Au travail!

When you have completed this unit, you will be able to socialise using some colloquial French, ask for and give help, give instructions and ask permission, give your opinion and describe your intentions.

1 A plus!

a Lisez la conversation entre deux jeunes qui travaillent dans un camping et trouvez dans le texte l'équivalent des expressions suivantes:

i	Qu'est-ce que tu fais comme travail?	**v**	On m'a donné.
ii	Où est-ce que tu vas travailler?	**vi**	C'est bien.
iii	Je dois partir.	**vii**	C'est horrible!
iv	Tu as de la chance!	**viii**	Les enfants.

Dominique	Salut, je m'appelle Dominique. Et toi?
Babette	Moi, c'est Babette.
Dominique	Tu vas bosser où?
Babette	A la crèche.
Dominique	Veinarde! C'est super d'être avec les mômes.
Babette	Et toi, c'est quoi ton boulot?
Dominique	Moi, on m'a refilé l'organisation des jeux le soir. C'est l'enfer! (...) Oh, il est trois heures! Bon, je me casse.
Babette	OK, à plus!

b Ecoutez le dialogue et notez la prononciation.

Au revoir!	A demain!
A tout de suite!	A la semaine prochaine!
A tout à l'heure! ("A tout!")	A bientôt!
A plus tard! ("A plus!")	A la prochaine!
A ce soir!	A un de ces jours! ("A un de ces quatre!")

10 Au travail!

2 Il est interdit de ...

Regardez les panneaux (signs) et trouvez les instructions correspondantes.

1 Interdit aux animaux 3 Défense de fumer 5 Attention au feu
2 Ne pas stationner 4 Accès interdit 6 Ne pas plonger

3 Vous ne pouvez pas ...

Ecoutez 5 conversations dans un camping et remplissez les cases. (NB: **courir** = to run)

	Endroit	Problème
a		
b		
c		
d		
e		

il est interdit de/il est défendu de fumer
interdit de/défense de plonger
ne pas stationner

4 Ce n'est pas indiqué!

Lisez le dialogue entre le propriétaire d'un camping et un touriste, et complétez les phrases. Ensuite, écoutez l'enregistrement pour vérifier vos réponses.
(NB: **déplacer** = to move)

Propriétaire   Monsieur, la voiture bleue là-bas, c'est à vous?

Touriste   Oui, c'est à _____ **(a)**. Il y a un problème?

Propriétaire   Oui, je suis _____ **(b)** mais il est _____ **(c)** de stationner devant la réception.

Touriste   Ah bon! Ce n'est pas indiqué.

Propriétaire   Ah si, monsieur, il y a un grand panneau devant la porte … vous voyez? _____ **(d)**-vous déplacer votre voiture, s'il vous plaît?

Touriste   Je _____ **(e)** rester quelques minutes?

Propriétaire   Désolé monsieur, mais c'est _____ **(f)**. Vous bloquez l'_____ **(g)** au camping!

5 Oh, pardon!

A deux, imaginez une autre situation dans un camping et écrivez un dialogue.

6 Mettez-la là

Un touriste ne trouve pas de place de parking. Ecoutez le dialogue et répondez aux questions en anglais.

a Why does the campsite owner ask the tourist to move his car again?
b Where does the owner suggest he move the car to?
c Why can't he park there?
d Where does he finally park his car?

grammaire

Place du pronom objet

Où est-ce que je mets <u>la voiture</u>?   Mettez-<u>la</u> là.
Je <u>la</u> mets ici?   Non, ne <u>la</u> mettez pas là, mettez-<u>la</u> ici.

7 Une note

Ecrivez la note suivante en français:

Could you move your car because I cannot get out. Please put it beside your caravan or in the car park. Thank you.

8 Un accident

Ecoutez Nathan expliquer pourquoi on a appelé une ambulance au camping et dites si les phrases ci-dessous sont vraies ou fausses.

(NB: **pas grand-chose** = not a lot; **le type** = the guy; **renverser** = to knock down; **grave** = serious; **reculer** = to reverse; **Je m'en vais** = I'm going (away))

a A serious accident has happened on the campsite.
b Nathan once helped the man described.
c A child has been knocked down but is now OK and sitting down.
d Nicolas attends the campsite's crèche.
e The parents are in a restaurant.
f The grandmother is looking after Nicolas.

---

grammaire

Les pronoms "qui" et "que"
C'est le type <u>que</u> tu as aidé l'autre jour.
C'est Nicolas <u>qui</u> vient à la crèche tous les matins. / Tu vois l'enfant <u>qui</u> est assis là?

---

9 Une urgence

Remettez les phrases ci-dessous dans l'ordre pour faire 2 dialogues. Ensuite, écoutez l'enregistrement pour vérifier vos réponses.

Conversation 1
a Vous êtes sûr? Je vais voir …
b Oh! C'est rien. C'est le résident qui fait un barbecue!
c Alors? Qu'est-ce qui s'est passé?
d Mademoiselle, il faut appeler les pompiers, j'ai vu de la fumée sortir de la caravane 12.

Conversation 2
a D'accord, je m'en occupe tout de suite.
b Appelez le SAMU, s'il vous plaît, ma fille a mangé des fruits de mer et elle est allergique.
c C'est grave?
d Oui, elle a perdu connaissance.

10 Au secours!

A deux, faites 2 dialogues basés sur les situations suivantes:
a Une voiture a renversé votre fille.
b Il y a un feu (= fire) dans une tente.

 **11 Un concert**

Ecoutez 3 amis échanger leurs impressions sur un concert et corrigez les erreurs dans la transcription ci-dessous (il y en a 10). (NB: **trop de monde** = too many people; **le groupe** = band)

Yvan   Eh bien, c'était pas génial, hein?

Emma   Moi, j'ai trouvé ça bien… Bon, ce ne sont pas des stars, mais ils jouent bien et leur musique est bonne, je trouve.

Simone   Vous ne pensez pas qu'il y avait trop de monde?

Emma   Oui, c'est vrai, la salle était vraiment trop petite.

Yvan   A mon avis, les concerts en province sont toujours mauvais. Il faut aller dans les grandes villes pour ça.

Simone   Ah non, je suis pas d'accord, j'ai vu de fantastiques concerts dans des petites villes de province, justement, c'était plus sympa et moins commercial.

Emma   Moi, je crois que si on aime un groupe, ça n'a pas d'importance l'endroit où on le voit.

Simone   Oui, c'est vrai.

A mon avis, …	
(Moi,) je trouve que …	… c'est/c'était très bien
je pense que …	
je crois que …	
(Moi,) j'ai trouvé ça super/formidable/génial/nul/mauvais/pas terrible/ ennuyeux/etc.	
Et toi, tu as aimé?	
Je suis d'accord./C'est vrai.	Je ne suis pas d'accord./Ce n'est pas vrai.

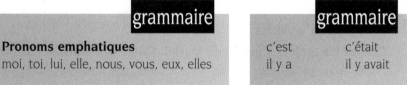

grammaire

Pronoms emphatiques
moi, toi, lui, elle, nous, vous, eux, elles

grammaire

c'est   c'était
il y a   il y avait

12 Je suis d'accord

A deux, lisez les phrases ci-dessous et dites si vous êtes d'accord. (Ex: – Moi, je trouve que les Parisiens ne sont pas très polis. Et toi? – Je suis d'accord.)

a Les Parisiens sont des gens très polis.

b Il y a de très bons restaurants à Londres.

c La musique folk, c'est pour les vieux!

d Il n'y a rien de bon au cinéma en ce moment.

e Edith Piaf est une excellente chanteuse.

f Le français est facile à apprendre.

13 Je voudrais partir …

Ecoutez quatre amis parler de leurs projets d'avenir et dites si les phrases ci-dessous sont vraies ou fausses.

a Micky n'a pas encore fini ses études.
b Serge ne veut pas aller en Thaïlande.
c Serge a l'intention de travailler dans une école.
d Isabelle n'a pas envie de travailler tout de suite.
e Isabelle va faire des études d'ingénieur.
f Alex va travailler dans un magasin de télévisions.

Je voudrais …	
J'aimerais …	
J'ai envie de …	(… faire le tour
Je pense …	du monde)
J'ai l'intention de …	

14 Projets d'avenir

Ecrivez les projets d'avenir de Muriel. Faites des phrases complètes. (Ex: *Muriel a l'intention de continuer ses études, elle voudrait faire …*) (NB: **à son compte** = freelance)

a continuer ses études / faire une maîtrise en traduction
b voyager pendant un an
c passer quelques mois en Angleterre / améliorer son anglais
d travailler à son compte / acquérir de l'expérience
e essayer d'obtenir un poste à la Commission européenne

15 Qu'est-ce que tu vas faire?

A deux, parlez et posez-vous des questions sur vos projets d'avenir.

Extra!

1 Travail de vacances

Listen to a conversation between four students at the campsite and note down the following information for each of them: how long they have been at the campsite / what job they do there / where they come from / what subject they are studying.

a Babette
b Richard
c Stéphanie
d Jean-Marc

2 Numéros d'urgence

Read the following information about what to do in case of emergency while in France and answer the questions below.

Les pharmacies
Pour un problème mineur, vous pouvez directement demander conseil dans les pharmacies. La nuit ou pendant le week-end, l'adresse de la pharmacie de garde est indiquée dans le journal local ou en vitrine dans les autres pharmacies.

Les pompiers *Numéro de téléphone: 18*
Les pompiers interviennent pour les feux, les accidents, les noyades, les blessures. Ils ont la réputation de pouvoir résoudre tous les problèmes domestiques! Par exemple: le chat qui ne peut plus descendre de l'arbre... Attention! Il ne faut pas abuser!

Le SAMU *Numéro de téléphone: 15*
Il s'agit du service d'aide médicale d'urgence. On les contacte pour les accidents graves. Ils sont en contact avec les hôpitaux.

La police et la gendarmerie *Numéro de téléphone: 17*
La police intervient pour les accidents, les cambriolages, les agressions. A la campagne, les gendarmes remplacent la police qui travaille principalement dans les villes.

a In which circumstances would you go directly to the chemist's in France?
b Where can you find out about emergency chemists at the weekend?
c How are firemen perceived in France?
d In which circumstances would you get in touch with the SAMU?
e What is the difference between the **police** and the **gendarmes**?

Grammaire

~ Object pronouns and the imperative

With the imperative (see Unit 4), object pronouns come after the verb.

E.g. **Où est-ce que je mets ma voiture? Mettez-<u>la</u> là.**

When there is a negative, object pronouns come before the verb.

E.g. **Je la mets là? Non, ne <u>la</u> mettez pas là, mettez-la ici.**

Note: when **me** and **te** come after the verb, they are replaced by **moi** and **toi**.

E.g. **Suivez-<u>moi</u>!** (But: **Vous me suivez?**) **Arrête-<u>toi</u>!** (But: **Tu t'arrêtes?**)

~ ne ... pas and the infinitive

With the infinitive, both parts of **ne ... pas** come in front of the verb.

E.g. **<u>Ne pas</u> fumer.**
Je préfère <u>ne pas</u> sortir.

~ qui and que

When explaining whom or what you are talking about, the relative pronouns **qui** and **que** can be used for linking the two parts of the sentence.

E.g. **C'est un enfant <u>qui</u> vient à la crèche.** (Rather than: **C'est un enfant. Il vient à la crèche.**)
C'est le type <u>que</u> tu as aidé. (Rather than: **C'est le type. Tu l'as aidé.**)

– **qui** is used when the person or thing referred to is the subject of the verb.

E.g. **C'est un enfant <u>qui</u> vient à la crèche.**
<u>l'enfant</u> vient à la crèche: enfant = subject of **vient**

– **que** is used when the person or thing referred to is the object of the verb.

E.g. **C'est le type <u>que</u> tu as aidé.**
Tu as aidé <u>le type</u>: type = object of **as aidé**
(Note: **que > qu'** in front of a vowel: e.g. **C'est le type <u>qu'</u>ils ont aidé.**)

~ moi, toi, lui ...

moi	nous
toi	vous
lui/elle	eux/elles

These pronouns are used:
– to emphasise the subject pronouns **je, tu, il, elle, nous, vous, ils, elles**.

E.g. **<u>Moi</u>, je trouve que c'est bien.**
<u>Lui</u>, il habite à Bordeaux.

– after prepositions like **chez, avec, pour**, etc.

E.g. **Je travaille avec <u>eux</u>.**
Pierre vient chez <u>nous</u> ce soir.

Exercices de grammaire

Object pronouns and the imperative

1 Answer the questions both in the positive and in the negative, replacing the words underlined with a pronoun: e.g. **Je mets <u>ma voiture</u> au parking? (Tu)**

> *Oui, mets-<u>la</u> au parking. / Non, ne <u>la</u> mets pas au parking.*

  a J'appelle <u>les pompiers?</u> (Vous)
  b Je ferme <u>la porte?</u> (Tu)
  c Je monte <u>la tente</u> là-bas? (Tu)
  d J'emmène <u>les enfants</u> à la piscine? (Vous)
  e Je laisse <u>le sac</u> dans la voiture ? (Tu)
  f Je finis <u>le dernier morceau de gâteau?</u> (Vous)

ne ... pas and the infinitive

2 Transform the following instructions, using **ne pas** + infinitive.
  E.g. **Défense de fumer. >** *Ne pas fumer.*

  a Défense de passer.
  b Il est interdit de stationner.
  c Défense d'ouvrir la fenêtre.
  d Il est défendu de jouer à la balle.
  e Il est interdit de nourrir les animaux.
  f Il est défendu de marcher sur la pelouse.

qui and que

3 Fill in the gaps, choosing between **qui** and **que** (or **qu'**).
  a C'est la voiture _____ tu aimes bien.
  b C'est un chanteur _____ vient du Québec.
  c Ce sont les gens _____ sont installés là-bas.
  d J'ai beaucoup aimé le concert _____ on a vu.
  e Tu as parlé à la fille _____ travaille au bar?
  f Vous avez vu le barbecue _____ ils ont acheté?

moi, toi, lui ...

4 Fill in the gaps in the dialogue, choosing **moi, toi, lui, elle, nous, vous, eux** or **elles**.
  – Tu as aimé la soirée chez Tom?
  – Bof! Je n'aime pas beaucoup aller chez _____**(a)**; ses parents sont toujours là et on ne peut pas s'amuser, avec _____**(b)**. Et _____**(c)**, tu as aimé?
  – _____**(d)**, je les trouve sympas, ses parents, surtout sa mère.
  – Oui, _____**(e)**, elle est cool, c'est vrai ... Tiens, je t'ai apporté ce CD.
  – C'est pour _____**(f)**?
  – Oui, oui, c'est pour _____**(g)**.

Vocabulaire

~ Dire au revoir
	Saying goodbye
A tout de suite!	See you in a minute!
A tout à l'heure!	See you later!
A plus tard!	See you later!
A ce soir!	See you this evening!
A demain!	See you tomorrow!
A la semaine prochaine!	See you next week!
A bientôt!	See you soon!
A la prochaine!	See you next time!
A un de ces jours!	See you around!

~ Langage familier
	Colloquial language
bosser	to work
refiler	to give
le (la) môme	kid
le type	guy
le boulot	job
le fric	money
veinard(e)	lucky
C'est l'enfer!	It's hell!
Je m'en vais.	I'm going away.
Je me casse!	I'm off!
J'en ai marre!	I'm fed up!
A tout!/A plus!	See you later!
pas grand-chose	not a lot
trop de monde	too many people

~ Instructions
	Instructions
Il est interdit de …/	Refrain from …/
Il est défendu de …	It is forbidden to …
Interdit de stationner/	No parking
Défense de stationner	
Ne pas fumer	No smoking
Attention (à)	Caution / Be careful

~ En cas d'urgence
	In case of emergency
le panneau	sign
l'accident (m)	accident
grave	serious
le feu	fire
la fumée	smoke
renverser	to knock down
déplacer	to move
reculer	to reverse
perdre connaissance	to lose consciousness
les pompiers	fire brigade
le SAMU	mobile accident unit
le poste de secours	first-aid post
au secours!/à l'aide!	help!

~ Opinions
	Opinions
A mon avis, …	In my opinion, …
Je trouve que …	I find that …
Je pense que …	I think that …
Je crois que …	I believe that …
(ne pas) être d'accord	to (dis)agree
formidable/génial(e)	great/super
pas terrible	not very good
ennuyeux(euse)	boring

~ Intentions
	Intentions
Je voudrais/J'aimerais …	I would like …
Je pense …	I am thinking of …
J'ai envie de …	I feel like …
J'ai l'intention de …	I intend to …
le projet	plan
l'avenir (m)	future

Travail à deux

1 Où garer la voiture?

It is Monday afternoon and you need to park your car. You are not sure about the parking restrictions in the area so you ask a passerby for help. Use the following prompts in your conversation. You start.

– Attract the attention of a passerby and ask if you can park here.
– Ask why not during the week?
– Ask if there is a car park nearby.
– Ask if s/he knows if you have to pay.
– Ask him/her to repeat the directions to the car park.
– Thank him/her appropriately.

2 Projets de vacances

You are discussing your holiday plans with a friend who has plans of his/her own. Using the following information, state your intentions and opinions and ask about your friend's plans. Your partner will start.

August

Going on holiday to West of France.
One of the best places for windsurfing.
Went there last year and enjoyed it.
Really liked the food.
Hope the weather is good.
Weather was excellent last year. Warm and windy, good for water sports.

December

Going to the States on a skiing holiday.
Have been to the States before.
Never been skiing before.
Think skiing is difficult.
Hope there is a lot of snow.

Travail à deux

1 Où garer la voiture?

You are stopped by someone in a car who wants to know about the parking restrictions in the area. Use the following information in your conversation. Your partner will start the conversation.

– Say that parking is not allowed between 0800 and 1800 on weekdays but it is allowed at the weekend.
– During the week parking is only permitted for residents.
– Tell him/her that there is a car park nearby and give directions; turn right at the end of the road, it is on the left by the supermarket.
– Say you are not sure if it is free, you think that you have to pay.
– Respond to his/her question.
– Finish the conversation appropriately.

2 Projets de vacances

You are discussing your holiday plans with a friend who has plans of his/her own. Using the following information, state your intentions and opinions and ask about your friend's plans. You start.

August

Going on holiday to Ireland for two weeks.
Went to Spain last year but didn't really enjoy it, it was too hot and there were too many people.
You have been to Ireland before, three years ago.
You really love the pubs and think in general that the night life is really good.
The people are also very friendly.

December

Not going on holiday.
Going to stay at home with friends and family.
Really like to be at home for Christmas.
Perhaps spend a weekend in Scotland.
Love the weather – it is always wet and windy!

Exercices supplémentaires
SUPPLEMENTARY EXERCISES

1 Toi et moi

 1 Questions

Lisez les questions et trouvez les réponses qui correspondent. The following questions may be used to find out information about someone. Match them with the appropriate response.

E.g. Tu t'appelles comment?
a Vous travaillez à Paris?
b Tu es belge ou suisse?
c Où travaillez-vous?
d Vous êtes française?
e Tu es vendeur?

1 A Paris.
2 Non, je suis belge.
3 Non, réceptionniste.
4 Je suis suisse.
5 Jeanne Meunier.
6 Non, à Calais.

2 Une rencontre

Mettez les phrases dans l'ordre pour faire un dialogue. Read a dialogue between two people meeting at a party in Paris and re-order the jumbled text. Then, listen to the recording to check your answer.

a – Ah! Et vous travaillez à Paris?
b – Moi, c'est Fiona.
c – Non, je suis irlandaise.
d – Bonsoir!
e – Je m'appelle Marc. Et vous?
f – Oui, je suis professeur d'anglais.
g – Bonsoir!
h – Ah! Vous êtes anglaise?

 3 Ça va?

Traduisez les phrases en français. Translate the following sentences into French.

a Hi! How are you?
b Goodbye, sir.
c I am German (*feminine*).
d Are you (*formal*) American (*masculine*)?
e Are you (*informal*) a student (*feminine*)?
f I live in London but I am from Glasgow.

4 Je m'appelle ...

Ré-écrivez les passages en utilisant "il" ou "elle". Transpose the following passages from the first person singular **je** to the third person singular **il** or **elle**.

E.g. **Je m'appelle Béatrice et je suis française.** > *Elle s'appelle Béatrice et elle est française.*

a Je m'appelle Natasha. Je suis américaine. J'habite à New York mais je suis de Chicago. Je suis étudiante en histoire de l'art.

b Je m'appelle Bob. Je suis irlandais. J'habite à Belfast mais je suis de Dublin. Je suis technicien.

c Je m'appelle Malika. Je suis marocaine. J'habite à Lille mais je suis de Paris. Je suis serveuse.

d Je m'appelle Luca. Je suis italien. Je suis de Milan mais j'habite à Rome. Je suis acteur.

5 Une conférence

Posez des questions. Listen to the prompts in English on the recording and practise asking the appropriate questions at a conference.

6 Une interview

Lisez l'interview et répondez aux questions. Read an interview with an exchange student, published in the student paper of a French university, and try to understand as much as you can without a dictionary.

> – Roberto, tu as vingt ans, tu es étudiant en philosophie, tu viens de Naples; pourquoi est-ce que tu étudies ici, en France?
> – Parce que j'adore la France! J'aime les Français, j'aime la cuisine française, la littérature, le cinéma, ... et bien sûr la philosophie: Descartes, Rousseau, Sartre, etc. Et je fais du français depuis l'âge de onze ans. Ma mère est suisse, mais elle ne parle pas français, elle vient de Zurich. Je suis très content en France, les études sont intéressantes et j'ai un travail: je suis serveur dans un restaurant italien!

a How old is Roberto?
b What is he studying?
c Where does he come from?
d Why does he like France?

e When did he start studying French?
f Why doesn't his mother speak French?
g Why does he like his studies?
h What sort of job does he do?

7 Un message

Ecrivez une petite description personnelle. Imagine: you have decided to join an internet chat-room for learners of French and you are sending your first message, introducing yourself to the other members. Write your message, giving as much information as possible.

2 Les autres

1 Encore des questions!

Faites correspondre les questions et les réponses. Listen to the recording to check your answers.

E.g. Tu as quel âge?

1 Tu es mariée?
2 Vous avez des enfants?
3 Il est divorcé?
4 Il a quel âge?
5 Tu as des amis ici?
6 Ah, tu as un fils?
7 Elle a dix ans?

a Oui, un fils.
b Oui, et il a deux enfants.
c Il a douze ans.
d Oui, trois ou quatre.
e Non, mais j'ai un copain.
f Non, douze ans.
g Oui, il s'appelle David.
h J'ai 20 ans.

2 Tu as des frères et des sœurs?

Lisez et complétez le dialogue. Ecoutez la conversation pour vérifier vos réponses.

Laurence	Ah, tu habites à Lyon?
Justin	Oui, et toi? Où _____ (a)-tu?
Laurence	A Lyon avec mon frère.
Justin	Il est _____ (b)?
Laurence	Non, il travaille dans un café. Et toi, tu as un frère?
Justin	Non, _____ (c) une sœur. Elle s'appelle Danielle.
Laurence	Elle est mariée?
Justin	Oui, _____ (d) mari s'appelle Henri.
Laurence	Il travaille?
Justin	Non, il _____ (e) étudiant en philosophie.
Laurence	Ah voici mon copain, au bar avec sa sœur!

3 La famille d'Hervé

Go back to exercise 10 (page 15) (about Hervé's family tree) and correct the false statements in that exercise, then write them out in full sentences. (There are six of them.)

4 J'ai deux enfants

Traduisez les phrases en français.

a He's nineteen years old.
b How old are they?
c Do you have brothers and sisters?
d We live with our brother.

e They have a son and a daughter.
f Her daughter is six.
g My boyfriend works with his father.
h Do you live with your parents?

5 Ma famille

Ecrivez quelques phrases sur votre famille. Using the language you have met so far, write a few sentences about your family.

E.g. *J'ai un fils ...*

 ### 6 Un sondage

You are studying town planning in France and you are conducting a survey (**un sondage**) in the streets of Calais. Listen to the prompts in English on the recording and then practise asking the appropriate questions about work, family and home.

(Note: flat = **un appartement**, house = **une maison**, sorry! = **pardon!**)

 ### 7 Une lettre

Lisez la lettre et écrivez une réponse. You have received the letter below from your new penfriend. Read it and write a suitable response.

> Cher.../Chère...,
>
> C'est moi, Alain, ton correspondant français. J'ai dix-huit ans, j'habite à Lille et je suis étudiant en informatique. J'habite avec mes parents, ma soeur Julie et ma grand-mère. J'ai une copine, elle s'appelle Tania, elle est russe et elle a dix-neuf ans. Elle est à l'université avec moi. Sa famille habite à Moscou. Et toi, quel âge as-tu? Tu as des frères et des soeurs? Tu habites avec tes parents? Tu as un copain/une copine? Ecris-moi vite!
>
> A bientôt,
>
> Alain

8 Qu'est-ce que tu veux?

Mettez les mots dans l'ordre pour faire des phrases.

a sandwich / vous / un / voulez?

b boire / chose / veux / quelque / à / tu?

c pour / merci / non / moi / pas.

d café / veux / un / tu?

e moi / chaud / un / chocolat / pour.

 ### 9 Une vieille amie

Imaginez une conversation avec une vieille amie. You are in a cafeteria and have just bumped into an old friend, Brigitte. Imagine what type of conversation might ensue, then write a dialogue in French between you and Brigitte.

Say hello. / Ask how she is.

Offer her a drink. / Ask if she would also like something to eat, etc.

La routine

1 Qui fait quoi?

Remplissez la grille. Around the world, different people are doing different things at different times. Listen to the recording to find out about them and fill in the grid below in English.

	Place	Time	Activity
a Mr and Mrs Durand			
b Marianne Pottier			
c Alain Laforêt			
d Michel Dubinge			
e Samia Tarouch			
f Marcel Dijan			

2 Un e-mail

Lisez l'e-mail et complétez les phrases. Read the email below from an English student to her French friend and fill in the gaps with the missing words. (NB: **les devoirs** = assignment.)

A: assia2@yahoo.fr
Objet: Bonjour!

Chère Assia,

Comment vas-tu? Bien, j'espère.

Je _____(a) étudiante depuis octobre et j'aime l'université. Le jeudi je _____(b) les cours à 11 heures et je _____(c) à 3 heures. Je prends _____(d) déjeuner à la cafétéria de l'université avec Daniel. Je mange toujours _____(e) spaghettis, c'est délicieux! L'_____(f)-midi nous allons à la bibliothèque pour finir _____(g) devoirs de la semaine. Ensuite, nous _____(h) le train pour aller à la piscine. Je vais à la piscine le lundi soir, le jeudi après-midi et le samedi matin. Aujourd'hui, je _____(i) le ménage et demain je _____(j) à Londres. Je prends le train à 6 heures et j'_____ (k) à 11 heures. J'aime beaucoup ma vie d'étudiante ici. Ecris-moi vite!

Sandy

---

3 Une petite annonce

a Lisez et écoutez les descriptions personnelles. Read through the descriptions below in a lonely hearts column, then listen to the same five people describing themselves and decide who is who.

1 Jeune femme, 22 ans, intelligente et active, aime lire, aller au théâtre et faire du sport (squash, aérobic).

2 Homme, 45 ans, intelligent et riche, aime le théâtre, l'opéra, la musique classique et les promenades dans la nature.

3 Jeune homme, 28 ans, tendre et sportif, aime écouter de la musique, faire du sport et sortir en boîte.

4 Femme, 39 ans, dynamique et aventureuse, aime le travail, les voyages, les hommes et l'aventure.

5 Homme, 62 ans, tendre, sens de l'humour, aime faire la cuisine et le ménage, aller au théâtre et à l'opéra.

b Lisez les descriptions encore une fois et trouvez le/la partenaire idéal(e). Play Cupid and find a suitable partner for the following people:

  i Jeanne, 29, very dynamic, loves sport.
  ii Louis, 40, hardworking, loves travelling.
  iii Jules, 25, very bright, loves culture.
  iv Marie, 59, very gentle, loves opera.
  v Isabelle, 42, sophisticated, loves playing the piano.

c Ecrivez votre propre petite annonce.

4 J'adore!

Look at the following sentences and according to the plus or minus signs, write in the correct form of **aimer bien** (+), **aimer** (++), **aimer beaucoup** (+++), **ne pas aimer beaucoup** (–), **ne pas aimer** (– –) or **détester** (– – –).

E.g. **Vous   +++   faire du vélo.** > *Vous aimez beaucoup faire du vélo.*

a Je   ++   jouer à la pétanque.

b Tu   – –   faire du sport.

c Elle   +   aller à la piscine.

d Vous   +++   faire des courses.

e Nous   – –   jouer au tennis.

f Ils   – – –   aller à la gym.

5 J'ai un problème!

Faites correspondre les phrases. Match the problem in English with the appropriate advice in French. (NB: **essayer** = to try.)

1 I watch too much television.

2 I have not got any food.

3 I can't do it.

4 I have not got any money.

5 I am not very fit.

6 I am really tired.

a Tu dois aller au supermarché.

b Vous devez aller au lit.

c Tu dois faire du sport.

d Vous devez arrêter.

e Vous devez aller à la banque.

f Vous devez essayer.

4 En ville

 1 C'est loin?

Mettez les phrases dans l'ordre pour faire un dialogue.

a C'est où, la rue George Sand?
b Non, c'est à dix minutes environ.
c Mais, je vous en prie.
d Pardon, monsieur?
e Oui, dans la rue George Sand.
f Oui?
g C'est loin?
h Alors, vous prenez la troisième rue à gauche, puis la première à droite, et c'est là.
i Merci beaucoup!
j Est-ce qu'il y a un supermarché près d'ici?

2 L'intrus

Trouvez l'intrus. Find the odd one out.

a rue / avenue / place / garage / boulevard
b tourner / lire / prendre / traverser / aller
c boulangerie / épicerie / supermarché / bibliothèque / boucherie
d entre / devant / puis / derrière / sur

3 Pardon madame!

Lisez les réponses et écrivez les questions.

E.g. **La rue des Mimosas? C'est la deuxième à droite.** > *Pardon, vous savez où est la rue des Mimosas?*

a L'office du tourisme? Alors, vous prenez la deuxième rue à gauche, et c'est en face, sur la gauche.
b Oui, il y a une poste à 2 minutes d'ici, dans la rue des Combattants.
c Ah non, elle n'est pas à côté de la gare, elle est en face.
d Non, c'est à 5 minutes.

 **4 En vacances**

On holiday in France, you have just arrived in a little town. You go into the tourist office to get a map and find out about a hotel, restaurants and other places of interest. Listen to the prompts in English before taking your turn in the conversation. (Note: a map of the town = **un plan de la ville**.)

5 Au magasin de vêtements

Lisez le dialogue et complétez les phrases. Ecoutez la conversation pour vérifier vos réponses. (NB: **la cabine (d'essayage)** = changing room)

– Bonjour, je peux vous _____ **(a)**?
– Oui, je _____ **(b)** essayer ce pantalon.
– Oui. Vous _____ **(c)** voulez en quelle _____ **(d)**: noir, bleu ou beige?
– Vous ne _____ **(e)** avez pas en blanc?
– Non, désolé.
– Bon, je vais essayer _____ **(f)** beige.
– Voilà. La cabine est _____ **(g)** côté de la caisse.
– Merci. (...)
– Ça va?
– Oui, il est parfait. Je le _____ **(h)**.

6 Je n'aime pas trop ...

Look at the following list of clothes and, using the (+) or (–) signs as indicators, state whether or not you like each item.

E.g. **Vous aimez la jupe? (+)** > *Oui, je l'aime bien.*
    Tu aimes le pantalon? (–) > *Non, je ne l'aime pas.*

a Vous aimez la chemise? (+)
b Tu aimes le manteau? (–)
c Est-ce qu'elle aime la veste? (–)
d Ils aiment l'écharpe? (+)
e Est-ce qu'il aime le gilet? (+)
f Vous aimez les chaussures? (–)

7 Tu aimes?

Traduisez les phrases en français. Utilisez "tu".

a The skirt? No, I do not like it.
b This dress? Yes, I prefer it.
c Do you like it?
d Yes, I like it.
e Do you like this pair of trousers?
f She likes the yellow shirt and I like it too.

8 Je l'adore!

Mettez les mots dans l'ordre pour faire des phrases.

a pantalon / j' / le / aime / noir / bien
b gris / pull / préfère / je / ce
c chaussures / jaunes / aimes / ces / tu / ?
d je / les / ne / pas / aime
e vous / jupe / préférez / cette / rose / ?
f verte / aime / cette / il / veste / pas / n'

5 En train

📖 1 Quelle est la question?

Reliez les questions avec les réponses ci-dessous.
(Ex: Seconde classe, SVP. > Première ou seconde classe?)

a Pendant les vacances? Eh bien, je vais aller en Espagne, chez mon copain.

b Oui, à San Francisco.

c Attendez … il part à 10h32.

d Alors … il arrive à Lille à 20h56.

e Ça fait 124 euros.

f Quai numéro 3.

g J'y vais en métro, en général.

h Vous devez aller à la porte numéro 12.

1 Comment allez-vous au travail?

2 C'est sur quel quai?

3 A quelle heure part le train?

4 Qu'est ce que tu vas faire pendant les vacances?

5 Je dois aller où?

6 Ça fait combien?

7 A quelle heure arrive le train?

8 Ils habitent aux Etats-Unis?

📖 2 Pêle-mêle!

Les phrases ci-dessous sont mélangées. Remettez-les dans l'ordre.

a Le train part à 14h35.

b Je voudrais un billet, aller-retour, pour Avignon, s'il vous plaît. C'est combien?

c Alors, 45 euros.

d Seconde classe, pardon.

e Alors, c'est le quai numéro 3.

f Alors, c'est un peu plus loin, sur votre gauche là-bas.

g Bon. Merci beaucoup. Au revoir.

h Oui. Et à quelle heure part le prochain train, s'il vous plaît?

i Un aller-retour pour Avignon, c'est …

j Et c'est quel quai?

k Quai 3 … où est-ce que c'est?

🎧 3 Un aller simple, s'il vous plaît

You are at the coach station in Limoges and you want to go to Guéret. Listen to the prompts in English before taking your turn in the conversation.

4 Cher Ben …

Voici une lettre qui est mélangée. Lisez-la et remettez les paragraphes dans l'ordre.

Cher Ben,

a Ensuite, nous allons voir un ami qui habite à Madrid, nous allons prendre le train rapide pour y aller. Il faut réserver à l'avance pour avoir une place. Matthias veut aller au Portugal pour voir son copain Carlos.

b Comment vas-tu?
Je suis à Paris jusqu'à dimanche et après … les vacances! Je suis très content. Je vais partir avec mes deux copains Dino et Matthias. Dino est de Rome et Matthias habite en Corse avec ses parents mais il étudie à Paris.

c Il habite à côté de Lisbonne, alors nous allons prendre le car, c'est moins cher! Carlos est en vacances et il va nous faire visiter les petits villages portugais en vélo. C'est une bonne idée mais je ne suis pas très sportif! Et toi? Qu'est-ce que tu vas faire et où vas-tu aller pendant les vacances? Tu peux venir avec nous si tu veux.

d Nous voulons aller dans le sud de l'Europe pour commencer. Je vais prendre le train avec Dino jusqu'à Irún en Espagne et Matthias va arriver en avion à Bilbao. Il faut aller le chercher à l'aéroport. Nous voulons visiter le Pays basque et aller à la plage pendant quelques jours.

À bientôt.
Stéphane

5 Problèmes de transport

Remplissez les blancs et puis écoutez pour vérifier vos réponses.

Ce soir je vais _____**(a)** au cinéma avec mes amis. D'habitude nous _____**(b)** allons _____**(c)** métro mais cette semaine il y a une _____**(d)** du métro à Paris. Alors il _____**(e)** trouver un autre moyen de transport et _____**(f)** pouvons y aller _____**(g)** voiture. Le film commence _____**(h)** 20h30 mais il _____**(i)** partir de la maison vers 19h parce qu'il y a beaucoup de circulation. Nous prenons la voiture de _____**(j)** copine Céline parce que ma voiture est _____**(k)** panne. J'espère que nous allons arriver _____**(l)** l'heure.

6 A l'hôtel

1 A la réception

Lisez le dialogue et remplissez les blancs. Ecoutez pour vérifier vos réponses.
Read the following dialogue and fill in the gaps. Listen to the recording to check your answers.

– Bonjour, je _____ **(a)** réserver trois chambres.
– C'est à _____ **(b)** nom?
– Au _____ **(c)** de Poussin.
– Pour _____ **(d)** de nuits?
– Pour trois nuits.
– Pour combien de _____ **(e)**?
– Pour six.
– Vous voulez des _____ **(f)** simples?
– Oui, s'il vous _____ **(g)**. Combien ça fait?
– La chambre _____ **(h)** 100 euros, alors 3 chambres ça _____ **(i)** 300 euros.
– Vous _____ **(j)** les cartes de crédit?
– Oui, pas de problème.

2 A l'hôtel

Ecrivez les phrases ci-dessous en français.

a Is there a private car park?
b Where is the lift, please?
c What time is breakfast?
d I have a problem with my room.
e There aren't any towels in the bathroom.
f The lift on the third floor does not work.

3 Où est l'intrus?

Lisez les listes de vocabulaire et trouvez l'intrus.

a chambre / douche / barbecue / téléphone
b salon / piscine / cuisine / wc
c janvier / printemps / juin / août
d réserver / prendre / se lever / vouloir
e réservation / piscine / sauna / parking

4 Comment ça s'écrit?

Ecoutez les conversations téléphoniques et notez comment les clients épellent leur nom.

a ...   c ...
b ...   d ...

5 Une réservation

Lisez la lettre ci-dessous, puis écrivez une lettre de réservation en utilisant les informations ci-dessous.

– one room for three people.
– one double bed/one single bed.
– bathroom if possible.
– from 3 August until 6 August.
– Is there satellite television/a restaurant in the hotel?
– How much is the set meal?

50 Bowlers Street
Londres

Londres, le 14 juin 2007

Monsieur,

Je voudrais réserver deux chambres pour deux personnes du 15 août au 23 août. Je voudrais une chambre avec deux lits simples et salle de bains et une chambre avec un lit pour deux personnes. Si possible avec vue sur la mer. Est-ce qu'il y a un parking dans l'hôtel?
Avec mes remerciements, je vous prie de croire, monsieur, à mes salutations distinguées.

Paula Daniels

6 Bienvenue chez moi!

Décrivez votre maison/appartement, les étages, les salles, les meubles ... Vous pouvez aussi décrire ce qui ne fonctionne pas!

7 Ça ne marche pas!

Take part in a conversation at a hotel reception. In the first part you will be making a booking and in the second part a complaint. Take your turn in the conversation when you are prompted in English.

7 Au restaurant

 1 Au téléphone

Traduisez les conversations téléphoniques ci-dessous.

a
– Hello.
– May I speak to Helen, please?
– Hold on, I'll pass you over.
– Thanks.

b
– Hello.
ˈ– Is Janet there?
– Sorry, she isn't here.
– Can I leave a message?

c
– Hello.
– Hello, I'd like to speak to Bruce, please.
– Sorry, he isn't here.
– Could he call me back?
– OK, I'll tell him.

d
– Hello.
– Could I speak to Emer, please?
– Speaking.
– Hello, it's Carol.

2 Tu veux sortir?

Remplissez les blancs, puis écoutez pour vérifier vos réponses. Attention: certains blancs peuvent contenir plusieurs mots.

– Allô.
– Salut, Carl, _____ (**a**) Claudia.
– Salut, ça va?
– Oui bien merci. _____ (**b**) tu fais ce week-end?
– Euh … rien.
– Ça te _____ (**c**) de sortir samedi soir?
– Oui, pourquoi pas.
– On _____ (**d**) aller au cinéma.
– Bonne idée.
– A quelle heure?
– On _____ (**e**) devant le cinéma à 7h?
– Entendu. A samedi soir.
– Oui, à samedi, au revoir.

3 Il est comment?

You are meeting some work colleagues at Charles de Gaulle airport. You have never met them before and do not know what they look like. You ask a work colleague to describe them.

Listen to the prompts in English before taking your turn.

4 Elle est très belle!

Lisez les descriptions ci-dessous et écrivez des phrases complètes.

a Isabelle: 25 ans, française, petite, cheveux blonds, longs, yeux bleus

b Alan: 33 ans, anglais, grand, mince, cheveux bruns, yeux verts, moustache, barbe

c Joshua: 50 ans, américain, très grand, gros, cheveux noirs, courts, yeux bleus, lunettes

d Juliette: 17 ans, irlandaise, grande, mince, cheveux roux, yeux verts, taches de rousseur

5 Au restaurant

Reliez les questions et les réponses.

1 Qu'est-ce que c'est l'entrée du jour?   **a** Non, je ne mange jamais de dessert.

2 Comment voulez-vous votre steak?   **b** Oui, un petit peu, s'il te plaît.

3 Vous avez choisi?   **c** Essayez l'assiette de crudités.

4 Vous voulez du gâteau?   **d** Oui, on en prend une bouteille.

5 Tu en veux?   **e** Pas encore.

6 Vous avez une entrée végétarienne?   **f** Saignant, s'il vous plaît.

7 Vous prenez du vin?   **g** C'est de la soupe.

6 Où est l'intrus?

Lisez chaque liste de vocabulaire et trouvez l'intrus!

a gâteau / steak / glace / pâtisserie / fruit

b saucisson / agneau / steak / truite / poulet

c tomate / pomme / carotte / oignon / salade

d dessert / addition / entrée / plat principal

7 Pêle-mêle!

Voici une conversation au restaurant, mais toutes les phrases sont mélangées. Mettez-les dans l'ordre. Ecoutez pour verifier vos réponses.

a Et comme plat principal, monsieur?

b D'accord, je la prends.

c Oui, monsieur, vous avez choisi?

d Et comme dessert?

e Je ne prends pas de dessert.

f Oui, euh … qu'est-ce que c'est l'entrée du jour?

g C'est une salade niçoise. C'est très bon.

h Très bien. Vous prenez du vin peut-être?

i Comme plat principal, je vais prendre la truite aux amandes, s'il vous plaît.

j Un verre de vin blanc, s'il vous plaît.

k Monsieur, s'il vous plaît?

8 Vacances et loisirs

1 Un week-end super!

Traduisez les phrases en français.

a We have had an excellent weekend.
b What did you (= **tu**) do on Saturday night?
c I couldn't come because I had to work.
d They (*m*) have had a problem with their car.
e Lucie loved Paris, she visited all the museums.
f I haven't seen the film, but I have read the book.

2 Ma semaine

Décrivez votre semaine: regardez votre agenda et écrivez quelques phrases. Utilisez les verbes "avoir", "étudier", "dîner", "travailler", "faire", "voir" et "jouer".

Lundi 17	10h00-12h00 cours d'anglais / 2h00-5h00 séminaire
Mardi 18	Etude à la bibliothèque
Mercredi 19	9h00-10h30 cours de chimie / 8h00 dîner chez Marc
Jeudi 20	Travail à la maison: dissertation
Vendredi 21	9h30-12h30 cours de maths / courses en ville
Samedi 22	3h00 match de foot
Dimanche 23	Tennis avec Mimi

3 J'ai eu un petit problème

Mettez les mots dans l'ordre pour faire des phrases.

a raté / ils / dernier / le / ont / métro
b restaurant / un / mangé / j' / bon / dans / ai
c as / que / qu' / tu / ce / fait / est / ?
d très / nous / week-end / passé / avons / bon / un
e voiture / il / sa / a / eu / avec / problème / un
f pas / a / venir / n' / pu / nous / elle / avec

4 Tu as reçu ma carte?

Lisez l'e-mail et complétez les phrases.

> **A: sylvie.lemercier@hotmail.fr**
> **Objet: Retour d'Inde**
> _____
>
> Salut Sylvie!
>
> Comment ça va? Est-ce que tu as reçu ma carte d'Inde? Je suis partie pendant un mois, avec _____ **(a)** copain Alex. On est d'abord _____ **(b)** à Delhi; c'est une ville fascinante mais très _____ **(c)** et polluée. On a aussi _____ **(d)** le Taj Mahal à Agra, à l'est de Delhi. Après, on a _____ **(e)** le train pour aller à Goa, sur la côte. C'est très touristique, mais on _____ **(f)** pu nager et se faire bronzer. Il a _____ **(g)** très chaud pendant deux semaines et puis la saison des pluies a commencé. On a _____ **(h)** les derniers jours à l'hôtel. On a lu, on a _____ **(i)** du poisson et des fruits de mer et on _____ **(j)** allés au marché: on a trouvé _____ **(k)** de jolies choses pour les amis. On a vraiment adoré _____ **(l)** Inde; on a _____ **(m)** d'y retourner l'année prochaine, peut-être dans le sud cette fois. Et toi, qu'est-ce que tu _____ **(n)** fait cet été?
>
> Bisous,
>
> Carole

5 Moi, j'ai travaillé …

Ecrivez une réponse à l'e-mail de Carole. Your email should contain the following:

– thank Carole for her email;
– you have also been to India, two years ago, and you loved it;
– this year, you stayed in Lille during the summer because you had to work;
– you found a job in a restaurant and you worked there for one month;
– in August, you had to study because you have exams next week;
– fortunately, you met an old friend and you did lots of things together in the evenings, so you had a good summer.

6 Je reviens de vacances

You have just come back from a holiday in Cornwall and you are talking about it with a friend who has also been away. Listen to the prompts in English before taking your turn in the conversation.

9 Education et expérience

 1 Une nouvelle vie en France

You have recently moved to Lille and are talking to a friend about your first impressions of life in France. Listen to the prompts in English before taking your turn.

 2 Je suis bien installé

Mettez les mots dans l'ordre pour faire des phrases.

a six / à / mois / travaillent / Brighton / ils / depuis.
b ans / à / habité / j' / Londres / ai / pendant / six.
c en / ai / commencé / études / 2005 / j' / mes.
d je / terminées / dernière / année / les / ai / l'.
e trouvées / ai / je / intéressantes / très / les.
f langues / je / inscrite / en / suis / me / de / cours.
g France / en / suis / bien / me / je / installé.

3 Entretiens

Ecoutez 3 entretiens et complétez la grille en anglais.

	Degree	Work experience	Plans for future
Nadine			
Kofi			
Elizabeth			

4 Un bon profil

Ecoutez une jeune femme parler de son éducation et de son expérience personnelle et complétez le texte.

J'ai _____ **(a)** mes études en juillet 2007. J'ai une _____ **(b)** de sciences naturelles et de 2005 à 2007, j'ai _____ **(c)** une maîtrise de biologie marine à l'université de Nice. _____ **(d)** septembre 2007 je travaille aux Etats-Unis comme chercheur. Je suis bilingue français-arabe, et j'ai aussi une bonne _____ **(e)** de l'anglais. Il y a trois ans, je _____ **(f)** suis _____ **(g)** en cours d'espagnol. J'ai _____ **(h)** à tous mes examens et je dirais que je le parle bien et je _____ **(i)** débrouille à l'écrit. J'aime aussi faire du sport, surtout de la planche à voile et de la natation.

5 Un CV

Ecrivez votre CV.

Nom:

Date de naissance:

Nationalité:

Adresse:

Formation:

Expérience professionnelle:

Divers:

Centres d'intérêt:

10 Au travail

1 Un style familier

Express the following sentences in more colloquial language, changing the words underlined.

a Je vais chercher <u>les enfants</u>.
b On m'a <u>donné</u> de l'argent.
c Je <u>m'en vais</u>.
d Je <u>travaille</u> au bar.
e A un de ces <u>jours</u>!
f Qu'est-ce que tu fais comme <u>travail</u>?
g A <u>plus tard</u>.
h C'est <u>horrible</u>.

2 Au camping

You are being introduced to a colleague who works in a campsite. Listen to the prompts in English before taking your turn in the conversation.
(Note: **poste de secours** = first-aid post.)

3 Renseignements

Ecoutez la conversation au camping et répondez aux questions.

a Where can tourists park their cars?
b What are the campsite restrictions regarding pets?
c What time does the restaurant shut?
d What are the restrictions on the use of the swimming pool?
e What is the restriction regarding music?

4 Interdictions

Mettez les mots dans l'ordre pour faire des phrases.

a de / ici / interdit / fumer / est / il
b voitures / derrière / la / les / mettez / autres
c est / indiqué / ce / pas / n'
d des / c' / travailler / est / de / mômes / sympa / avec
e au / désolé / monsieur / bloquez / l' / accès / camping / vous
f défendu / est / jouer / de / il / la / de / musique
g la / là / mettez / ne / pas

5 J'en ai marre!

Dennis a presque fini ses études et écrit un mail à son ami Alain. Lisez-le et répondez aux questions en anglais. (NB: **un mémoire** = dissertation; **j'en ai marre (de)** = I'm fed up (with); **le fric** = money (slang))

A: alaingodet@orange.fr
Object: Presque la fin!

Salut Alain!

Comment ça va? Moi, je bosse dur en ce moment: les examens commencent bientôt et en plus, j'ai deux dissertations à finir et je dois rendre mon mémoire de fin d'études! Mais, encore deux mois, et c'est FINI! J'ai des difficultés à imaginer la vie après l'université, mais je suis vraiment impatient de faire autre chose. Je trouve que les études universitaires durent trop longtemps. J'en ai marre d'étudier, j'ai envie de voir le monde et de travailler, de gagner de l'argent et d'être enfin indépendant! J'espère trouver du boulot dans une autre ville, plus petite que Londres. Ici, c'est trop grand, il y a trop de gens, trop de pollution et tout coûte cher. Mais avant ça, j'ai l'intention de prendre de longues, longues vacances! Le seul problème, c'est le fric. Il va falloir que je travaille pendant l'été pour gagner assez d'argent pour acheter un billet d'avion pour une destination exotique … Et toi, quelles nouvelles? Est-ce que tu en as aussi marre de la fac? Quels sont tes projets pour l'année prochaine?

A bientôt,
Dennis

---

a Why is Dennis very busy at the moment?
b When is he going to finish his studies?
c How does he feel about his studies?
d What does he want to do afterwards?
e What does he think about London?
f What does he need to do during the summer? Why?

6 Eh bien moi …

Ecrivez une réponse au mail de Dennis. Dans votre email:

– parlez de vos études, par exemple: intéressantes/difficiles/quelle année/etc.
– dites où vous voulez habiter après vos études (dans la même ville ou ailleurs) et pourquoi
– parlez de vos projets d'avenir: ce que vous allez faire pendant les vacances et après l'université.

GUIDE TO GRAMMATICAL TERMS

Language learners often feel unsure about grammatical terms. The following list gives some simple definitions. Examples are underlined, terms used which are defined elsewhere in the list are given in bold. Examples are drawn from English: reference is made to French only when something distinctive about that language needs to be noted. This Guide is concerned only with the meanings of grammatical terms: there is a French Grammar Summary beginning on page 148.

Adjective   A word used to describe a **noun** ('an interesting woman'; 'the curry is hot'). See also **demonstrative adjective**, **possessive adjective**.

Adverb   A word which describes the action of a **verb** ('she sings beautifully', 'he cooks well') or modifies (= gives further information about) an **adjective** ('it's a really expensive car') or another adverb ('she sings really well').

Agree   In English, **adjectives** don't change their form but in French they have to agree with the **noun** they are describing in **gender** and **number**: if the noun is feminine, the adjective must be in the feminine form, if the noun is plural, so is the adjective.

Article   The (called the definite article), a or an (the indefinite article).

Auxiliary verb   A **verb** combining with another verb to form a compound tense. ('She has gone' = auxiliary verb 'to have' here used to form the perfect tense by combining with the **past participle** of the verb 'to go'.)

Comparative   Form of an **adjective** ('that room is bigger than this one'; 'they've bought a more expensive car') or adverb ('it happens more often than you think') expressing a greater degree.

Conjunction   A word which joins parts of a sentence ('he was tired and he wanted to go home'; 'they arrived early because they wanted a good place').

Demonstrative adjective   These 'point out' **nouns** (this chair/these chairs; that house/those houses).

Direct object   The word which directly undergoes the action of the verb. In the sentence 'she sent her mother a present', what she sent was a present, so that is the direct object. She didn't send her mother! See also **indirect object**.

Gender   In French, all **nouns** have a grammatical **gender**, masculine or feminine, and **adjectives** have to **agree**.

Imperative   **Verb** form used in giving commands and instructions ('Turn left now!').

Indirect object   A secondary **object**. In the sentence 'she sent her mother a present', the **direct object**, the thing which is sent, is the present. It was sent to her mother, the indirect object.

Infinitive   The basic form of a **verb** ('to sing'; 'to write').

Irregular verb   **Verb** that doesn't follow a standard pattern.

Noun   Word denoting a person ('student'), thing ('book') or abstract idea ('happiness').

Number   Whether a word is **singular** or **plural**.

Object   The **noun** or **pronoun** which undergoes the action of the **verb**. 'We bought a <u>house</u>'; 'I saw <u>him</u>'.

Object pronoun   **Pronoun** used when it's the **object** of the **verb**. <u>Me</u>, <u>you</u>, <u>him</u>, <u>her</u>, <u>it</u>, <u>us</u>, <u>them</u>.

Past participle   Part of the **verb** which combines with an **auxiliary verb** to form the perfect tense ('they have arrived'; 'I have seen').

Plural   More than one: the plural of 'man' is '<u>men</u>'.

Possessive adjective   e.g. '<u>my</u> house', '<u>your</u> friend', '<u>his</u> car' etc.

Preposition   e.g. '<u>on</u> the table', '<u>under</u> the chair', '<u>to</u> the station', '<u>for</u> the teacher' etc.

Pronoun   Word taking the place of a **noun**. 'Peter saw the waitress' becomes '<u>he</u> saw <u>her</u>'.

Reflexive verb   In French, a **verb** formed with an extra pronoun (called a reflexive pronoun). E.g. <u>se laver</u> (to get washed): je <u>me</u> lave, il <u>se</u> lave, vous <u>vous</u> lavez etc.

Regular verb   **Verb** that follows a standard pattern.

Relative pronoun   **Pronoun** used to refer back to a noun earlier in the sentence, e.g. 'the man <u>who</u> lives there is very old'; 'the book <u>which</u> he chose …'; 'the woman/film <u>that</u> he saw…'.

Singular   One rather than many: the singular of 'bananas' is '<u>banana</u>'.

Subject   Who or what carries out the action of the verb. '<u>A student</u> sent me this email'; '<u>we</u> are travelling next week'; '<u>the letter</u> arrived yesterday'.

Subject pronoun   Pronoun used when it's the **subject** of the **verb**: <u>I</u>, <u>you</u>, <u>he</u>, <u>she</u>, <u>it</u>, <u>we</u>, <u>they</u>.

Tense   Form taken by a **verb** to show when the action takes place, e.g. Present tense: 'they <u>live</u> in New York'; Past tense: 'they <u>lived</u> in New York'; Future tense: 'they <u>will live</u> in New York' etc.

Verb   Word indicating an action ('they <u>ate</u> their dinner') or state ('the book <u>lay</u> on the table'). Different **tenses** are used to show when something happened. See also **irregular verb**, **reflexive verb**, **regular verb**.

GRAMMAR SUMMARY

In this section, you will find a summary of the grammar points covered in the book, as well as some supplementary information and verb tables. For a more detailed explanation of the different points, please refer to the grammar pages in each unit (given in brackets). If you are not familiar with grammatical terms, you will probably find the 'Guide to Grammatical Terms' on the previous two pages very useful as an introduction to this section.

The noun group

Nouns

1. Masculine and feminine (see page 8)

In French, nouns are masculine (m) (e.g. **le jour**) or feminine (f) (e.g. **la nuit**). Their ending can sometimes give an indication of their gender. The following are generally <u>feminine</u>:
- most nouns ending in **-e**: e.g. **la piscin<u>e</u>, la chos<u>e</u>**;
- nouns ending in   **-ie**: e.g. **l'épiceri<u>e</u>, la biologi<u>e</u>**;
                          -ion: e.g. **l'opin<u>ion</u>, l'éducat<u>ion</u>**;
                          -té: e.g. **la nationali<u>té</u>, la socié<u>té</u>**.

The following are generally <u>masculine</u>:
- nouns ending in   **-c, -f, -l, -r**: e.g. **le vo<u>l</u>, le ba<u>r</u>**;
                          -age: e.g. **le chôm<u>age</u>, le gar<u>age</u>**;
                          -ment: e.g. **le renseigne<u>ment</u>, le change<u>ment</u>**.

But there are many exceptions: e.g. **<u>le</u> musé<u>e</u>, <u>la</u> me<u>r</u>**, etc.
Most words used to refer to people have a masculine and a feminine form, the feminine form usually having an extra **-e** at the end: e.g. **l'ami, l'amie**.

2. Plural

Most nouns form their plural (i.e. when they refer to more than one person or thing) by adding an **-s** (e.g. **le livre, les livre<u>s</u>**).
Notable exceptions are:
- nouns ending in **-s, -x**, or **-z**, which do not change: e.g. **le pay<u>s</u>, les pay<u>s</u>**;
- nouns ending in **-au, -eau** or **-eu**, which take an **-x**: e.g. **le bat<u>eau</u>, les bat<u>eaux</u>**;
- many nouns ending in **-al**, which have their plural in **-aux**: e.g. **le journ<u>al</u>, les journ<u>aux</u>**.

Determiners

3. Articles (see pages 20, 32 and 72)

There are three main kinds of articles:
Le is used to refer to a person or thing which is known by the person you are talking to, either because it is specific (e.g. **<u>la</u> France; <u>le</u> livre qui est sur la table**) or because it is generic (e.g. **<u>le</u> mardi** – every Tuesday; **j'aime <u>les</u> maths** – maths in general). The different forms are:

- **le** with a masculine word (e.g. **le pain**);
- **la** with a feminine word (e.g. **la chemise**);
- **l'** with a word starting with a vowel, masculine or feminine (e.g. **l'enfant**);
- **les** with a plural word, masculine or feminine (e.g. **les lunettes**).

Un is used when the person or thing referred to is not specified (e.g. **un livre**; **il a des amis français**). The different forms are:
- **un** with a masculine word (e.g. **un cours**);
- **une** with a feminine word (e.g. **une lettre**);
- **des** with a plural word, masculine or feminine (e.g. **des chaussures**).

Du is used to refer to an uncountable quantity (e.g. **j'ai mangé du poulet** – compare with **j'aime le poulet** and **j'ai acheté un poulet**). The different forms are:
- **du** with a masculine word (e.g. **du vent**);
- **de la** with a feminine word (e.g. **de la chance**);
- **de l'** with a word starting with a vowel, masculine or feminine (e.g. **de l'eau**);
- **des** with a plural word, masculine or feminine (e.g. **des frites**).

4. Demonstratives (see page 46)

Ce is used when referring to a person or thing by pointing them out. The different forms are:
- **ce** with a masculine word (e.g. **ce pull**);
- **cet** with a masculine word starting with a vowel (e.g. **cet après-midi**);
- **cette** with a feminine word (e.g. **cette année**);
- **ces** with a plural word, masculine or feminine (e.g. **ces gens**).

5. Possessives (see page 20)

Like the articles and the demonstratives, they agree with the noun that follows, i.e. the person or thing they refer to (e.g. **mon vélo**, **mes disques**). For the different forms, see page 20. Note: possession can also be expressed using **le**, **la**, **l'**, **les** + **de**: e.g. **C'est la copine de Paul? Non, c'est sa soeur.**

6. Interrogatives

Quel is used to ask information about someone or something. The different forms are:
- **quel** with a masculine word (e.g. **Quel âge as-tu?**);
- **quelle** with a feminine word (e.g. **Quelle heure est-il?**);
- **quels** with a masculine word in the plural (e.g. **Quels sont tes plats préférés?**);
- **quelles** with a feminine word in the plural (e.g. **Quelles boucles d'oreille voulez-vous essayer?**).

7. Adjectives (see pages 46 and 72)

Adjectives are used to describe a person or a thing (e.g. **un type sympa**, **un travail ennuyeux**). Most adjectives come after the noun in French, but there are many exceptions. For example, a number of short and common adjectives come before the noun:

bon(ne)	**grand(e)**	**long(ue)**	**vieux(vieille)**	**beau(belle)**
mauvais(e)	**petit(e)**	**court(e)**	**jeune**	**joli(e)**
nouveau(elle)	**gentil(le)**	**premier(ère)**		
gros(se)	**haut(e)**	**deuxième**		

Some adjectives can be placed before the noun to give a particular emphasis: e.g. **C'est une excellente idée!**

Adjectives agree in gender (masculine or feminine) and number (singular or plural) with the noun they describe (e.g. **des étudiantes chinoises**). The most common patterns for the endings of adjectives (and nouns used as adjectives) are as follows:

masculine singular	feminine singular	masculine plural	feminine plural
grand	grande	grands	grandes
jeune	jeune	jeunes	jeunes
premier	première	premiers	premières
anglais	anglaise	anglais	anglaises
furieux	furieuse	furieux	furieuses
ancien	ancienne	anciens	anciennes

But many common adjectives are irregular: e.g. **long, longue**; **blanc, blanche**.

Note: the following adjectives, which come before the noun, have a different form in the masculine singular when the noun starts with a vowel or a silent **h**:
- **beau** > **bel** (e.g. **un bel homme**)
- **nouveau** > **nouvel** (e.g. **le nouvel an**)
- **vieux** > **vieil** (e.g. **un vieil ordinateur**)

Comparisons: to compare one person or thing with another, the following structure is used:

plus (more) / **moins** (less) / **aussi** (as) + adjective + **que**

For example, **Ce film est plus long** (longer) **que l'autre.**

A la campagne, la vie est moins chère (less expensive) **qu'à Paris.**

Tu trouves que le vin italien est aussi bon (as good) **que le vin français?**

Note that **plus** and **bon** cannot be used together, **meilleur** (better) is used instead: e.g. **Elle a eu de meilleurs résultats que l'année passée.** (Similarly, **mieux** is used instead of **plus** and the adverb **bien**: e.g. **Je travaille mieux à la bibliothèque qu'à la maison.**)

8. Pronouns (see pages 46, 60, 84, 108 and 120)

Pronouns are used instead of nouns to avoid:
- mentioning the noun if it is obvious who or what is being talked about: e.g. **Tu habites à Paris?**
- repeating the noun if it has already been mentioned: e.g. **Tu connais Marie? Oui, bien sûr, je la** (= Marie) **connais bien.**

There are many pronouns to choose from, depending on their function in the sentence, the words that introduce them and the person or thing they refer to.

Here are those covered in this book:

function	singular	plural	examples
subject	**je, tu, il, elle, on**	**nous, vous, ils, elles**	**<u>On</u> va au cinéma.** **<u>Vous</u> venez avec nous?**
object – direct (i.e. not introduced by a preposition)	**me, te, le, la**	**nous, vous, les**	**Je <u>la</u> vois tous les jours.** **Tu peux <u>nous</u> appeler la semaine prochaine?**
object – indirect introduced by **à** <u>person</u> <u>thing</u> or <u>place</u>	**me, te, lui** **y**	**nous, vous, leur** **y**	**Il <u>t</u>'a parlé?** **Nous <u>y</u> allons demain.**
object – indirect introduced by an expression of quantity <u>person</u> or <u>thing</u>	**en**	**en**	**J'<u>en</u> ai trois, et vous?**
introduced by a preposition like **chez, pour, avec,** etc. (come <u>after</u> the verb) <u>person</u>	preposition + **moi, toi, lui, elle**	preposition + **nous, vous, eux, elles**	**Je ne suis jamais allée chez <u>eux</u>.** **C'est pour <u>moi</u> ou pour <u>lui</u>?**

Qui and **que** are called <u>relative pronouns</u> and are used to give details about a person or a thing without repeating the noun in a separate sentence. For example, **On a logé chez un ami. <u>Cet ami</u> habite à Paris depuis dix ans.** > **On a logé chez un ami <u>qui</u> habite à Paris depuis dix ans.**

• **Qui** is used when the person or thing being referred to is the subject of the verb following the relative pronoun. For example, **Elle travaille dans une <u>école</u>. <u>L'école</u> est près de chez elle.** > **Elle travaille dans une école <u>qui</u> est près de chez elle.**
• **Que** is used when the person or thing being referred to is the object of the verb following the relative pronoun. For example, **Hier, on a vu un <u>film</u>. On a adoré <u>ce film</u>.** > **Hier, on a vu un film <u>qu'</u>on a adoré.**

The verb group

Verbs

9. Verb conjugation (see pages 8, 20 and 32)

Verbs are made of two parts: a stem and an ending: e.g. **aim-er**, **je regard-e**, **vous sort-ez**.

Different endings are used depending on the person (1st, 2nd, 3rd), the number (singular, plural), the tense (present, past, future), etc. Some verbs follow a regular pattern of endings, but many don't.

It can be helpful to classify verbs in four groups, according to their ending in the infinitive (the form you would find in the dictionary, e.g. **habiter**):
* verbs ending in **-er**: all regular, except for **aller**;
* verbs ending in **-ir**: regular verbs follow either the **finir** pattern or the **partir** pattern; there are also some irregular verbs;
* verbs ending in **-re**: some follow the **perdre** pattern, but many are irregular;
* verbs ending in **-oir**: all irregular.

See the verb tables pages 154 to 157 for the different patterns.

10. Verb construction (see pages 60, 72 and 108)

Verbs can be constructed in different ways. They can:
* come on their own: e.g. **Elle dort. Mes amis sont arrivés.**
* come with: – a direct object: e.g. **Je prends le bus. Marc la connait.**
    – an indirect object: e.g. **Ils parlent à leurs amis. Tu lui a téléphoné?**
    – an infinitive: e.g. **Nous devons partir. Le film va commencer.**
* be reflexive: e.g. **Vous vous levez à quelle heure? Je m'ennuie!**
* be impersonal (only used with **il**): e.g. **Il pleut. Il faut réussir!**

11. The present tense (see pages 32 and 60)

The present tense is used to refer to:
* a current or usual action / situation: e.g. **J'habite à Bruxelles.**
* an action / situation in the process of happening: e.g. **Anne n'est pas là, elle fait des courses.**
* an action / situation in the future: e.g. **Le train part dans cinq minutes.**
* instructions: e.g. **Vous prenez la première à droite.**

So, depending on the context, it will be translated in different ways. For example,
– **En général, on mange à une heure.** > We usually <u>eat</u> at one o'clock.
– **On mange!** > We're <u>eating</u>!
– **Ce soir, on mange au restaurant.** > Tonight, we<u>'re eating</u> at the restaurant.

For the different forms of the present tense, see the verb tables pages 154 to 157 and the unit pages mentioned above.

12. The perfect tense (see pages 96 and 108)

The perfect tense (**passé composé**) is used to refer to a past event, seen as completed. It is generally made up of the present tense of **avoir** (the auxiliary), followed by the past participle of the verb: e.g. **Hier, j'ai joué au football. Ils ont voyagé pendant deux mois.**

A few verbs form the perfect tense with **être**. They are:
- the following 14 verbs (most easily remembered in pairs):

aller – **venir**

arriver – **partir**

entrer – **sortir**

monter – **descendre**

passer – **retourner**

tomber – **rester**

mourir – **naître**

- all reflexive verbs.

When the auxiliary **être** is used, the past participle must agree with the subject of the verb: e.g.
Ta mère est arrivée. Ils se sont bien amusés au Portugal.

For the different forms of the perfect tense and use with negatives and pronouns, see the unit pages mentioned above as well as the verb tables pages 154 to 157.

13. The imperative (see pages 46 and 120)

The imperative is used to give instructions or tell someone to do something. It is generally formed like the present tense, but without the pronouns **tu** or **vous**: e.g. **Attends! Continuez tout droit!**

14. Adverbs

Adverbs can be used to describe an action / situation: e.g. **Il vient rarement ici.** Many adverbs end in **-ment** (similarly in English, many end in -ly). This ending is usually added to the feminine form of the adjective: e.g. **lente-ment, heureuse-ment.**

However, many adverbs do not end in **-ment**, including some very common ones: e.g. **bien, mal, beaucoup, peu, souvent, vite**, etc.

15. Prepositions (see pages 32 and 60)

Prepositions are used to introduce a complement:
- to a verb: e.g. **jouer de la guitare, aller chez quelqu'un;**
- to a noun: e.g. **une chambre avec salle de bains; un verre de vin;**
- to an adjective: e.g. **content(e) de quelque chose, facile à faire.**

When **le** and **les** follow **à** and **de**, they always combine to form **au / aux** and **du / des** – see page 32.

Verb tables

Auxiliaries

Infinitive	Present	Perfect	Imperfect	Future	Conditional
être	je suis tu es il/elle/on est nous sommes vous êtes ils/elles sont	j'ai été tu as été il/elle/on a été nous avons été vous avez été ils/elles ont été	j'étais tu étais il/elle/on était nous étions vous étiez ils/elles étaient	je serai tu seras il/elle/on sera nous serons vous serez ils/elles seront	je serais tu serais il/elle/on serait nous serions vous seriez ils/elles seraient
avoir	j'ai tu as il/elle/on a nous avons vous avez ils/elles ont	j'ai eu tu as eu il/elle/on a eu nous avons eu vous avez eu ils/elles ont eu	j'avais tu avais il/elle/on avait nous avions vous aviez ils/elles avaient	j'aurai tu auras il/elle/on aura nous aurons vous aurez ils/elles auront	j'aurais tu aurais il/elle/on aurait nous aurions vous auriez ils/elles auraient

Regular verbs

Infinitive	Present	Perfect	Imperfect	Future	Conditional
aimer	j'aime tu aimes il/elle/on aime nous aimons vous aimez ils/elles aiment	j'ai aimé tu as aimé il/elle/on a aimé nous avons aimé vous avez aimé ils/elles ont aimé	j'aimais tu aimais il/elle/on aimait nous aimions vous aimiez ils/elles aimaient	j'aimerai tu aimeras il/elle/on aimera nous aimerons vous aimerez ils/elles aimeront	j'aimerais tu aimerais il/elle/on aimerait nous aimerions vous aimeriez ils/elles aimeraient
finir	je finis tu finis il/elle/on finit nous finissons vous finissez ils/elles finissent	j'ai fini tu as fini il/elle/on a fini nous avons fini vous avez fini ils/elles ont fini	je finissais tu finissais il/elle/on finissait nous finissions vous finissiez ils/elles finissaient	je finirai tu finiras il/elle/on finira nous finirons vous finirez ils/elles finiront	je finirais tu finirais il/elle/on finirait nous finirions vous finiriez ils/elles finiraient

partir	je pars
	tu pars
	il/elle/on part
	
	nous partons
	
	vous partez
	ils/elles partent
		je suis parti(e)
		tu es parti(e)
		il/elle/on est
		  parti(e)(s)
		nous sommes
		  parti(e)s
		vous êtes parti(e)s
		ils/elles sont
		  parti(e)s
			je partais
			tu partais
			il/elle/on partait
			
			nous partions
			
			vous partiez
			ils/elles partaient
				je partirai
				tu partiras
				il/elle/on partira
				
				nous partirons
				
				vous partirez
				ils/elles partiront
					je partirais
					tu partirais
					il/elle/on partirait
					
					nous partirions
					
					vous partiriez
					ils/elles partiraient

Infinitive	Present	Perfect	Imperfect	Future	Conditional
perdre	je perds tu perds il/elle/on perd nous perdons vous perdez ils/elles perdent	j'ai perdu tu as perdu il/elle/on a perdu nous avons perdu vous avez perdu ils/elles ont perdu	je perdais tu perdais il/elle/on perdait nous perdions vous perdiez ils/elles perdaient	je perdrai tu perdras il/elle/on perdra nous perdrons vous perdrez ils/elles perdront	je perdrais tu perdrais il/elle/on perdrait nous perdrions vous perdriez ils/elles perdraient

Irregular verbs

Infinitive	Present	Perfect	Imperfect	Future	Conditional
aller	je vais tu vas il/elle/on va nous allons vous allez ils/elles vont	je suis allé(e) tu es allé(e) il/elle/on est allé(e)(s) nous sommes allé(e)s vous êtes allé(e)s ils/elles sont allé(e)s	j'allais tu allais il/elle/on allait nous allions vous alliez ils/elles allaient	j'irai tu iras il/elle/on ira nous irons vous irez ils/elles iront	j'irais tu irais il/elle/on irait nous irions vous iriez ils/elles iraient
appeler	j'appelle tu appelles il/elle/on appelle nous appelons vous appelez ils/elles appellent	j'ai appelé tu as appelé il/elle/on a appelé nous avons appelé vous avez appelé ils/elles ont appelé	j'appelais tu appelais il/elle/on appelait nous appelions vous appeliez ils/elles appelaient	j'appellerai tu appelleras il/elle/on appellera nous appellerons vous appellerez ils/elles appelleront	j'appellerais tu appellerais il/elle/on appellerait nous appellerions vous appelleriez ils/elles appelleraient
boire	je bois tu bois il/elle/on boit nous buvons vous buvez ils/elles boivent	j'ai bu tu as bu il/elle/on a bu nous avons bu vous avez bu ils/elles ont bu	je buvais tu buvais il/elle/on buvait nous buvions vous buviez ils/elles buvaient	je boirai tu boiras il/elle/on boira nous boirons vous boirez ils/elles boiront	je boirais tu boirais il/elle/on boirait nous boirions vous boiriez ils/elles boiraient
connaître	je connais tu connais il/elle/on connaît nous connaissons vous connaissez ils/elles connaissent	j'ai connu tu as connu il/elle/on a connu nous avons connu vous avez connu ils/elles ont connu	je connaissais tu connaissais il/elle/on connaissait nous connaissions vous connaissiez ils/elles connaissaient	je connaîtrai tu connaîtras il/elle/on connaîtra nous connaîtrons vous connaîtrez ils/elles connaîtront	je connaîtrais tu connaîtrais il/elle/on connaîtrait nous connaîtrions vous connaîtriez ils/elles connaîtraient
devoir	je dois tu dois il/elle/on doit nous devons vous devez ils/elles doivent	j'ai dû tu as dû il/elle/on a dû nous avons dû vous avez dû ils/elles ont dû	je devais tu devais il/elle/on devait nous devions vous deviez ils/elles devaient	je devrai tu devras il/elle/on devra nous devrons vous devrez ils/elles devront	je devrais tu devrais il/elle/on devrait nous devrions vous devriez ils/elles devraient

Infinitive	Present	Perfect	Imperfect	Future	Conditional
dire	je dis tu dis il/elle/on dit nous disons vous dites ils/elles disent	j'ai dit tu as dit il/elle/on a dit nous avons dit vous avez dit ils/elles ont dit	je disais tu disais il/elle/on disait nous disions vous disiez ils/elles disaient	je dirai tu diras il/elle/on dira nous dirons vous direz ils/elles diront	je dirais tu dirais il/elle/on dirait nous dirions vous diriez ils/elles diraient
écrire	j'écris tu écris il/elle/on écrit nous écrivons vous écrivez ils/elles écrivent	j'ai écrit tu as écrit il/elle/on a écrit nous avons écrit vous avez écrit ils/elles ont écrit	j'écrivais tu écrivais il/elle/on écrivait nous écrivions vous écriviez ils/elles écrivaient	j'écrirai tu écriras il/elle/on écrira nous écrirons vous écrirez ils/elles écriront	j'écrirais tu écrirais il/elle/on écrirait nous écririons vous écririez ils/elles écriraient
faire	je fais tu fais il/elle/on fait nous faisons vous faites ils/elles font	j'ai fait tu as fait il/elle/on a fait nous avons fait vous avez fait ils/elles ont fait	je faisais tu faisais il/elle/on faisait nous faisions vous faisiez ils/elles faisaient	je ferai tu feras il/elle/on fera nous ferons vous ferez ils/elles feront	je ferais tu ferais il/elle/on ferait nous ferions vous feriez ils/elles feraient
lire	je lis tu lis il/elle/on lit nous lisons vous lisez ils/elles lisent	j'ai lu tu as lu il/elle/on a lu nous avons lu vous avez lu ils/elles ont lu	je lisais tu lisais il/elle/on lisait nous lisions vous lisiez ils/elles lisaient	je lirai tu liras il/elle/on lira nous lirons vous lirez ils/elles liront	je lirais tu lirais il/elle/on lirait nous lirions vous liriez ils/elles liraient
mettre	je mets tu mets il/elle/on met nous mettons vous mettez ils/elles mettent	j'ai mis tu as mis il/elle/on a mis nous avons mis vous avez mis ils/elles ont mis	je mettais tu mettais il/elle/on mettait nous mettions vous mettiez ils/elles mettaient	je mettrai tu mettras il/elle/on mettra nous mettrons vous mettrez ils/elles mettront	je mettrais tu mettrais il/elle/on mettrait nous mettrions vous mettriez ils/elles mettraient
pouvoir	je peux tu peux il/elle/on peut nous pouvons vous pouvez ils/elles peuvent	j'ai pu tu as pu il/elle/on a pu nous avons pu vous avez pu ils/elles ont pu	je pouvais tu pouvais il/elle/on pouvait nous pouvions vous pouviez ils/elles pouvaient	je pourrai tu pourras il/elle/on pourra nous pourrons vous pourrez ils/elles pourront	je pourrais tu pourrais il/elle/on pourrait nous pourrions vous pourriez ils/elles pourraient
prendre	je prends tu prends il/elle/on prend nous prenons vous prenez ils/elles prennent	j'ai pris tu as pris il/elle/on a pris nous avons pris vous avez pris ils/elles ont pris	je prenais tu prenais il/elle/on prenait nous prenions vous preniez ils/elles prenaient	je prendrai tu prendras il/elle/on prendra nous prendrons vous prendrez ils/elles prendront	je prendrais tu prendrais il/elle/on prendrait nous prendrions vous prendriez ils/elles prendraient

Infinitive	Present	Perfect	Imperfect	Future	Conditional
savoir	je sais tu sais il/elle/on sait nous savons vous savez ils/elles savent	j'ai su tu as su il/elle/on a su nous avons su vous avez su ils/elles ont su	je savais tu savais il/elle/on savait nous savions vous saviez ils/elles savaient	je saurai tu sauras il/elle/on saura nous saurons vous saurez ils/elles sauront	je saurais tu saurais il/elle/on saurait nous saurions vous sauriez ils/elles sauraient

venir	je viens
	tu viens
	il/elle/on vient
	
	nous venons
	
	vous venez
	ils/elles viennent
		je suis venu(e)
		tu es venu(e)
		il/elle/on est
		  venu(e)(s)
		nous sommes
		  venu(e)s
		vous êtes venu(e)s
		ils/elles sont
		  venu(e)s
			je venais
			tu venais
			il/elle/on venait
			
			nous venions
			
			vous veniez
			ils/elles venaient
				je viendrai
				tu viendras
				il/elle/on viendra
				
				nous viendrons
				
				vous viendrez
				ils/elles viendront
					je viendrais
					tu viendrais
					il/elle/on viendrait
					
					nous viendrions
					
					vous viendriez
					ils/elles viendraient

voir	je vois tu vois il/elle/on voit nous voyons vous voyez ils/elles voient	j'ai vu tu as vu il/elle/on a vu nous avons vu vous avez vu ils/elles ont vu	je voyais tu voyais il/elle/on voyait nous voyions vous voyiez ils/elles voyaient	je verrai tu verras il/elle/on verra nous verrons vous verrez ils/elles verront	je verrais tu verrais il/elle/on verrait nous verrions vous verriez ils/elles verraient
vouloir	je veux tu veux il/elle/on veut nous voulons vous voulez ils/elles veulent	j'ai voulu tu as voulu il/elle/on a voulu nous avons voulu vous avez voulu ils/elles ont voulu	je voulais tu voulais il/elle/on voulait nous voulions vous vouliez ils/elles voulaient	je voudrai tu voudras il/elle/on voudra nous voudrons vous voudrez ils/elles voudront	je voudrais tu voudrais il/elle/on voudrait nous voudrions vous voudriez ils/elles voudraient

VOCABULARY

à	to, at	annoncér	to announce
d'abord	(at) first	annuler	to cancel
tout d'abord	first of all	Antilles (f. pl.)	West Indies
accès (m.)	access	août	August
accident (m.)	accident	apéritif (m.)	aperitif
d'accord	fine, OK	appareil (m.)	appliance, telephone
être d'accord	to agree	appartement (m.)	flat, apartment
ne pas être d'accord	to disagree	appel (m.)	call, phone call
acheter	to buy	appeler	to call, to telephone
acteur (trice)	actor, actress	s'appeler	to be called
actuellement	at the moment	appétit (m.)	appetite
addition	the bill	bon appétit	enjoy your meal
adorer	to adore, to love	apprendre	to learn
adresse (f.)	address	appuyer	to push, to press
aérobic (m.)	aerobics	après	after, afterwards
aéroport (m.)	airport	d'après	according to
affaires (f.)	business	après-midi (m.or f.)	afternoon
africain(e)	African	architecte	architect
Afrique (f.)	Africa	architecture (f.)	architecture
Afrique du Sud (f.)	South Africa	argent (m.)	money
âge (m.)	age	argent de poche (m.)	pocket money
agence (f.)	agency	Argentine (f.)	Argentina
agneau (m.)	lamb	argentin(e)	Argentinian
agréable	pleasant	armoire (f.)	wardrobe
aider	to help	s'arrêter	to stop
aimer	to like, to love	arrivée (f)	arrival
alcool (m.)	alcohol	arriver	to arrive, to happen
Algérie (f.)	Algeria	ascenseur (m.)	lift
algérien(ne)	Algerian	assez	enough, rather
Allemagne (f.)	Germany	assiette (f.)	plate
allemand(e)	German	assistant(e)	assistant
aller	to go	athlétisme (m.)	athletics
aller simple (m.)	single ticket	attendre	to wait for
allergique à	allergic	faire attention	to be careful
aller-retour (m.)	return ticket	aucun(e)	any, more, no
allô	hello (on the phone)	aujourd'hui	today
améliorer	to improve	au revoir	goodbye
ami(e)	friend	aussi	also, too
s'amuser	to have fun, enjoy oneself	aussi … que	as … as
an (m.)	year	autobus (m.)	bus
ancien(ne)	former, ancient	automne (m.)	autumn
anglais(e)	English	autour de	around
Angleterre (f.)	England	autre	other
animal (m)	animal	être en avance	to be early
animal domestique	pet	avant	before
animé(e)	lively	avec	with
année (f.)	year	avenir (m.)	future
anniversaire (m.)	birthday	à l'avenir	in the future

avenue (f.)	avenue	boire	to drink
avion (m.)	airplane	boisson (f.)	drink
avis (m.)	opinion	boîte de nuit (f.)	nightclub
à mon avis	in my opinion	aller en boîte	to go clubbing
avocat(e)	lawyer	bon(ne)	good, mild (weather)
avoir	to have	bonjour	hello
avril	April	bonne nuit	good night
		bonsoir	good evening
baccalauréat (bac) (m.)	A-levels (equivalent)	bord (m.)	edge, side
se baigner	to bathe, swim	au bord de la mer	at the seaside
baignoire (f.)	bathtub	bosser (coll.)	to work
bain (m.)	bath	boucher(ère)	butcher
salle de bains (f.)	bathroom	boucherie (f.)	butcher's shop
balade (f.)	walk, stroll, ride	boucles d'oreille (f. pl.)	earrings
banque (f.)	bank	boulanger(ère)	baker
bar (m.)	bar	boulangerie (f.)	baker's shop
bar-tabac (m.)	newsagent, tobacconist's shop	boule (f.)	scoop, ball
		boulevard (m.)	boulevard
barbe (f.)	beard	boulot (m.) (coll.)	job, work
bas(se)	low	bout (m.)	end, tip
en bas	downstairs, at the bottom	bouteille (f.)	bottle
bateau (m.)	boat	bricolage (m.)	DIY
bâtiment (m.)	building	faire du bricolage	to do DIY
beau (belle)	beautiful, handsome	briller	to shine
beau-fils (m.)	son-in-law, step-son	britannique	British
beau-frère (m.)	brother-in-law, step-brother	bronzer	to tan
		se faire bronzer	to sunbathe
beau-père (m.)	stepfather/father-in-law	brouillard (m.)	fog
belle-fille (f.)	daughter-in-law, step-daughter	bruit (m.)	noise
		brûlure (f.)	burn
belle-mère (f.)	mother-in-law, step-mother	brun(e)	brown (hair)
		bureau (m.)	office
belle-sœur (f.)	sister-in-law, step-sister	bureau de tourisme (m.)	tourist information office
beaucoup	a lot	bus (m.)	bus
bébé (m.)	baby		
beige	beige	c'est ça	that's right
belge	Belgian	ça	that, it
Belgique (f.)	Belgium	ça va?, ça va	how are you?, (I'm) fine
besoin (m.)	need	cabine d'essayage (f.)	changing room
avoir besoin (de)	to need	café (m.)	black coffee, pub
beurre (m.)	butter	café crème (m.)	white coffee
bibliothèque (f.)	library	caisse (f.)	check-out, till
bien	well, good	calme	quiet
bien sûr	of course	campagne (f.)	countryside
bientôt	soon	camping (m.)	campsite
à bientôt!	see you soon!	faire du camping	to go camping
bienvenue!	welcome!	Canada (m.)	Canada
bière (f.)	beer	canadien(ne)	Canadian
bilingue	bilingual	canapé-lit (m.)	sofa bed
billet (m.)	ticket	canard (m.)	duck
biologie (f.)	biology	car (m.)	coach
biscuit (m.)	biscuit	carré (m.)	square
blanc(he)	white	carrefour (m.)	crossroads
bleu(e)	blue	carte (f.)	map, card, menu
blond(e)	blond	en cas de	in the event of

159

casquette (f.)	cap	chocolat chaud (m.)	hot chocolate
casser	to break	choisir	to choose
se casser (coll.)	to leave	choix (m.)	choice
Je me casse! (coll.)	I'm off!	chômage (m.)	unemployment
cathédrale (f.)	cathedral	être au chômage	to be unemployed
cause (f.)	cause	chômeur(euse)	unemployed person
à cause de	because of	chose (f.)	thing
ce (cet, cette), ces	it, this, that, these, those	cigarette (f.)	cigarette
ceci	this	ciel (m.)	sky
cela	that	cinéma (m.)	cinema
célibataire	single	cinq	five
celui-ci, celui-là	this one, that one	cinquante	fifty
(celle-ci, celle-là)		circulation (f.)	traffic
cent	one hundred	circuler	to run (trains)
centre (m.)	centre	citron (m.)	lemon
centre-ville (m.)	town centre	citron pressé (m.)	fresh lemon juice
certificat (m.)	certificate	clair(e)	light, clear
chacun(e)	each one	classe (f.)	class
chaise (f.)	chair	client(e)	customer
chaise roulante (f.)	wheelchair	climat (m.)	climate
chambre (f.)	bedroom	cocher	to tick
champignon (m.)	mushroom	coca (m.)	Coca-Cola
chance (f.)	luck	coin (m.)	corner
bonne chance	good luck!	au coin de	at the corner of
changement (m.)	change	collège (m.)	(lower) secondary school
changer	to change	collègue	colleague
chanter	to sing	commander	to order
chanteur(euse)	singer	comme	like, as
chaque	each	commencer	to begin, to start
charcuterie (f.)	cold meats, delicatessen	comment	how
château (m.)	castle	commerce (m.)	trade, business, shop
chaud	hot, warm	centre commercial (m.)	shopping centre
avoir chaud	to be hot	commode (f.)	chest of drawers
chauffage (m.)	heating	complet(ète)	full, complete
chauffeur (m.)	driver	complètement	completely
chaussettes (f. pl.)	socks	composter	to validate, to punch
chaussures (f. pl.)	shoes		(ticket)
chemin (m.)	path, way	comprendre	to understand, to include
cheminée (f.)	fireplace	compris(e)	included
chemise (f.)	shirt	comptable (m.)	accountant
chemisier (m.)	blouse	comptabilité (f.)	accountancy
chèque (m.)	cheque	compte (m.)	account
chèque de voyage (m.)	traveller's cheque	à son compte	freelance
cher(ère)	expensive	compter	to count
chercher	to look for	conduire	to drive
chercheur(euse)	researcher	confortable	comfortable
cheveux (m. pl.)	hair	congé (m.)	leave, time off
chèvre (m.)	goat's cheese	connaissance (f.)	knowledge
chez	at somebody's house	connaître	to know (someone)
chez moi	at my house	continuer	to continue
chic	smart	contre	against
chimie (f.)	chemistry	par contre	however
Chine (f.)	China	copain (m.)	boyfriend, friend
chinois(e)	Chinese	copine (f.)	girlfriend, friend
chocolat (m.)	chocolate	correspondance (f)	connection (tube, train)

Corse (f.)	Corsica	demi-frère (m.)	half-brother
costume (m.)	suit	demi-sœur (f.)	half-sister
côte (f.)	coast, chop	dentiste	dentist
côté (m.)	side	départ (m.)	departure
à côté de	next to	département (m.)	department (administrative area)
côté couloir	aisle seat		
côté fenêtre	window seat	déplacer	to move
se coucher	to go to bed, to lie down	depuis	for, since
couleur (f.)	colour	dernier(ère)	last
couramment	fluently	derrière	behind
courir	to run	descendre	to go down
cours (m.)	lecture, course	désirer	to want
cours intensif (m.)	intensive course	désolé(e)	sorry
courses (f. pl.)	shopping	dessert (m.)	dessert
faire des courses	to go shopping	au-dessous de	below, underneath
court(e)	short	au-dessus de	above
cousin(e)	cousin	destination (f.)	destination
coûter	to cost	à destination de	going to
couverture (f.)	cover, blanket	détester	to detest
crèche (f.)	nursery	deux	two
crème (f.)	cream	deuxième	second
crèmerie (f.)	dairy shop	devant	in front of
croire	to believe	devenir	to become
croissant (m.)	croissant	devoir	to have to, must
croque-monsieur (m.)	toasted ham and cheese sandwich	différent(e)	different
		difficile	difficult
crudités (f. pl.)	raw vegetables	dimanche (m.)	Sunday
cuiller (f.)	spoon	dîner	to dine, to have dinner
cuisine (f.)	kitchen	dîner (m.)	evening meal
cuisiner	to cook	diplôme (m.)	diploma, certificate
cuisinier(ère)	cook	dire	to say
cuisinière (f.)	cooker	directeur(trice)	director, manager
cuit(e)	cooked	direction (f.)	management
bien cuit	well done (steak)	disponible	available
culturel(le)	cultural	disque (m.)	disc, record
curieux(euse)	nosy	dissertation (f.)	essay
curriculum vitae (m.)	CV	divers(e)	miscellaneous
		divorcé(e)	divorced
dame (f.)	lady	dix	ten
Danemark (m.)	Denmark	dix-huit	eighteen
danois(e)	Danish	dix-neuf	nineteen
dans	in	dix-sept	seventeen
danse (f.)	dance	docteur (m.)	doctor
danser	to dance	doctorat (m.)	PhD doctorate
date (f.)	date	domicile (m.)	residence
de	of, from	c'est dommage	it's a pity
se débrouiller	to cope, to manage	donc	therefore, so
décembre	December	dormir	to sleep
décider	to decide	dormir à la belle étoile	to sleep out in the open
décrire	to describe	douche (f.)	shower
déjeuner (m.)	lunch	se doucher	to shower
demain	tomorrow	douze	twelve
à demain!	see you tomorrow!	draps (m. pl.)	bed linen
demander	to ask for	droit (m.)	law
déménager	to move house	droit(e)	straight

droite (f.)	right	équipé(e)	equipped
à droite	on the right	équitation (f.)	horse-riding
du, de la, des	of the, some	escalade (f.)	climbing
durer	to last	escargot (m.)	snail
		Espagne (f.)	Spain
eau (f.)	water	espagnol(e)	Spanish
eau minérale (f.)	mineral water	espérer	to hope
échouer	to fail	essayer	to try
école (f.)	school	essence (f.)	petrol
écologie (f.)	ecology	est (m.)	east
économie (f.)	economics	Estonie (f.)	Estonia
écossais(e)	Scottish	estonien(ne)	Estonian
Ecosse	Scotland	étage (m.)	floor
écouter	to listen to	Etats-Unis (m. pl.)	United States
écrire	to write	été (m.)	summer
éducation (f.)	education	étoile (f.)	star
église (f.)	church	étranger(ère)	foreign
Egypte (f.)	Egypt	être	to be
électricien(ne)	electrician	étude (f.)	study
elle (f.)	she, her	études (f. pl.)	studies
elles (f. pl.)	they, them	études (f.) commerciales	business studies
emmener	to take	étudiant(e)	student
emploi (m.)	job	étudier	to study
employé(e)	employee	euro (m.)	euro
en	in, of it, of them	Europe (f.)	Europe
encore	more, yet, still	européen(ne)	European
endroit (m.)	a place	évier (m.)	sink
enfant	child	examen (m.)	exam
enfant unique	only child	exemple (m.)	example
enfer (m.)	hell	expérience (f.)	
c'est l'enfer! (coll.)	it's hell!	professionnelle	work experience
enfin	finally, well	exposition (f.)	exhibition
s'ennuyer	to be bored	exprès	on purpose
ennuyeux(euse)	boring		
enseignement (m.)	teaching	fac (f.) (coll.)	university
enseigner	to teach	en face de	opposite
ensemble	together	de toute façon	in any case, anyway
ensuite	next, then	faim (f.)	hunger
entendre	to hear	avoir faim	to be hungry
entier(ère)	entire, whole	faire	to do, to make
entre	between	ça fait	it is, it comes to
entrée (f.)	starter, entrance	famille (f.)	family
entreprise (f.)	firm, company	fatigué(e)	tired
entrer	to come in, to go in	se fatiguer	to get tired
entretien (m.)	interview	il faut	it is necessary
envie (f.)	urge, craving	fauteuil (m.)	armchair
avoir envie (de)	to feel like, to fancy, to want	faux(sse)	false, untrue
		femme (f.)	woman, wife
envoyer	to send	fenêtre (f.)	window
épeler	to spell	jour (m.) férié	public holiday
épice (f.)	spice	fermer	to close
épicé(e)	spicy	fermeture (f.) annuelle	annual closure
épicerie (f.)	grocer's shop	fête (f.)	party, public holiday
épicier(ère)	grocer	feu (m.)	fire
équipe (f.)	team	feux (m. pl.)	traffic lights

février	February	grands-parents (m. pl.)	grandparents
fille (f.)	girl, daughter	gratuit(e)	free (no charge)
fils (m.)	son	grave	serious
fin (f.)	end	grec(que)	Greek
finalement	finally, in the end	Grèce (f.)	Greece
finir	to finish	grève (f.)	strike
fléchettes (f. pl.)	darts	grillé(e)	grilled
flic (m.) (coll.)	policeman	gris(e)	grey
fois (f.)	time	gros(se)	big, fat
foncé(e)	dark	groupe (m.)	group
football (m.)	football	guichet (m.)	ticket office
footing (m.)	jogging	guitare (f.)	guitar
formation (f.)	education/training	gym (f.)	gym
formidable	great		
fort(e)	strong, loud	s'habiller	to get dressed
fournir	to provide/supply	habiter	to live
fraise (f.)	strawberry	comme d'habitude	as usual
franc (m.)	franc	haut(e)	high
français(e)	French	heure (f.)	hour
France (f.)	France	être à l'heure	to be on time
francophone	French-speaking	à quelle heure?	at what time?
frère (m.)	brother	heureusement	fortunately
fric (m.) (coll.)	money	heureux(se)	happy
frites (f. pl.)	chips	hier	yesterday
froid(e)	cold	histoire (f.)	history
avoir froid	to be cold	hiver (m.)	winter
fromage (m.)	cheese	homme (m.)	man
fruit (m.)	fruit	Hongrie (f.)	Hungary
fumée (f.)	smoke	hongrois(e)	Hungarian
fumé(e)	smoked	hôpital (m.)	hospital
fumer	to smoke	horaire (m.)	timetable
furieux(euse)	furious	hôtel (m.)	hotel
		Hôtel (m.) de ville	town hall
gagner	to earn, to win	huile (f.)	oil
gallois(e)	Welsh	huit	eight
garage (m.)	garage		
gare (f.)	station	ici	here
gare routière (f.)	coach station	idéal(e)	ideal
gâteau (m.)	cake	idée (f.)	idea
gauche	left	bonne idée!	good idea!
à gauche	on the left	identité (f.)	identity
génial(e)	great, super	il (m.)	he, it
gens (m. pl.)	people	il y a	ago, there is, there are
gentil(le)	kind, nice	ils (m. pl.)	they
géographie (f.)	geography	image (f.)	image
gestion (f.)	management	imperméable (m.)	rain coat
gestion (f.) d'entreprise	business management	important(e)	important
gilet (m.)	cardigan	impossible	impossible
gîte (m.)	holiday cottage	Inde (f.)	Indian
glace (f.)	ice cream	indien(ne)	Indian
goûter	to taste	infirmier(ère)	nurse
grand(e)	big, tall	information (f.)	information
Grande-Bretagne (f.)	Great Britain	informatique (f.)	computing
grand-mère (f.)	grandmother	ingéniérie (f.)	engineering
grand-père (m.)	grandfather	ingénieur (m.)	engineer

s'inscrire	to enrol	laisser	to leave
s'installer	to settle	laisser un message	to leave a message
intelligent(e)	intelligent	lait (m.)	milk
intention (f.)	intention	langage (m.) familier	colloquial language
avoir l'intention (de)	to intend to	langue (f.) étrangère	foreign language
interdire	to forbid	lapin (m.)	rabbit
intéressant(e)	interesting	lavabo (m.)	washbasin
internet (m.)	internet	lave-linge (m.)	washing machine
interrupteur (m.)	switch	lave-vaisselle (m.)	dishwasher
inviter	to invite	laver	to wash
Irak (m.)	Irak	se laver	to get washed
iraquien(ne)	Iraqi	le (la, les)	the
irlandais(e)	Irish	le, la	it, him, her
Irlande (f.)	Ireland	les	them
Italie (f.)	Italy	lecture (f.)	reading
italien(ne)	Italian	léger(ère)	light
		légume (m.)	vegetable
jamaïcain(e)	Jamaican	lendemain (m.)	the day after
Jamaïque (f.)	Jamaica	lequel?/laquelle?	which one?
jamais	never	letton(ne)	Latvian
jambon (m.)	ham	Lettonie (f.)	Latvia
janvier	January	lettre (f.)	letter
Japon (m.)	Japan	lettre de	reference letter
japonais(e)	Japanese	recommandation (f.)	
jardin (m.)	garden	lettres modernes (f. pl.)	humanities
jaune	yellow	se lever	to get up
je	I	Liban (m.)	Lebanon
jean (m.)	jeans	librairie (f.)	bookshop
jeu (m.)	game	libre	free
jeudi	Thursday	licence (f.)	Bachelor's degree
jeune	young	lieu (m.)	place
joli(e)	pretty	au lieu de	instead of
jouer	to play	ligne (f.)	line
jour (m.)	day	limonade (f.)	lemonade
à un de ces jours (coll.)	see you around!	linguistique (f.)	linguistics
journal (m.)	newspaper	lire	to read
journaliste	journalist	liste (f.)	list
journée (f.)	day	lit (m.)	bed
bonne journée!	have a good day!	lit double (m.)	double bed
juillet	July	lit simple (m.)	single bed
juin	June	litre (m.)	litre
jupe (f.)	skirt	littérature (f.)	literature
jus (m.)	juice	Lituanie (f.)	Lithuania
jusqu'à	until, up to	lituanien(ne)	Lithuanian
juste	just, correct	livre (m.)	book
		livre (f.)	pound
kilo (m.)	kilo	location (f.)	hire, rental
kilomètre (m.)	kilometer	loger	to accommodate, to stay
kilométrage (m.)	mileage	loin	far, far away
kir (m.)	Kir (white wine and	loisir (m.)	leisure
	blackcurrant)	Londres	London
		long(ue)	long
là	there	longtemps	a long time
là-bas	over there	lotte (f.)	monkfish
lac (m.)	lake	louer	to rent, to hire

lourd(e)	heavy
lui, leur	(to) him, (to) her, (to) them
lundi (m.)	Monday
lune (f.)	moon
lunettes (f. pl.)	glasses
lycée (m.)	upper secondary school
madame (f.)	madam, Mrs
mademoiselle (f.)	miss
magasin (m.)	shop
grand magasin (m.)	department store
magazine (m.)	magazine
magnifique	brilliant
mai	May
main (f.)	hand
maintenant	now
mais	but
maison (f.)	house
à la maison	at home
maîtrise (f.)	Master's degree
mal (m.)	pain, bad
mal	badly
pas mal	not bad (pretty good)
malade	ill
malheureusement	unfortunately
manger	to eat
manteau (m.)	coat
marchand(e)	shopkeeper
marche (f.)	step
marché (m.)	market
marcher	to walk, to function
ça marche?	does it work?
mardi (m.)	Tuesday
mari (m.)	husband
marié(e)	married
marketing (m.)	marketing
Maroc (m.)	Morroco
marocain(e)	Moroccan
marrant(e)	funny
en avoir marre (coll.)	to be fed up
marron	brown (eyes)
mars	March
match (m.)	match
mathématiques (f. pl.)	mathematics
matin (m.)	morning
matinée (f.)	morning
mauvais(e)	bad
me	(to) me, myself
mécanicien(ne)	mechanic
médecin (m.)	doctor
médicament (m.)	medicine, medication
meilleur(e)	better
même	same, even
ménage (m.)	housework, household
menthe (f.)	mint

mention (f.)	distinction
menu (m.)	set menu
mer (f.)	sea, seaside
au bord de la mer	at the seaside
merci	thank you
mercredi (m.)	Wednesday
mère (f.)	mother
météo (f.)	weather forecast
métier	job, career
mètre (m.)	metre
métro (m.)	tube, underground
mettre	to put
se mettre à (faire)	to start (doing)
meuble (m.)	a piece of furniture
à mi-temps	part-time
midi	midday, noon
mignon(ne)	cute, attractive
milieu (m.)	middle
mille	thousand
million (m.)	million
mince	slim
minuit	midnight
minute (f.)	minute
mode (f.)	fashion
moderne	modern
moi	me
moins	less
mois (m.)	month
moitié (f.)	half
môme	kid
mon, ma, mes	my
monde (m.)	world
beaucoup de monde	a lot of people
monsieur (m.)	Sir, Mr
montagne (f.)	mountain
monter	to go up
montrer	to show
morceau (m.)	piece, bit
mot (m)	word
moto (f.)	motorbike
mourir	to die
moustache (f.)	moustache
moyen(ne)	average
moyen (m.) de transport	means of transport
musée (m.)	museum
musique (f.)	music
nager	to swim
naissance (f.)	birth
naître	to be born
natation (f.)	swimming
faire de la natation	to go swimming
nationalité (f.)	nationality
ne ... jamais	never
ne ... pas	not

ne ... plus	no longer, no more	ouest (m.)	west
ne ... que	only	Ouganda (m.)	Uganda
ne ... rien	nothing	ougandais(e)	Ugandan
né(e)	born	oui	yes
neige (f.)	snow	outil informatique (m.)	computer package
il neige	it snows, it is snowing	ouvert(e)	open
neuf	nine	ouvrir	to open
neveu (m.)	nephew		
ni	neither	pain (m.)	bread
nièce (f.)	niece	pamplemousse (m.)	grapefruit
Noël (m.)	Christmas	en panne	broken down, out of order
noir(e)	black	pantalon (m.)	trousers
noix (f.)	walnut	papeterie (f.)	stationer's
nom (m.)	name	papier (m.)	paper
nom (m.) de famille	surname	Pâques (m.)	Easter
au nom (de)	in the name of	par	through
nombre (m.)	number	parc (m.)	park
non	no	parce que	because
nord (m.)	north	pardon	excuse me, sorry, pardon
Norvège (f.)	Norway	parents (m. pl.)	parents
norvégien(ne)	Norwegian	parfois	sometimes
note (f.)	mark	parking (m.)	car park
notre, nos	our	parler	to speak
nous	we, (to) us, ourselves	partir	to leave
nouveau(elle)	new	pas (m.)	step
novembre	November	pas	not
nuage (m.)	cloud	pas du tout	not at all
nuit (f.)	night	pas grand-chose	not a lot
nul(le) (coll.)	not nice	pas mal de	quite a lot of
numéro (m.)	number	passer	to pass by, through
		passer un coup de fil (coll.)	to make a phone call
objet (m.)	object	passer un examen	to sit an exam
objet (m.) de valeur	valuable	pâtisserie (f.)	pastry / cake shop
être obligé(e) de	to have to	payer	to pay
obtenir	to gain, to get	pays (m.)	country
s'occuper de	to deal with, to take care of	Pays-Bas (m. pl.)	Netherlands
octobre	October	Pays de Galles (m.)	Wales
œil (m.) (yeux pl.)	eye	pendant	for, during
œuf (m.)	egg	penser	to think
offrir	to offer	pension (f.)	guest house
oiseau (m.)	bird	demi-pension (f.)	half-board
on	one/we	perdre	to lose
oncle (m.)	uncle	perdre connnaisance	to lose consciousness, to faint
onze	eleven		
opéra (m.)	opera	père (m.)	father
opinion (f.)	opinion	permettre	to allow
orage (m.)	storm	permis (m.) de conduire	driving licence
orange (f.)	orange	personne (f.)	person
orange (f.) pressée	fresh orange juice	personnes (f. pl.) handicapées	disabled people
ordinateur (m.)	computer		
oreille (f.)	ear	pétanque (f.)	boules
oreiller (m.)	pillow	petit(e)	little, small, short (person)
ou	or	petit déjeuner (m.)	breakfast
où	where	petit-fils (m.)	grandson
oublier	to forget		

petite-fille (f.)	granddaughter	Portugal (m.)	Portugal
peu	not much	portugais(e)	Portuguese
un (petit) peu	a (little) bit	possible	possible
à peu près	more or less, about	poste (f.)	post office
peut-être	perhaps	poste (m.)	job, position
pharmacie (f.)	chemist's shop	poste (m.) de secours	first-aid post
pharmacien(ne)	chemist	pot (m.) (coll.)	drink
philosophie (f.)	philosophy	poulet (m.)	chicken
photographie (f.)	photography	pour	for
piano (m.)	piano	pourboire (m.)	tip (money)
pièce (f.)	room/play	pourquoi	why
pied (m.)	foot	pousser	to push
à pied	on foot	pouvoir	to be able, can
ping-pong (m.)	table tennis	préférer	to prefer
pique-nique (m.)	picnic	premier(ère)	first
piquer (coll.)	to steal	prendre	to take
piscine (f.)	swimming pool	prénom (m.)	first name
pittoresque	picturesque	près	near
place (f.)	seat, square	se présenter	to introduce oneself
se plaindre	to complain	prêt(e)	ready
plan (m.)	street map	prêter	to lend
planche (f.) à voile	windsurfing	printemps (m.)	spring
plat(e)	flat, smooth	prix (m.)	price
plat (m.)	dish	problème (m.)	problem
plat (m.) du jour	dish of the day	prochain(e)	next
plat (m.) principal	main course	à la prochaine!	see you next time!
plein(e)	full	proche	near
plein de	lots of	professeur (m.)	teacher
à plein temps	full-time	profession (f.)	occupation
il pleut	it rains, it's raining	projet (m.)	plan, project
pluie (f.)	rain	promenade (f.)	walk
plus	more	se promener	to go for a walk
plus ou moins	more or less	proposer	to suggest
plus tard	later	propre	clean
à plus tard!	see you later!	en provenance de	coming from
plusieurs	several	psychologie (f.)	psychology
pneu (m.) crevé	flat tyre	puis	then
poêlé(e)	pan-fried	pull (m.)	jumper
à point	medium done		
pointure (f.)	shoe size	quai (m.)	platform
poisson (m.)	fish	qualification (f.)	qualification
poissonnerie (f.)	fishmonger's	quand	when
poivre (m.)	pepper	quarante	forty
police (f.)	police	quart (m.)	quarter
policier(ère)	policeman (woman)	quart (m.) d'heure	quarter of an hour
politique (f.)	politics	quartier (m.)	neighbourhood, area
pollué(e)	polluted	quatorze	fourteen
Pologne (f.)	Poland	quatre	four
polonais(e)	Polish	à un de ces quatres!	see you around!
pomme (f.)	apple	(coll.)	
pompiers (m. pl.)	fire brigade	quatre-vingt-dix	ninety
pont (m.)	bridge	quatre-vingts	eighty
porte (f.)	door	quatrième	fourth
portefeuille (m.)	wallet	que (conjunction)	that, than
porter	to carry, to wear	que (pronoun)	that, what, which

167

qu'est-ce que c'est?	what is it?	retard (m.)	delay
Québec (m.)	Quebec	être en retard	to be late
québécois(e)	Quebecois	retourner	to go back
quel(le)	what, which	retraite (f.)	retirement
quelque	some	être à la retraite	to be retired
quelque chose	something	se retrouver	to meet up
quelquefois	sometimes	réussir	to succeed, to pass
quelques	a few	se réveiller	to wake up
quelqu'un	someone	réveil (m.) automatique	early morning call
question (f.)	question·	revenir	to come back
qui	who, whom	rez-de-chaussée (m.)	ground floor
quincaillerie (f.)	hardware shop	rien	nothing
quinze	fifteen	de rien	don't mention it, that's OK
quitter	to leave	rivière (f.)	river
quoi	what	robe (f.)	dress
		rond(e)	round
radio (f.)	radio	rond-point (m.)	roundabout
randonnée (f.) (à pied)	walking, hiking	rose	pink
rapide	fast	rouge	red
rappeler	to call back, to call again	route (f.)	road
se raser	to shave	roux(sse)	ginger (hair)
rater	to miss	Royaume-Uni (m.)	United Kingdom
réceptionniste	receptionist	rue (f.)	road, street
recevoir	to receive	rugby (m.)	rugby
recommander	to recommend	russe	Russian
refiler (coll.)	to give	Russie (f.)	Russia
réfrigérateur (m.)	fridge		
refuser	to refuse	sac (m.)	bag
regarder	to watch, to look at	saignant(e)	rare (steak)
région (f.)	region	saison (f.)	season
relax (m.)	garden lounger	basse saison (f.)	low season
relaxant(e)	relaxing	demi-saison (f.)	mid-season
remplir un formulaire	to fill in a form	haute saison (f.)	high season
rencontrer	to meet	salade (f.)	salad
rendez-vous (m.)	appointment	sale	dirty·
renseignements (m. pl.)	information	salle (f.)	room
se renseigner	to find out, make enquiries	salle (f.) à manger	dining room
rentrer	to come, go back (home)	salle (f.) de bains	bathroom
renverser	to knock down	salle (f.) de séjour	living room
réparer	to repair	salon (m.)	sitting room
repas (m.)	meal	salut!	hi!, goodbye! (informal)
répéter	to repeat	samedi (m.)	Saturday
répondre	to answer	SAMU (m.)	mobile accident unit
réponse (f.)	answer	sandwich (m.)	sandwich
se reposer	to rest, to relax	sans	without
République tchèque (f.)	Czech Republic	sauce (f.)	sauce
réservation (f.)	booking	sauce (f.) au poivre	pepper sauce
réserver	to book	saucisse (f.)	sausage
responsable	person in charge	saucisson (m.)	salami, cured meat
responsable de	responsible (for)	sauf	except
restaurant (m.)	restaurant	saumon (m.)	salmon
reste (m.)	remainder, rest	savoir	to know (something)
rester	to stay	savon (m.)	soap
résultat (m.)	result	science (f.)	science
résumé (m.)	summary		

sciences (f. pl.) commerciales	business studies	son, sa, ses	his, her
sciences (f. pl.) de l'éducation	education	sortie (f.)	exit, way out
		sortir	to come/go out
sciences (f. pl.) politiques	politics	souligner	to underline
		soupe (f.)	soup
se	himself, herself, themselves	sous	under
		souvent	often
sec (sèche)	dry	se spécialiser	to specialise
second(e)	second	sport (m.)	sport
secours (m.)	help	faire du sport	to play sport
secrétaire	secretary	sportif(ve)	keen on sport, good at sport
seize	sixteen		
séjour (m.)	stay, living room	stage (m.)	work placement
séjour (m.) à l'étranger	stay abroad	stagiaire	person on work placement
sel (m.)	salt	station (f.) de métro	underground station
selon	according to	station (f.) service	petrol station
semaine (f.)	week	steak (m.)	steak
à la semaine prochaine!	see you next week!	sucre (m.)	sugar
Sénégal (m.)	Senegal	sud (m.)	south
sénégalais(e)	Senegalese	Suède (f.)	Sweden
sens (m.)	direction, sense	suédois(e)	Swedish
sentir	to feel	suffisant(e)	sufficient
se sentir à l'aise	to feel at ease	suggérer	to suggest
séparé(e)	separated	Suisse (f.)	Switzerland
sept	seven	suisse	Swiss
septembre	September	suivant(e)	next, following
serré(e)	tight	suivre	to follow
serveur(euse)	waiter(tress)	suivre un cours	to do a course
serviette (f.)	towel	super	super, brilliant, great
servir	to serve	supermarché (m.)	supermarket
seul(e)	alone	sur	on
seulement	only	sûr(e)	sure, certain
si	if	bien sûr	of course
s'il te plaît, s'il vous plaît	please (informal, formal)	surtout	above all, especially
		sympa	nice, friendly
simple	simple		
sinon	otherwise, or else	tableau (m.)	picture
six	six	taches (f. pl.) de rousseur	freckles
ski (m.)	ski, skiing		
faire du ski	to go skiing	taille (f.)	size
ski (m.) nautique	water skiing	tante (f.)	aunt
snack bar (m.)	snack bar	taper	to type
SNCF (f.)	French national railways	tard	late
société (f.)	company	tarte (f.)	pie
sociologie (f.)	sociology	tarte (f.) aux pommes	apple pie
sœur (f.)	sister	tartiflette (f.)	potato gratin
soif (f.)	thirst	tartine (f.)	buttered bread
avoir soif	to be thirsty	tasse (f.)	cup
soir (m.)	evening	taxi (m.)	taxi
à ce soir	see you this evening	tchèque	Czech
soirée (f.)	evening	te	(to) you, yourself
soixante	sixty	technicien(ne)	technician
soixante-dix	seventy	tee-shirt (m.)	tee-shirt
soleil (m.)	sun	téléphone (m.)	telephone
		téléphoner à	to telephone

télévision (f.)	television	se trouver	to be situated, to find oneself
télévision (f.) par satellite	satellite television	truite (f.)	trout
tellement	so much	tu	you (singular, informal)
temps (m.)	time, weather	type (m.) (coll.)	guy
de temps en temps	from time to time		
tenir	to hold, to keep	un(e)	a, one
tennis (m.)	tennis	une fois	once
tente (f.)	tent	uniforme (m.)	uniform
terminer	to finish	université (f.)	university
terrasse (f.)	terrace	usine (f.)	factory
terre (f.)	ground	utile	useful
pas terrible	not very good	utiliser	to use
test (m.)	test		
tête (f.)	head	vacances (f.pl.)	holidays
TGV (m.)	high speed train	vanille (f.)	vanilla
thé (m.)	tea	varié(e)	varied
théâtre (m.)	theatre	végétarien(ne)	vegetarian
ticket (m.)	ticket	veille (f.)	day before
timbre (m.)	postage stamp	veinard(e) (coll.)	lucky
toi	you	vélo (m.)	bike
toilettes (f. pl.)	toilet(s)	en vélo	by bike
faire sa toilette	to wash	vendeur(euse)	sales assistant
tomate (f.)	tomato	vendre	to sell
tomber	to fall	vendredi (m.)	Friday
ton, ta, tes	your (singular, informal)	venir	to come
tôt	early	vent (m.)	wind
toujours	always	vérifier	to check
tour (m.)	turn, tour (of a city)	verre (m.)	glass
tour (f.)	tower	vers	towards
tour (m.) du monde	world trip	vert(e)	green
tourisme (m.)	tourism	veste (f.)	jacket
tous les jours	everyday	vêtements (m. pl.)	clothes
tout(e), tous(tes)	every, all	vétérinaire	vet
tout de suite	immediately	viande (f.)	meat
à tout de suite	see you in a minute	vie (f.)	life
tout droit	straight ahead	vieux (vieille)	old
tout le monde	everyone	village (m.)	village
traducteur(trice)	translator	ville (f.)	town, city
traduction (f.)	translation	vin (m.)	wine
train (m.)	train	vingt	twenty
trajet (m.)	journey, route	vingtième	twentieth
tranquille	quiet	violon (m.)	violin
transport (m.)	transport	visite (f.)	visit
travail (m.)	work	visiter	to visit
travailler	to work	vitesse (f.)	speed
traverser	to cross	vivre	to live
treize	thirteen	vocabulaire (m.)	vocabulary
trente	thirty	voici	here is, here are, here you are
très	very	voilà	there you are, here you are
trois	three		
trop (de)	too (much)	voile (f.)	sailing
trop de monde	too many people	voir	to see
trouver	to find	voisin(e)	neighbour

voiture (f.)	car, carriage	vrai(e)	real, true
vol (m.)	flight	vraiment	really
volley (m.)	volleyball	vue (f.)	view
à volonté	help yourself	vue sur la mer (f.)	sea view
votre, vos	your (formal or plural)		
à votre disposition	available	week-end (m.)	weekend
à votre service	you are welcome		
vouloir	to want, to wish	y	there
vous	you (formal or plural), yourselves	yaourt (m.)	yoghurt
		yoga (m.)	yoga
voyage (m.)	trip		
voyager	to travel	zéro	zero, nought

ANSWERS

Answers

UNIT 1

1 b 1c; 2a; 3b.

3   je suis; je m'appelle; c'est

4   Spanish; French; Irish; African; Italian;
Indian; Senegalese; Scottish; Greek;
German; Welsh.
secretary; nurse; doctor; teacher; director;
student; lawyer; journalist; waiter/waitress;
technician; sales assistant

5   **a** italien/avocat; **b** espagnol/technicien;
c grecque/professeur; **d** indien/journaliste;
e galloise/étudiante; **f** irlandaise/secrétaire

7   **a** améric<u>ain</u>; **b** ind<u>ienne</u>; **c** écoss<u>aise</u>;
d bel<u>ge</u>; **e** alle<u>mand</u>; **f** secré<u>taire</u>;
g étud<u>iant</u>; **h** technic<u>ien</u>; **i** vend<u>euse</u>;
j infirm<u>ier</u>

8   **a** grecque/étudiante en philosophie/
Londres; **b** indien/Bombay/Manchester;
c sénégalais/étudiant en physique/Dakar;
d suisse/Zürich/Londres;
e espagnole/étudiante en anglais/Oxford;
f serveur/Cardiff/Bruxelles

9 b 1; 3; 4; 7; 9; 12; 14; 15; 18; 25; 30; 44; 60

10 **a** appelle; **b** moi; **c** suis; **d** à; **e** suis;
f de; **g** directeur; **h** vendeuse

11 **a** Oui, c'est moi. **b** Je suis sénégalaise.
c Je suis de Dakar. **d** Je suis vendeuse.

12 **a** Vous êtes/Vous vous appelez Joseph
Toure? **b** Vous êtes français? **c** Vous êtes
d'où? **d** Qu'est-ce que vous faites?

13 f; d; b; c; a; e; h; g.

14 **a** Comment tu t'appelles? **b** Qu'est-ce que
tu fais? **c** Tu es anglaise? **d** Tu es d'où?
e Tu habites où? **f** Tu travailles?

16 **a** Jacques Vandevelde; **b** belge;
c à Liège; **d** étudiant; **e** Isabelle
Chamfraud; **f** canadienne; **g** à Montréal;
h étudiante

Extra!

1   **a** Clément Dufond/français/Bastia (Corse)/
sciences politiques/ne travaille pas;
b Gérard Denis/belge/Bruxelles/anglais
(langues)/le soir dans un bar; **c** Nathalie
Martin/française/Nice/biologie/ne travaille
pas; **d** Sylvie Lebon/française/Poitiers/
langues étrangères (anglais et espagnol)/
ne travaille pas; **e** Arthur Dumarre/
suisse/Lausanne/allemand et économie/
stage à mi-temps; **f** Béatrice Lemercier/
suisse/Genève/histoire/serveuse dans un
restaurant

2   **a** Paris; **b** law; **c** waitress; **d** engineer;
e Versailles.

Exercices de grammaire

1   **a** espagnol; **b** irlandaise; **c** sénégalais;
d galloise; **e** suisse; **f** belge; **g** grec;
h infirmière; **i** réceptionniste;
j secrétaire; **k** directeur; **l** vendeuse;
m professeur; **n** étudiante

2   **a** Elle ne s'appelle pas Mary. Elle est
étudiante. Elle n'est pas américaine. Elle
habite à Rome. Elle ne travaille pas au
bureau.
b Il s'appelle Laurent. Il n'est pas infirmier.
Il est français. Il n'habite pas à Toulouse. Il
travaille dans un café.

3   **a** Tu es Hélène? **b** Tu viens d'où?
c Qu'est-ce qu'elle fait? **d** Est-ce qu'il
travaille? **e** Tu habites où? **f** Tu es
américaine? **g** Qu'est-ce que tu étudies?
h Comment elle s'appelle?

4   **a** Elle habite à Marseille? **b** Qu'est-ce qu'il
fait? **c** Tu es étudiant à Londres?
d Est-ce que vous êtes de Rome?
e Comment tu t'appelles? **f** Il travaille
dans un café? **g** Vous êtes d'où? **h** Elle
n'est pas anglaise?

UNIT 2

3 salut!; tu travailles; j'ai un copain; une copine; congolais; français

4 **a** married/divorced/a son/a daughter/a wife/a husband/children **b** parce que leurs familles ne sont pas traditionnelles

5 **a** her son; **b** her boyfriend and his daughter; **c** doctor; **d** four years old

6 **a** ta; **b** quel; **c** ans; **d** où; **e** à; **f** est; **g** étudiante; **h** travaille

8 **a** V; **b** F; **c** F; **d** F; **e** V; **f** F; **g** F; **h** V; **i** V; **j** F

9 f; b; d; a; c; e

10 **a** Ce sont mes copines; **b** Ils travaillent à Londres; **c** Ils habitent à Paris; **d** Ce sont tes copains?; **e** Ils ont treize ans; **f** Mes amies sont étudiantes.

11 **a** F; **b** F; **c** F; **d** V; **e** V; **f** F

12 **a** 2; **b** 1; **c** 3

13 **a** ça; **b** ma; **c** veux; **d** un; **e** un; **f** manger; **g** merci; **h** un

Extra!

1 Possible answers
François: 1 brother/1 sister Isabelle lives in Belgium/lots of friends in Brussels
Anne-Marie: 1 younger sister/lots of friends everywhere: Bordeaux, Lille, Limoges, Nancy, Lyon/1 brother Arnaud from Lyon
Gabriella: 1 sister goes to university in Lyon/2 brothers still at school (college)/ mother does not work/father works at the train station/not many friends/best friend lives near her

2 **a** 21; **b** She is a student there; **c** four; **d** no; **e** four sisters; **f** Southport.

Exercices de grammaire

1 **a** habite; **b** ont; **c** s'appelle; **d** a; **e** est; **f** travaille; **g** s'appelle; **h** a;

i est; **j** est; **k** habite; **l** travaille; **m** a.

2 **a** ma; **b** nos (plural); **c** notre/mon; **d** sa; **e** leurs (plural); **f** ton; **g** son

3 **a** ta; **b** notre; **c** des; **d** un; **e** le/mon; **f** son; **g** un/le; **h** un/mon; **i** votre; **j** un/ton

UNIT 3

2 **a** Je fais la cuisine; **b** Nous regardons la télé; **c** Je fais une dissertation pour le cours de philo; **d** Rien de spécial, nous lisons; **e** J'écoute de la musique; **f** Je mange.

4 **1** e; **2** g; **3** d; **4** h; **5** a; **6** j; **7** b; **8** f; **9** c; **10** i

5 **a** Bertrand; **b** the swimming pool; **c** guitar lesson; **d** going clubbing; **e** Alain, his sister and a girlfriend; **f** cycling

8a **a** il est deux heures et quart; **b** il est onze heures moins vingt-cinq; **c** il est cinq heures et demie; **d** il est minuit moins le quart; **e** il est huit heures dix; **f** il est neuf heures

8b Il est quelle heure?/Quelle heure est-il (s'il vous plaît)?/Tu as l'heure (s'il te plaît)?/ Vous avez l'heure (s'il vous plaît)?

10 lundi; mardi; mercredi; jeudi; vendredi; samedi; dimanche

11 **a** open from 9 a.m. to 1 p.m., from Monday to Friday; **b** closed at the weekend; **c** open from midday to 4 p.m. on Tuesdays and Thursdays; **d** closed on Sunday afternoon from 1 p.m. to 3 p.m. **e** open in the evening from 6 p.m. to 9 p.m.

12 **a** je prends; je commence; je termine; je travaille; je vais; je pars; j'arrive; je finis; je mange
b **i** V; **ii** F; **iii** V; **iv** F; **v** V; **vi** V; **vii** F; **viii** V

14 **a** j'aime bien le sport; **b** j'aime beaucoup la planche à voile; **c** je n'aime pas beaucoup le football; **d** j'aime beaucoup le théâtre

175

15 a aller; **b** jouer; **c** jouer; **d** faire; **e** faire;
f jouer

16 a does not like going swimming, likes to
play football and rugby, likes to go to the
cinema; **b** does not like to dance, likes
to play sport a lot, likes cycling and windsurfing; **c** likes to go to the gym, to go
shopping, to listen to music, hates going
to the theatre; **d** does not like to watch
television, likes to play cards, really likes to
do yoga but does not like cooking

Extra!

1 Possible answers
Ricardo: lots of work/does sport/phones
his friends/goes for walks/goes cycling
Anne: nurse, works nights/will go to
friend's birthday party/will go to a club/will
go to a restaurant
Daniella: lots of work/student of German
and Italian/gets home late/only goes out
at the weekend/goes swimming with her
boyfriend

2 a to go shopping with her friends; **b** at
nine o'clock; **c** has lunch; **d** goes to the
gym; goes swimming; **e** She goes to a
restaurant and then to see a film or to a
bar or nightclub; **f** at midday

Exercices de grammaire

1 a Nous jouons du piano; **b** Tu joues au
tennis; **c** Je vais au cinéma; **d** Vous allez à
l'université? **e** Ils/elles jouent aux cartes;
f Tu vas à la piscine?

2 a aime; **b** vais; **c** faire; **d** n'aime pas;
e sors; **f** allons; **g** aimons; **h** n'est pas;
i préfère; **j** aime; **k** adore.

3 a Vous aimez faire du sport?; **b** Elle n'aime
pas faire de la natation; **c** Nous aimons
bien jouer aux cartes; **d** Il n'aime pas aller
au cinéma; **e** J'aime regarder la télévision.

4 a Il doit aller à l'église le dimanche matin;
b Je dois sortir ce soir; **c** Ils doivent aller
au lit; **d** Tu dois boire quelque chose;
e Nous devons travailler cet après-midi;
f Vous devez faire du sport.

UNIT 4

1 a 6; **b** 3; **c** 4; **d** 5; **e** 7; **f** 8; **g** 1; **h** 2

2 a droit; **b** gauche; **c** première; **d** droite

3 a bibliothèque; supermarché; bar-tabac.
b Vous prenez la deuxième rue à droite, et
c'est là, à gauche; Vous prenez la première
rue à gauche, et c'est là à droite.

4 a Statue du Petit Quinquin; **b** hôpital
militaire; **c** Eglise St Maurice; **d** la gare

6 a next to; **b** between; **c** opposite; **d** in
front of; **e** on the corner of; **f** behind

7 a F: Le restaurant est à côté de la
boucherie; **b** F: La bibliothèque est dans
la rue des Alliés; **c** F: Entre la poste et le
musée, il y a un théâtre; **d** V; **e** F: Le bar-
tabac est au coin de la rue Dauphine et de
l'avenue Gambetta; **f** V; **g** V; **h** F: Il y a un
arrêt d'autobus devant la gare.

9 a a black coat; **b** a white or green shirt;
c He doesn't like it; **d** blue, pink, red and
yellow; **e** the coat, the green shirt and the
pink shirt.

10 a €75; **b** chemise; **c** €95; **d** gilet rouge;
e €250; **f** chemise bleue; **g** chemise
blanche; **h** €180

11 Je voudrais ce pull **rouge**; **90** euros; Moi,
je voudrais cette **jupe** bleue et ces deux
tee-shirts **blancs**; Et ce **manteau**; Et tu
n'aimes pas la **veste** verte là?; Non, je
n'aime pas beaucoup les **vestes**; elle coûte
200 euros.

12 a i a pair of trousers, a shirt and maybe
shoes; **ii** black trousers, a grey shirt and
black shoes; **b i** Tu aimes ce pantalon?;
ii Moi aussi; **iii** J'aime les deux; **iv** Je

préfère les noires; **v** Tu veux les essayer?

14 de la charcuterie; du pain; du poisson; des fruits; de l'huile; du saucisson; de la viande; du fromage; de l'alcool; des légumes; des épices

15 **a** boulangerie-pâtisserie; marchand de fruits et légumes; boucherie; un marchand de journaux; **b** check your answers in the vocabulary section p.48

Extra!

1 **a** T; **b** T; **c** F; **d** T; **e** F; **f** F

2 **a** blue dress and pink dress; **b** jumper and skirt; **c** 65 euros; **d** blue dress

Exercices de grammaire

1 **a** prenez; **b** allez; **c** tournez; **d** traversez; **e** prenez; **f** continuez

2 **a** la; **b** de la; **c** de l'; **d** du; **e** de l'; **f** du; **g** la; **h** la; **i** le

3 **a** l'; **b** la; **c** la; **d** les; **e** l'

4 **a** cette; **b** ces; **c** ce; **d** cette; **e** ces; **f** cet

5 **a** les chemises roses; **b** les tee-shirts blancs; **c** les pantalons rouges; **d** les jupes bleues; **e** les gilets gris; **f** les robes jaunes

UNIT 5

1 le Portugal; Porto; la Suisse; l'Italie; Rome; la Grèce; les Pays-Bas; le Danemark; l'Espagne; Madrid

2 **a** à; **b** au; **c** en; **d** en; **e** en; **f** aux; **g** à; **h** en

4 **a** 10.11; **b** three 2nd class tickets; **c** 10.52; **d** platform 2

6 **a** réservation; **b** deux; **c** à; **d** partir; **e** 9 heures; **f** correspondance; **g** arrive; **h** 226; **i** réservation; **j** composter

9 **1** d; **2** e; **3** b; **4** g; **5** c; **6** f; **7** a

10 **a** le 07.58 de Paris-Nord; **b** le 0.800 ou le 08.09; **c** le 07.58 ou le 08.28

11 **1** b; **2** a; **3** c

12 **a** vas; **b** partir; **c** train; **d** cher; **e** vendredi; **f** 100; **g** aéroport; **h** beaucoup

15 **a** 3; **b** 6; **c** 5; **d** 1; **e** 2; **f** 4

16 c; g; d; b; a; f; e

17 **a** la voiture est en panne; **b** elle est en retard; **c** elle n'a plus d'essence; **d** il y a une grève/le train est annulé

Extra!

1

	train no.	from	to	platform	track	delay
a	993	Nantes	–	2	4	–
b	625	–	Marseille	6	8	–
c	289	–	Lyon	–	–	25 mins
d	418	Paris	Avignon	7	14	–
e	472	–	Grenoble	–	–	10 mins
f	325	Mâcon	Valence	–	–	15 mins
g	591	Saint-Etienne	–	8	10	–

2 **a** 4; **b** underground and bus; **c** Saturdays 9 a.m.–5 p.m.; **d** 0.12; **e** one every minute

Exercices de grammaire

1 **a** au; **b** aux; **c** en; **d** en; **e** au; **f** en; **g** au; **h** aux; **i** en; **j** en; **k** en; **l** au; **m** en; **n** en

2 **a** Je vais prendre le train pour Milan; **b** Nous allons prendre l'avion pour Rome; **c** Ils vont partir pour Naples; **d** Elle va prendre le bateau pour la Corse; **e** Tu vas visiter la ville pour acheter des souvenirs?; **f** Vous allez sortir avec Pierre ce soir?

3 **a** veulent; **b** peut; **c** faut; **d** voulez; **e** veut; **f** pouvons; **g** faut; **h** peuvent

4 **a** Comment est-ce que tu vas à Bordeaux? J'y vais en voiture; **b** Est-ce qu'ils vont en France mardi? Ils y vont lundi; **c** Est-ce qu'elle va au supermarché tous les jours? Elle y va tous les jours;

d Comment est-ce que vous allez au travail? Nous y allons à pied; **e** Est-ce que tu vas à Paris en avion? J'y vais en Eurostar.

UNIT 6

1 **a** voudrais; **b** vous; **c** combien; **d** deux; **e** une; **f** fait

2 **conversation 1:** 1; 2; 2; 85; **conversation 2:** 1; 1; 1; 95; **conversation 3:** 3; 6; 4; 97

4 Stankevitch; Herbolin; Rebayi

5 **3** a; **1** f; **2** e; **6** b; **5** d; **4** c

6 **a** 4; **b** 6; **c** 5; **d** 1; **e** 7; **f** 3; **g** 8; **h** 2

7 **a** shower not working/water cold/press red switch; **b** no pillows/normally are in the wardrobe/also problem with satellite/will check

8 La douche ne marche pas./ Il n'y a pas d'eau chaude./ Le chauffage ne fonctionne pas. / Il n'y a pas assez de serviettes. / Il n'y a pas de couvertures.

9 **a** Elle se lève tard, elle se lave et il y a un problème avec la douche; **b** Elle va à la réception. Elle se plaint; **c** Elle se promène près de la Tour Eiffel et de Notre-Dame; **d** Elle s'amuse beaucoup; **e** Elle rentre à l'hôtel. Elle se couche tard.

10 **a** de 6h à 9h; **b** chambre ou restaurant; **c** 8,30 euros

11 **a** morning call/available; **b** swimming-pool is open; **c** the following cards; **d** traveller's cheques and cash; **e** 24 hours a day; **f** is served; **g** satellite TV is available; **h** management is not responsible

12 **a** F; **b** V; **c** V

13 **a** ouvert; **b** décembre; **c** janvier; **d** du; **e** au; **f** basse; **g** septembre; **h** novembre.

15 dans la brochure; entre les deux; est plus grand; le premier

16 extra sofa in the lounge/washing machine is not in the kitchen any more, it is in the bathroom/added a TV set and a phone in the first bedroom/ added a cot in the second bedroom/ swimming pool open between 9 a.m. and 8 p.m.

Extra

1 **1** Saint Denis; **2** Beau site; **3** Beau site; **4** Saint Denis; **5** Les Pinsons; **6** Saint Denis/Les Pinsons.

2 Possible answers
Customer 1: wants to book rooms for next week for three days (Friday to Sunday)/ one double room with toilet and one single room/wants sea view, satellite TV and fridge/ will arrive Friday around 3 p.m.
Customer 2: problems/shower is not working/no hot water/only cold/window does not close/noisy in the street/wife can't sleep/TV is not working

Exercices de grammaire

1 **a** me; **b** me; **c** nous; **d** nous; **e** nous; **f** se; **g** se; **h** se; **i** nous

2 **a** Nous ne nous réveillons pas avant dix heures; **b** Tu te lèves tôt aujourd'hui!; **c** Vous ne vous habillez pas?; **d** Elles se promènent dans le jardin; **e** Elle ne se douche pas tous les matins; **f** Je vais me réveiller tôt demain.

3 **a** La deuxième maison est plus agréable que la première maison; **b** La cuisine dans la première maison est moins spacieuse que dans la deuxième maison; **c** La salle de bains est aussi moderne dans la première maison que dans la deuxième maison; **d** Le jardin est plus pratique dans la première maison; **e** La deuxième maison est moins tranquille; **f** Les chambres sont plus grandes dans la deuxième maison.

4 **a** une; **b** de; **c** une; **d** de; **e** de; **f** une.

UNIT 7

1 **a** 3; **b** 10; **c** 9; **d** 7; **e** 8; **f** 6;
   g 2; **h** 5; **i** 1; **j** 4

2 **1 a** pourrais lui parler; **b** peux lui laisser
   2 a pourrais-je; **b** n'est pas là; **c** pourrait
   me; **d** le lui

3 **a** going out at the weekend; **b** to go
   dancing – to go to a restaurant and then
   to a nightclub; **c** She is going to telephone
   them this evening; **d** Saturday evening at
   8 p.m. in front of the railway station

5 **a** tall and fat/short brown hair/blue eyes/
   wearing glasses/beard and moustache;
   b short and slim/long blond hair/green
   eyes/freckles/wearing earrings

6 **a** Raphaël – very tall, slim, short brown
   hair and green eyes; **b** Pierre, shorter than
   Raphaël, long blond hair and blue eyes,
   beard and glasses

7 **a** veux; **b** cours; **c** quart; **d** encore;
   e connais; **f** comment; **g** grand;
   h cheveux; **i** courts **j** barbe; **k** yeux

9 **a** Man: Starter: raw vegetables; Main
   course: vegetarian dish; Dessert: cheese;
   Drink with meal: beer and bottle of red
   wine; Woman: Starter: snails; Main course:
   steak (medium done) with pepper sauce
   (dish of the day); Dessert: ice cream,
   two scoops of vanilla and one scoop of
   chocolate; Drink with meal: kir and bottle
   of mineral water; **b** plat du jour **c** Meat:
   steak with pepper sauce; Fish: trout with
   almonds; Vegetarian: raw vegetables,
   vegetarian dish; onion soup

10 **a** V; **b** F; **c** F; **d** F; **e** V; **f** V

11 je voudrais commander; je prends la salade
   verte; je vais prendre le steak-frites; bien
   cuit; la tarte aux pommes; vin rouge; après
   mon dessert

12 **a** 3; **b** 5; **c** 4; **d** 1; **e** 7; **f** 8; **g** 6; **h** 2

Extra

1 **a** Etienne for Solange; **b** 7 p.m. on
   Thursday, café du Commerce, opposite the
   cinema; **c** have a drink and then go to see
   a film

2 **a** She has a new boyfriend; **b** 1m 80 tall,
   curly black hair and blue eyes; **c** two
   weeks; **d** south-west France; **e** Jacques:
   windsurfing; Stéphanie: sunbathing

Exercices de grammaire

1 **a** Je voudrais …; **b** On pourrait …;
   c Elle voudrait …; **d** Il pourrait …;
   e Je pourrais ….

2 **a** Tu vas lui téléphoner; **b** Ils vont leur
   parler?; **c** Elle va lui dire quelque chose;
   d Vous lui donnez de l'argent?; **e** Elles
   vont leur donner des bonbons?

3 on aime sortir; on va au restaurant; on
   adore; on va au cinéma; on rentre; on fait;
   on joue.

4 **a** Oui, j'en prends; **b** Non, ils n'en ont
   pas; **c** Oui, elle en a; **d** Non, je n'en veux
   pas; **e** Oui, il en mange; **f** Non, il n'y en a
   pas.

UNIT 8

1b ai vu; a mangé; a dansé; ai dormi; ai pris;
   ai lu; as fait; ai fait; ai perdu; ai dû; ont
   retrouvé; ai passé; ont acheté; avez fait;
   ont préféré; avons regardé

1c voir; manger; danser; dormir; prendre;
   lire; faire; faire; perdre; devoir; retrouver;
   passer; acheter; faire; préférer; regarder

2a 1 with her English friend; **2** They visited
   museums, saw a play and a film; **3** He
   finished an essay; **4** He ate and drank a lot
   on Saturday evening.

2b a ai fait; **b** a visité; **c** a vu; **d** ai fini;
   e ai invité; **f** a fait; **g** a bu; **h** a dormi

3 Elise a fait plein de choses avec sa copine
   anglaise; elles ont visité des musées, elles

ont vu une pièce de théâtre et un film. Jean-Marc a fini sa dissertation samedi. Le soir, il a invité des amis à dîner. Sa copine Isabelle a fait un plat indien très épicé. Ils ont bu plein de bière et ils ont dormi toute la journée dimanche.

5 **1** d; **2** a; **3** e; **4** c; **5** b

6a c; i; d; b; h; e; a; g; j; f

7 Rami a dû travailler pour son père; son téléphone ne marche pas

8 **a** Je n'ai pas pu venir à la soirée; **b** parce que j'ai rencontré un vieux copain dans la rue; **c** il a proposé d'aller dans un bar; **d** on a beaucoup bu; **e** je n'ai pas vu l'heure; **f** j'ai raté le dernier bus

9 **a** F; **b** V; **c** F; **d** F; **e** F.

11 **a** vacances; **b** suis; **c** Où; **d** combien; **e** semaine; **f** promenades; **g** allé; **h** fait; **i** Quand; **j** trois

12 **Benoît:** Normandie/2 semaines/mauvais/ lire et dormir; **Sarah et Michel:** Corse/ 1 semaine/beau/plage, ski nautique

14 **1** il y a du soleil; **2** il y a des nuages; **3** il pleut; **4** il neige; **5** il y a du vent; **6** il y a du brouillard; **7** il y a de l'orage

15 **hiver** il fait très froid et il neige beaucoup; **printemps** il pleut souvent; **été** il fait très chaud et très humide; **automne** il fait beau et il y a de belles couleurs

Extra!

1 Possible answers
Muriel: spent weekend with parents/ Saturday went shopping/went to the restaurant/Sunday worked at the baker's/ had lunch with Jean in the village restaurant/watched TV in the afternoon
Stéphane: had a good weekend/Saturday did some DIY/Sunday invited neighbours around for a drink

Loulou: went rock climbing with friends/ camped outside/problem with mosquito bites and heavy rucksacks/backache but happy
Bernard: Saturday played the guitar with his band/evening concert in a bar/ celebrated their success till late/slept late on Sunday/did not work

2 **a** to the Alps for three weeks; **b** went on cycle trips – hard but they saw wonderful countryside; **c** they followed its route; **d** fine, but not too hot and with some clouds; **e** good, traditional and not expensive; **f** fit; **g** He is working in his father's office because he has no money left.

Exercices de grammaire

1 **a** avons; **b** suis; **c** est; **d** ont; **e** sont; **f** as

2 **a** J'ai fait de la planche à voile; **b** Vous avez aimé ce film?; **c** Elles n'ont pas pris l'avion; **d** Mes amis sont restés ici pendant une semaine; **e** Tu es allée en vacances?; **f** On a dû partir à dix heures; **g** Nous sommes rentrés le 20 juillet; **h** Elle n'est pas partie aux Etats-Unis.

3 **a** ai parlé; **b** a passé; **c** est allée; **d** sont restés; **e** ont loué; **f** ont fait; **g** ont vu; **h** ont adoré; **i** ont décidé

4 **a** pendant; **b** il y a; **c** pendant; **d** pendant; **e** il y a; **f** Il y a

UNIT 9

1 1980 > 1990; trois > quatre; ans > mois; 1998 > 1999; j'habite > je travaille

2 **a** pendant; **b** depuis; **c** pendant; **d** depuis

3 Past:
Il est né en 1975. Il a habité en Tunisie pendant 3 ans avec ses parents. Il a déménagé en France en 1978. Ses parents ont travaillé à Marseille pendant 10 ans.

Present:
Son père est à la retraite. Sa famille habite à Toulouse depuis 4 ans. Mustapha et son frère étudient l'anglais depuis 3 ans. Son frère travaille depuis 6 mois dans une entreprise en informatique.

5 a two weeks; **b** As soon as she arrived she felt happy/at ease; **c** English and Japanese; **d** yesterday morning

6 a s'inscrire, remplir, se renseigner, s'installer; **b i** Journalism, **ii** Humanities Degree – English literature, **iii** one week

7 a depuis; **b** sens; **c** installée; **d** m'; **e** suis; **f** inscrite; **g** me

8a i Florence: 1 mois; Hugo: 2 semaines; Beate: 1 an; **ii** Florence: dans un appartement avec 2 étudiantes, 1 espagnole et 1 allemande; Hugo: à l'hôtel; Beate: dans un appartement, pas loin de Victoria, avec son copain anglais; **iii** Florence s'est fait beaucoup d'amis et s'amuse bien; Hugo trouve que les Anglais sont sympa mais que Londres est sale et polluée et qu'il y a trop de monde; Beate trouve qu'il y a beaucoup de choses à faire à Londres mais préfère les Français

b a Elle s'appelle Florence, elle est italienne. Elle est en Angleterre depuis un mois et elle se sent déjà bien à l'aise. Elle a trouvé un appartement où elle habite avec d'autres étudiantes, une espagnole et une allemande. Elles sont obligées de parler anglais, et Florence a l'impression que son anglais s'est beaucoup amélioré. Elle s'est déjà fait beaucoup d'amis et elle s'amuse bien, elle ne s'ennuie pas une minute.
b Il s'appelle Hugo, c'est un étudiant français. Il est en Angleterre depuis deux semaines et il va y rester pendant trois mois. Il est venu pour travailler et apprendre l'anglais. Il n'a pas rencontré beaucoup de gens et son anglais ne s'est pas beaucoup amélioré. En ce moment, il loge à l'hôtel mais il espère trouver bientôt un appartement avec des étudiants anglais. Il croit que les Anglais sont sympa mais il n'a pas vraiment eu l'occasion de leur parler! Il n'aime pas trop Londres parce qu'il trouve qu'il y a trop de monde et que la ville est très sale et polluée. **c** Elle s'appelle Beate, elle vient d'Allemagne. Elle est à Londres depuis un an. Elle travaille au bureau de tourisme à la gare de Victoria. Elle rencontre beaucoup de touristes et elle a l'occasion de pratiquer son anglais et son français. Beate habite avec son copain anglais dans un appartement, pas loin de Victoria. Ils y sont depuis six mois. Beate aime bien Londres, parce qu'elle trouve qu'il y a beaucoup de choses à faire mais elle croit qu'elle va préférer la France: elle pense que les Français sont plus sympa et plus marrants, et que leur cuisine est meilleure!

10 a F; **b** F; **c** F; **d** V; **e** F

11 a nom; **b** lieu de naissance; **c** Baccalauréat; **d** licence; **e** maîtrise; **f** mention; **g** connaissances en informatique; **h** employée de bureau; **i** bilingue; **j** un stage; **k** date de naissance, **l** société

12 c; e; i; b; a; g; f; h; d; k; j

13 1 Julia est de Birmingham. Elle a une licence en littérature italienne. En 2005 elle s'est inscrite pour faire une formation d'enseignante. Elle l'a réussie avec mention. Elle a déménagé à Londres il y a six mois et elle enseigne depuis deux mois. **2** John est né à Manchester. Il a une licence en littérature anglaise et il a passé cinq ans en Europe. Il a travaillé comme serveur et professeur d'anglais. Il travaille à Londres comme professeur depuis deux ans. **3** Carmen est bilingue espagnol-anglais. Elle a fait une maîtrise et elle s'est inscrite pour faire une formation d'enseignante l'année dernière. Elle l'a réussie avec mention. Elle n'a pas d'expérience de l'enseignement.

14 **a** 4; **b** 1; **c** 2; **d** 3

15 **a** reçu; **b** passer; **c** travaillé; **d** depuis; **e** stage; **f** obtenu; **g** fini; **h** encore; **i** économie; **j** maîtrise, **k** bonne

Extra!

1 **a** marketing manager; **b** degree in business studies with distinction; marketing diploma; **c** marketing studies; **d** six months with Nestlé at Vevey in Switzerland; **e** did a one-year intensive course in French and speaks it fluently.

2 **Homme:** licence de commerce/2 mois dans le service import-export de la société + 1 an dans une société française à Londres/anglais – couramment; **Femme:** maîtrise de commerce/6 mois dans le service marketing de la société/italien – couramment + un peu de russe/stage de 3 mois en informatique

Exercices de grammaire

1 **a** J'ai habité en Australie pendant trois ans; **b** Ils travaillent en Angleterre depuis deux mois; **c** Elle a étudié l'anglais à l'école pendant cinq ans; **d** Ils apprennent le français depuis trois mois; **e** Vous y avez habité pendant combien de temps?

2 **a** Claudia s'est inscrite à l'université en 2005; **b** Aziz s'est renseigné pour entrer dans l'école de commerce; **c** Ils se sont beaucoup amusés à Paris; **d** Claudia s'est mise à apprendre l'espagnol; **e** Aziz s'est mis à faire de la natation; **f** Claudia et Aziz se sont installés dans un appartement près de la Sorbonne.

3 **a** Non, je ne me suis pas inscrit(e) à l'université; **b** Non, elle ne s'est pas renseignée pour les cours de japonais;

c Non, nous ne sommes pas installés dans notre nouvelle maison; **d** Non, elles ne se sont pas ennuyées; **e** Non, il ne s'est pas amusé; **f** Non, elles ne se sont pas senties à l'aise en France.

4 **a** Oui, je l'ai passé; **b** Oui, je l'ai envoyé; **c** Oui, elle l'a obtenu; **d** Oui, il les a réussis; **e** Oui, elles l'ont contactée; **f** Oui, je l'ai rencontrée.

UNIT 10

1 a **i** C'est quoi ton boulot? **ii** Tu vas bosser où? **iii** Je me casse; **iv** Veinarde! **v** On m'a refilé; **vi** C'est super; **vii** C'est l'enfer! **viii** Les mômes

2 **a** 3; **b** 4; **c** 2; **d** 6; **e** 1; **f** 5.

3 **a** bar/animaux interdits; **b** piscine/interdit de courir; **c** accès à la maison/interdit au public; **d** devant la porte de l'hôtel/ stationnement interdit; **e** restaurant/pique-nique interdit

4 **a** moi; **b** desolé; **c** interdit; **d** Pourriez; **e** peux; **f** défendu; **g** accès

6 **a** other cars cannot gain access; **b** to the car park; **c** There are no spaces left; **d** next to the tennis court

7 Pourriez-vous déplacer votre voiture parce que je ne peux pas sortir. Mettez-la à côté de votre caravane ou dans le parking (*or* au parking), s'il vous plaît. Merci.

8 **a** F; **b** V; **c** V; **d** V; **e** F; **f** V

9 **1** d; a; c; b; **2** b; c; d; a

11 terrible>génial; pas mal>bien; chantent>jouent; sympa>bonne; trouvez>pensez; beaucoup>vraiment; nuls>mauvais; super>fantastiques; intime>sympa; musicien>groupe

13 **a** F; **b** F; **c** V; **d** V; **e** F; **f** F

Extra!

1 **Babette:** since the weekend/works in the bar/comes from near Nice/economics – third year

Richard: two weeks/works at the swimming pool/comes from Lille/business studies

Stéphanie: two weeks/works in the crèche/comes from Paris/accounting and languages

Jean-Marc: two weeks/waiter lunchtime and barman evening/comes from Nantes/engineering school

2 **a** for minor problems; **b** in the local newspaper or in the window of pharmacies; **c** They have the reputation of being able to solve all domestic problems; **d** In the case of a medical emergency or a serious accident; **e** Police are in towns, **gendarmes** are in the country.

Exercices de grammaire

1 **a** Oui, appelez-les. / Non, ne les appelez pas; **b** Oui, ferme-la. / Non, ne la ferme pas; **c** Oui, monte-la là bas. / Non, ne la monte pas là-bas; **d** Oui, emmenez-les à la piscine. / Non, ne les emmenez pas à la piscine; **e** Oui, laisse-le dans la voiture. / Non, ne le laisse pas dans la voiture; **f** Oui, finissez-le. / Non, ne le finissez pas.

2 **a** Ne pas passer; **b** Ne pas stationner; **c** Ne pas ouvrir la fenêtre; **d** Ne pas jouer à la balle; **e** Ne pas nourrir les animaux; **f** Ne pas marcher sur la pelouse.

3 **a** que; **b** qui; **c** qui; **d** qu'; **e** qui; **f** qu'

4 **a** lui; **b** eux; **c** toi; **d** Moi; **e** elle; **f** moi; **g** toi

SUPPLEMENTARY EXERCISES
Unit 1

1 **a** 6; **b** 4; **c** 1; **d** 2; **e** 3

2 d; g; e; b; h; c; a; f

3 **a** Bonjour! Ça va? **b** Au revoir, monsieur; **c** Je suis allemande; **d** Vous êtes américain? **e** Tu es étudiante? **f** J'habite à Londres mais je suis de Glasgow.

4 **a** Elle s'appelle Natasha. Elle est américaine. Elle habite à New York mais elle est de Chicago. Elle est étudiante en histoire de l'art; **b** Il s'appelle Bob. Il est irlandais. Il habite à Belfast mais il est de Dublin. Il est technicien; **c** Elle s'appelle Malika. Elle est marocaine. Elle habite à Lille mais elle est de Paris. Elle est serveuse; **d** Il s'appelle Luca. Il est italien. Il est de Milan mais il habite à Rome. Il est acteur.

6 **a** 20; **b** philosophy; **c** Naples; **d** because he likes French people, French food, literature, cinema and philosophy; **e** when he was 11; **f** because she is from Zurich; **g** because they are very interesting; **h** He is a waiter in an Italian restaurant.

Unit 2

1 1e; 2a; 3b; 4c; 5d; 6g; 7f

2 **a** habites; **b** étudiant; **c** j'ai; **d** son; **e** est

3 **b** Sa grand-mère a 75 ans; **c** Il a une nièce; **d** Son grand-père s'appelle Robert; **f** La copine de son cousin a 21 ans; **g** Le frère de Luc s'appelle Michel; **j** Sa tante a 44 ans.

4 **a** Il a 19 ans; **b** Ils ont quel âge?; **c** (Est-ce que) tu as des frères et des sœurs?; **d** Nous habitons avec notre frère; **e** Ils ont un fils et une fille; **f** Sa fille a six ans; **g** Mon copain travaille avec son père; **h** (Est-ce que) tu habites avec tes parents?

8 **a** Vous voulez un sandwich?; **b** Tu veux quelque chose à boire?; **c** Non, pas pour moi merci; **d** Tu veux un café?; **e** Un chocolat chaud pour moi.

Answers

Unit 3

1 **a** Paris, 12.30 p.m., having lunch;
   b Brussels, 12.30 p.m., eating a sandwich
   in the office; **c** Quebec, 7.30 a.m., having
   breakfast after having been jogging;
   d Kinshasa, 1.30 p.m., university law
   lecture; **e** Beirut, 2.30 p.m., swimming pool
   with her brother and her cousin; **f** Tahiti,
   11.30 p.m., night club with friends.

2 **a** suis; **b** commence; **c** termine/finis;
   d mon/le; **e** des; **f** après; **g** les/nos;
   h prenons; **i** fais; **j** vais; **k** arrive

3a 1 3rd speaker; 2 5th speaker; 3 1st
   speaker; 4 4th speaker; 5 2nd speaker

3b **i** 3; **ii** 4; **iii** 1; **iv** 5; **v** 2

4 **a** j'aime; **b** tu n'aimes pas; **c** elle aime
   bien; **d** vous aimez beaucoup; **e** nous
   n'aimons pas; **f** ils détestent…

5 1 d; 2 a; 3 f; 4 e; 5 c; 6 b

Unit 4

1 d; f; j; e; a; h; g; b; i; c

2 **a** garage; **b** lire; **c** bibliothèque; **d** puis

3 **a** Pardon, vous savez où est l'office de
   tourisme? **b** Est-ce qu'il y a une poste
   près d'ici? **c** Est-ce que la bibliothèque est
   à côté de la gare? **d** C'est loin?

5 **a** aider; **b** voudrais; **c** le; **d** couleur;
   e l'; **f** le; **g** à; **h** prends

6 **a** Oui, je l'aime; **b** Non, je ne l'aime pas;
   c Non, elle ne l'aime pas; **d** Oui, ils
   l'aiment; **e** Oui, il l'aime; **f** Oui, je les
   aime.

7 **a** La jupe? Non, je ne l'aime pas; **b** Cette
   robe? Oui, je la préfère; **c** Tu l'aimes?
   d Oui, je l'aime bien; **e** Tu aimes ce
   pantalon? **f** Elle aime la chemise jaune, et
   moi aussi, je l'aime.

8 **a** J'aime bien le pantalon noir; **b** Je préfère
   ce pull gris; **c** Tu aimes ces chaussures

jaunes? **d** Je ne les aime pas; **e** Vous
préférez cette jupe rose? **f** Il n'aime pas
cette veste verte.

Unit 5

1 **a** 4; **b** 8; **c** 3; **d** 7; **e** 6; **f** 2; **g** 1; **h** 5

2 b; i; d; c; h; a; j; e; k; f; g

4 b; d; a; c

5 **a** aller; **b** y; **c** en; **d** grève; **e** faut;
   f nous; **g** en; **h** à; **i** faut; **j** ma; **k** en; **l** là

Unit 6

1 **a** voudrais; **b** quel; **c** nom; **d** combien;
   e personnes; **f** lits; **g** plaît; **h** fait; **i** fait;
   j prenez

2 **a** (Est-ce qu') il y a un parking privé
   dans l'hôtel?; **b** Où est l'ascenseur, s'il
   vous plaît?; **c** A quelle heure est-ce que
   vous servez le petit déjeuner?; **d** J'ai un
   problème dans/avec ma chambre; **e** Il n'y
   a pas de serviettes dans la salle de bains;
   f L'ascenseur au troisième étage ne marche
   pas.

3 **a** barbecue; **b** piscine; **c** printemps; **d** se
   lever; **e** réservation

4 **a** Constantopoulou; **b** Tamelikecht;
   c Wolfreys; **d** Lavillatte

Unit 7

1 **a** Allô; Pourrais-je parler à Helen, s'il vous
   plaît?; Ne quittez pas, je vous la passe;
   Merci. **b** Allô; Janet est là?; Désolé, elle
   n'est pas ici; Est-ce que je peux laisser un
   message? **c** Allô; Allô, je voudrais parler à
   Bruce, s'il vous plaît; Désolé, il n'est pas là;
   Il pourrait me rappeler?; D'accord, je vais
   le lui dire. **d** Allô; Je pourrais parler à Emer,
   s'il vous plaît?; C'est moi; Allô, c'est Carol.

2 **a** c'est; **b** Qu'est-ce que; **c** dit/dirait;
   d va; **e** se voit/retrouve

4 **a** Isabelle est française et elle a vingt-cinq ans. Elle est petite et elle a les cheveux blonds et longs et les yeux bleus. **b** Alain est anglais et il a trente-trois ans. Il est grand et mince et il les cheveux bruns. Il a les yeux verts, une moustache et une barbe. **c** Joshua est américain et il a cinquante ans. Il est très grand et gros. Il a les cheveux noirs et courts et les yeux bleus. Il porte des lunettes. **d** Juliette est irlandaise et elle a dix-sept ans. Elle est grande et mince et elle a les cheveux roux. Elle a les yeux verts et des taches de rousseur.

5 **1** g; **2** f; **3** e; **4** a; **5** b; **6** c; **7** d

6 **a** steak; **b** truite; **c** pomme; **d** addition

7 k; c; f; g; b; a; i; d; e; h; j

Unit 8

1 **a** Nous avons passé un week-end excellent; **b** Qu'est-ce que tu as fait samedi soir? **c** Je n'ai pas pu venir parce que j'ai dû travailler; **d** Ils ont eu un problème avec leur voiture; **e** Lucie a adoré Paris, elle a visité tous les musées; **f** Je n'ai pas vu le film, mais j'ai lu le livre.

3 **a** Ils ont raté le dernier métro; **b** J'ai mangé dans un bon restaurant; **c** Qu'est-ce que tu as fait? **d** Nous avons passé un très bon week-end; **e** Il a eu un problème avec sa voiture; **f** Elle n'a pas pu venir avec nous.

4 **a** mon; **b** allés; **c** sale; **d** vu/visité; **e** pris; **f** a; **g** fait; **h** passé; **i** mangé; **j** est; **k** beaucoup; **l** l'; **m** décidé; **n** as

5 Chère Carole,

Merci pour ta lettre. Tu as de la chance d'avoir passé tes vacances d'été en Inde. Veinarde! Il y a deux ans je suis allée en Inde aussi et j'ai beaucoup aimé. Vraiment, je trouve ce pays superbe.

Malheureusement, cet été je n'ai pas pu partir en vacances et j'ai dû rester à Lille pour travailler. C'est la vie! En juillet, j'ai trouvé un travail dans un restaurant qui n'est pas loin de chez moi. J'y ai travaillé pendant un mois. Pendant le mois d'août, j'ai dû étudier pour préparer mes examens et je vais les passer la semaine prochaine. Heureusement, j'ai aussi eu un peu de temps pour me relaxer. En juillet une vieille amie est venue me voir à Lille et on a fait plein de choses ensemble.

A bientôt j'espère.

Sylvie

Unit 9

2 **a** Ils travaillent à Brighton depuis six mois; **b** J'ai habité à Londres pendant six ans; **c** J'ai commencé mes études en 2005; **d** Je les ai terminées l'année dernière; **e** Je les ai trouvées très intéressantes; **f** Je me suis inscrite en cours de langues; **g** Je me suis bien installé en France.

3 **1 Nadine**: English degree from Manchester University; graduated in 2005. Went to India in 2006 and worked in a primary school for a year. Currently working in a secondary school in Dakar. Been in post for two years. Next year she is going to return to England to do a Master's degree in education; **2 Kofi**: Has a Master's degree in computing. Finished in 2005. From 2006 to 2008 worked for a bank in Lille. Has been working for an internet company for two years and is starting to get bored and would like to find a different job; **c Elizabeth**: Has a degree in maths. When she finished her degree she decided to go travelling. She went to New York and spent nine months there. She has worked as a waitress in a bar, and as a receptionist in a hotel and even done some babysitting. She would like to find a permanent job in

London and would like to do a Master's degree in statistics.

4 **a** fini; **b** licence; **c** fait; **d** depuis;
   e connaissance; **f** me; **g** inscrite;
   h réussi; **i** me

Unit 10

1 **a** les mômes; **b** refilé; **c** me casse;
   d bosse; **e** quatre; **f** boulot; **g** plus;
   h l'enfer

3 **a** in the car park; **b** They are not allowed
   in the bar or the restaurant; **c** midnight;
   d Children must be accompanied by an
   adult; **e** no music after 10 p.m.

4 **a** Il est interdit de fumer ici; **b** Mettez-la
   derrière les autres voitures; **c** Ce n'est

pas indiqué; **d** C'est sympa de travailler
avec des mômes; **e** Désolé monsieur,
vous bloquez l'accès au camping; **f** Il est
défendu de jouer de la musique; **g** Ne la
mettez pas là.

5 **a** The exams are starting soon and he
   has to finish two essays and hand in his
   dissertation; **b** in two months' time; **c** He
   thinks that they last too long; **d** He hopes
   to find work in another town, but before
   that he intends to go on a long holiday;
   e It's too big, there are too many people,
   too much pollution and everything is
   expensive; **f** work to earn enough to travel
   somewhere exotic

Index

ALSO IN THIS SERIES

French 2, Second Edition
Kate Beeching & Annie Fontaine Lewis

Spanish 1, Second Edition
Cathy Holden & María del Carmen Gil Ortega

Spanish 2
María Eugenia Greco & Gabriel Sánchez-Sánchez

Italian 1, Second Edition
Mara Benetti, Carmela Murtas & Caterina Varchetta (project co-ordinator
Roberto Di Napoli)

Italian 2
Mara Benetti, Cristina Testi & Caterina Varchetta

German 1
Tom Carty & Ilse Wührer